The Trustus Plays

The Trustus Plays

Jon Tuttle

intellect Bristol, UK / Chicago, USA

For Jim and Kay

First published in the UK in 2009 by
Intellect, The Mill, Parnall Road, Fishponds, Bristol, BS16 3JG, UK

First published in the USA in 2009 by
Intellect, The University of Chicago Press, 1427 E. 60th Street, Chicago,
IL 60637, USA

A catalogue record for this book is available from the British Library.

Cover Design: Holly Rose
Copy Editor: Jennifer Alluisi
Typesetting: John Teehan

ISBN: 978-1-84150-224-3
ISSN: 1754-0933

Printed in Canada by Friesens.

Series: Playtext Series
Series Editor: Roberta Mock
Photo of Jon Tuttle on back cover © Lynne Druschel

Contents

Preface

This book is a chronicle of Trustus Theatre's collaboration with Jon Tuttle over the last fifteen years and is in some ways a testament to the theatre's mission. Trustus began in a second-floor walkup in 1985 and has since evolved into a half-million dollar enterprise whose mainstage and studio spaces are home to three production companies. It is the only professional theatre in South Carolina to receive funding from the National Endowment of the Arts and to become a constituent member of the Theatre Communications Group.

What hasn't changed is our mission, which is to bring our audiences professional productions of new, original, and challenging plays. In 1988, we began our Playwrights' Festival to cultivate new voices for the stage, which has given me the privilege to work with many young playwrights. Most have gone on to successful careers, including Tony Awards, major motion pictures and a Pulitzer Prize, but Jon Tuttle impressed me in such a way that I jumped at the chance to make him Trustus' Playwright-in-Residence and then its Literary Manager.

Jon is a superb craftsman. Even his most eccentric characters are believable, and his dialogue is never self-conscious. Having directed two of his plays, I know my actors have found his characters highly fulfilling to inhabit and his dialogue easy to deliver. He knows what to listen for, how to take advice, and when to take a stand.

Jon's experience as a scholar and teacher shows in the way he deals with other playwrights. He has great empathy and appreciation for their hard work and treats them with the utmost respect. His leadership with our Playwrights' Festival has led to its international recognition as one of the best festivals in the world.

Trustus Theatre's long and productive relationship with Jon has been a great benefit to the theatre, the staff, and to me personally. We are proud that our collaboration has now borne this book and that now the rest of the theatre world can know about the good work we've done together.

Jim Thigpen
Founder/Artistic Director
Trustus Theatre

Through the Dark, Glassily

Yes, now I see it all perfectly; there are two possible situations—one can do either this or that. My honest opinion and my friendly advice is this: Do it or do not do it—you will regret both.

– Soren Kierkegaard[1]

I

Pirandello's Manager insists that "Drama is action, sir, action and not confounded philsophophy!"[2] and I couldn't agree more. There is no –ism that ever salvaged a play that was boring the hell out of me, no –ism that ever helped me hear what my own play was trying to tell me as I sat writing it. Indeed, when I began writing *The Hammerstone*, the first of the three plays gathered here, I no idea what it would even be about. All I knew was that it would be set in a ruin.

I had visited the cliff dwellings at Mesa Verde, Colorado, several times. These are whole, small towns carved into sandstone escarpments by the Anasazi Indians and then, about 1300 AD, inexplicably abandoned, as if the citizenry had simply vanished and time abruptly stopped. The rumors said cannibalism. (A hammerstone, by the way, is exactly what it sounds like: a rock used for grinding things like flesh and bone.) Standing amid the ruins, I was visited by that strange teleological twinge one gets around graveyards and shipwrecks. And I thought: there's a play here.

There wasn't. There was only a scene design and metaphor that became compatible with the story *The Hammerstone* finally told to me, which is a story of regeneration

1

and renewal. And as I look back through these plays now, I "see it all perfectly": each is a variation of that same story. I chose the epigram from Kierkegaard's "Judge William," above, because in very simple terms it describes (prescribes?) the basic structure of each play: the protagonist arrives at a moment when he must choose to do this or do that, but each choice is freighted with ontological implications. From that I conclude, with some surprise, that I must be some sort of existentialist.

Surprise because, like most academics, I'm never really sure what existentialism *is*. But I'm going to talk about it anyway, because I'm an academic. And because I'm a playwright, I think I must be drawn to the inherently dramatic tensions that to my understanding characterize existentialism.

Take for instance Kierkegaard's notion of the "anguish of Abraham."[3] How many good plays do *not* deal with a character's need to make complex and self-defining choices (should I kill my son or defy God?) on no other moral authority than his own narrow and unique experience? Existentialism reminds us that while our identities are formed by such choices, there is no single light—no universal principle or common wisdom—by which we can make them. We can proceed only by making what Kierkegaard and later Albert Camus termed a "leap" into an acceptance of our absurdity.

For Murray, the lusty and somewhat baffled professor in *The Hammerstone*, that leap occurs when he must decide whether to sign Woody's withdrawal slip. That moment is a crossroads: signing would mean abandoning his principles, surrendering to futility and beginning to hate, as his colleague Victor did, its agents. But Murray's "principles" are dubious. For him, the primary object of teaching is ego-gratification; it feeds his delusions of perpetual youth and virility, and *not* to sign would necessitate abandoning *them* and capitulating to a new, less appealing sense of himself. It took only a few months to write Murray into this jam, but almost a year of head-scratching to fully appreciate what I was asking of him and complete the play.

In fact, the play was not originally Murray's. While I was writing, I recalled that breathtaking moment in *To The Lighthouse* when, "Mr. Ramsay, stumbling along a passage one dark morning, stretched his arms out, but Mrs. Ramsay having died rather suddenly the night before, his arms, though stretched out, remained empty."[4] I forthwith decided to perpetrate, like Woolf, a bit of bait-and-switch by killing my original protagonist—Victor—and replacing him with another. At first it was just a gadget I couldn't resist, but later it helped articulate the dramatic question that compels the play.

That question comes straight out of Camus, who begins his essay, "An Absurd Reasoning," with his most famous passage:

> There is but one truly serious philosophical problem, and that is suicide.
> Judging whether life is or is not worth living amounts to answering the
> fundamental question of philosophy. All the rest—whether or not the world
> has three dimensions, whether the mind has nine or twelve categories—
> comes afterwards. These are games; one must first answer.[5]

The Hammerstone presumes nothing less than to answer the question of what gives
life value, and here's why: while I was writing it, someone close to me was talking
seriously about killing himself. I didn't know whether I should be afraid for him
or furious. Suddenly, I found Murray saying things I wanted to say to him—very
existential things—like this in Act II:

> Living. Just, just *living*. It's all just an act of *will*. Happiness, it isn't
> something you, you *get*, it isn't a reward, there are no rewards! You are
> happy, your life is happy, by the *force* of your *will*. Over time, over, over
> *pain*, that's *living*, you get the life, the *happiness*, that you *create*. And
> you *keep* creating it!

I knew when I wrote that speech that it articulated the play's one moral imperative,
and I believe in it still. What I didn't know at the time was that I was confusing clinical
depression with unhappiness, which are of course two very different things. At any
rate, it became necessary to the point of the play that Murray preach by example
when, in refusing to sign Woody's withdrawal slip, he makes his crucial choice and
thereby re-invents and restores himself to wholeness.

Murray and Victor, it needs pointing out, are not simply an Odd Couple. I conceived
them as exemplars of psychomachia, the medieval notion of a personality divided
into two co-dependent and complementary halves, and of Freud's concept of Eros
and Thanatos, the co-existing life and death instincts. These bifurcations echo through
Tennessee Williams and Herman Hesse and other heroes of my youth. I also see in
Murray and Victor, respectively, approximate embodiments of the two spheres of
consciousness Kierkegaard called (in *Either/Or*) the Aesthetic and Ethical, the former
being a refined hedonism or searching after pleasure, the latter being a commitment
to duty. One might also argue that by the time he makes his leap, Murray achieves
Kierkegaard's more paradoxical and vaguely Buddhist third stage: the Religious.

Other characters in the play are Voices in His Ear who help or push Murray along
his journey. Through any professor's door comes a multitude of Woodys and Kristis,
and into the profession pours a constant quantity of Dottys. Grace Berger, however,
is more than just the comic relief she appears to be. In her I discovered a goofy
raisonneur, a person committed, despite the calamities in her life, and however
ridiculous they may be, to muscling past absurd consciousness and, like Camus'
Sisyphus, embracing a "higher fidelity that negates the gods and raises rocks."[6] She

functions as (I can't believe I'm typing this) an existential Bodhisattva, coaxing first Victor and then Murray toward the Enlightenment she has achieved and a genuine sense of what makes life worth living. Hence her name.

II

It's 1991. I walk into Trustus Theatre for an evening of Stoppard. In the auditorium are over a hundred Barcaloungers arrayed around coffee tables, and out front is a bar. Great joint. I ask the nice lady if I can take my beer to my seat. She says, "We *insist.*" This is my first exchange with Kay Thigpen, the Managing Director, who founded Trustus with her husband Jim in 1985. Their mission was and remains to bring edgy, professional theatre to South Carolina. In 1988, they created the annual South Carolina (later Trustus) Playwrights' Festival award, a national contest which has annually premiered original plays, many of which have moved to off-Broadway, Hollywood or the Actors' Theatre of Louisville and were written by such now prominent writers as David Lindsay-Abaire, Stephen Belber, Toni Press-Coffman and Sarah Hammond. So anyway, before the lights come down, as I'm sitting there drinking my beer and eating my free popcorn, Jim bounds onto the stage for his nightly meet-and-greet, and everybody feels like family, and I think to myself, wouldn't it be something to get a production here?

Imagine my delight when, three years later, I get a call from Trustus informing me that *The Hammerstone* has won the 1994 Festival award and will be produced that August. That opening night marked the beginning of our relationship and will remain one of the fondest memories of my life. But I'll come back to that.

Skip ahead to Valentine's Day, 1995. The cover story of *Time* that week was a depressingly clinical investigation into the chemical origins of love. Turns out our deepest and noblest affections for one another are merely our wolfish pheromones goading us to procreate. Turns out there's a perfectly Darwinian explanation for the seven-year-itch and the spiraling divorce rate. Turns out Thornton Wilder had it all wrong: monogamy is unnatural, marriage a great cultural lie. I could dig it. I just got divorced. So I thought: there's a play here.

I dug in for several months researching the anthropological origins of mating and matrimony, particularly in Helen Fisher's excellent *Anatomy of Love*. I interviewed divorce lawyers and private investigators, one of whom was so jaded that he had surveilled his own fiancé for several years before finally marrying her. (It didn't last.) My play, I decided at the outset, would be impudently anti-romantic. I would call it *Drift*, because I liked the tectonic implications. It would be about the collapse of a marriage, of all marriages, forever and ever. It would be a dirge, a howl, a *cri de coeur*. Nice people would come see it and then not discuss it all the long way home.

What came out instead was a love story. The awful facts and figures spewing from Lee, my Machiavellian PI, were so odious even to me that I couldn't follow their implications through to their natural end by allowing my protagonist, Barbara, to leave her faithless husband. The climactic choice she makes at the end of the play—to stay with Arthur—is not the choice I had intended for her. It's weak, it's wrong, and it rubs against the grain of the rest of the play. And still it felt inevitable; I sensed it in every strand of the play's DNA. Why?

Because Oscar Brownstein was right. In *Strategies of Drama*, Brownstein proposed a definition of the dramatic climax very different from our traditional notion of a "turning point." To Brownstein, the climax occurs not on the stage, but in the audience, as "an actual event in the life of the spectator" in the form of a "perception shift." More than "a moment in the present or a collection of impressions," it is "an expanding sphere of discovered significance" which demands "a revision of our understanding of [the central character], of his motives, and therefore of the significance of the play."[7]

Reading that for the first time was a revelation, and while finishing *Drift*, I had my own perception shift: if marriage is a lie, most people still want to believe it, and I was no exception. I didn't want Lee to be right, even if he *was* right, and neither, I figured, would anybody else. Barbara didn't want the knowledge she'd spent the whole play pursuing, and I didn't want it for her. That's how her wrong choice became the right one for the play.

Barbara's choice is also a demonstration of what Jean Paul Sartre called "negation," the self-directed vacancy we all employ to detach ourselves from distasteful roles or to convince ourselves of something precisely because we don't believe it.[8] In *Being and Nothingness*, Sartre posited that identity formation—the "fundamental project" of one's life—is a continuing process during which a person is free to choose that personal moral construct that is her Self, but when she makes her choices, she is also choosing the image of what mankind "ought to be." And so it is, I think, that when Barbara ultimately decides to rejoin her husband in their home, she willingly submits, in exchange for the illusion of love and belonging, to an altered identity and asks us all to share in it. And if the play works, we do.

It was important that the atmosphere of *Drift* stayed spare, airless, more aural than visual and increasingly claustrophobic. I was inspired to attempt this by two theatrical gauntlets thrown unknowingly by others. One came from Lawrence Harbison, then general editor at Samuel French, Inc., who in a speaking engagement warned a group of us playwrights to "never begin your play with two people sitting at a table talking." He meant, of course, that the days of the smart-servant convention ("The young master's home from the continent, but his beloved is sworn to another!") were long over. The other came from Frank McGuinness, whose *Someone Who'll*

Watch Over Me was produced by Trustus in 1994. The play is a dramatization of Plato's Allegory of the Cave: the characters stay chained to a wall from beginning to end, save for one who escapes (along with the folks not having a good time) at intermission. There is therefore no opportunity for the conflict to escalate physically— no way anybody can even move. My God, the gall of it! And it worked! Duly taunted, I contrived to begin a play with two people sitting at a table talking, after which nobody would move. Much.

Jim selected *Drift* as the winner of the 1998 Festival award and during rehearsals asked me to be the theatre's Playwright-in-Residence. After the run, he invited me to serve as Literary Manager. But I'll come back to that.

III

It's 1991 again. There's an article in the newspaper about a little-known moment in American history: the warehousing of German and other prisoners-of-war in South Carolina during World War II. These prisoners, many of them Nazis, were forced to build rail lines, process lumber or—most deliciously—pick cotton, and were typically guarded by soldiers kept out of combat because they were black. The ironies pour forth: the prisoners became local celebrities, were praised for their industry and deportment and were welcomed by the very business establishments that prohibited their guards. As the war was nearing its end, escape attempts escalated, not because the prisoners were longing for Germany, but because they didn't want to go back. So off they went, in a perfect inversion of the Fugitive Slave Act: white slaves running north to America, pursued by their black overseers. And I think to myself: there are at least five plays here.

It took fourteen years of trying to write all five before I arrived at *Holy Ghost.* It took a few weeks after the 2005 Trustus premiere to realize that "Jon, it's so ambitious!" meant the play was still overpacked. For this I prefer to blame Timberlake Wertenbaker, whose brilliant *Our Country's Good* served as a template. I wanted my play, like hers, to be a sprawling canvas painted with rich oils, to portray not just individuals but an entire civilization. And I wanted to boldly defy caveats in the trade journals like "cast limit seven" or "simple set," which is one reason the play doesn't get produced much.

During my research, I learned that the prisoners were subjected to a secret re-education program meant to intellectually rewire them and to belie Nazi charges of American decadence and hypocrisy.[9] Granted, this program began after V-E Day—May 8, 1945—and not the autumn before, as *Holy Ghost* has it. Otherwise, the play stays fairly true to the particulars of the program, which looked a lot like

Goebbels' propaganda machine. Certain authors who might affirm notions of genetic supremacy—Rand, Shaw, London—were blacklisted in favor of others—Saroyan, Benet, a bit of Hemingway—more appropriate to the American mythos. The prisoners were also deviously brainwashed by Jane Russell movies. It was all too exquisite, and it occurred to me that the form of my play could better serve its function if along the way I deconstructed a few classic American texts.

Of course, as an academic, I'm never sure what deconstruction means. But this did not deter me from imbedding in *Holy Ghost* references to familiar and topical texts as a way of exploiting or subverting them. I knew my primary protagonist, a black army private, would follow the same trajectory from bloodlust to pacifism as did Stephen Crane's hero in *Red Badge of Courage*, so I named him Henry. I drew the names of my auxiliary protagonist (Bergen), villain (Reiker) and femme fatale (Patty) from Bette Greene's chipper young-adult novel *Summer of My German Soldier*. My self-hating Sergeant Waters is an incarnation of the eponymous character in Charles Fuller's *A Soldier's Play*. Marks, Loker and the whole tavern scene (II.6) come straight out of George Aiken's adaptation of *Uncle Tom's Cabin*, as does my runaway slave, Juraj Eras, ("George Harris"). The "Little Formless Fears" scene (II.3) is a borrowed moment from Eugene O'Neill's *The Emperor Jones*; the "Dutchmen" scene (II.4) takes its title and some of its particulars from Amiri Baraka's *Dutchman*, and King and Duke are lifted straight from Mark Twain's *The Adventures of Huckleberry Finn*, as is the "On the River" scene (II.7). And oh: I couldn't resist using the most famous line from *The Diary of Anne Frank*.

It was bloody commodious of President George W. Bush to plunge America into the Iraqi quagmire shortly before *Holy Ghost* premiered. In times of war, ideological reorientation goes hand-in-hand with ethnic purification. Patriotism is a code word for jingoism and, particularly in America, the cultural melting pot becomes a crucible. It was the perfect climate for a play about war and the various political, cultural and religious camps into which it distills us.

Language is a function of that distillation, or perhaps vice-versa. Upon moving to the American South, I heard for myself the many dialects subsecting the region according to race, culture, geography, and class. Some of them I can hardly understand, though a few, like Gullah, which one hears in the lowcountry and sea islands, are utterly beautiful. Nick Olcott, who directed a staged reading of the play in Washington, D.C., noted quite correctly that the play "is really about the intricate ways in which human beings establish signals to define the group that is 'us' and to differentiate from the group that is 'them,' and how meaningless and confused these signals can become when the context is changed and the assumptions negated."[10] I was thinking something like that when I had my Gullah woman propose that "Ef us lussen...ef us *lussen*, eh? Us onduhstan' one'nuddah."

Structurally, there are two trains running through *Holy Ghost*. (This may be another reason it doesn't get produced much.) To my mind, the play is Henry's, but Bergen's story occupies almost as much stage time. And while the tracks laid out for each man lead very different directions, they arrive at about the same place.

On Henry, *Holy Ghost* plays an elaborate dirty trick. To create him I drew on such worthy dramatic forebears as David Rabe's Pavlo Hummel and Charles Gordone's Johnny Williams, two GI's who are subsumed by forces beyond their control or even comprehension and who never really stand a chance. Early in the play, Henry overestimates himself or the force of his own will-to-power; he expects to fight Nazism with (I can't believe I'm typing this) Nietzsche-ism. All along his journey, he is asked to choose between allegiances conditioned by his race, nationality and personal affections, but every choice he makes is somehow wrong, every commitment a dead end, and he ends up behind bars, unworthy of his volk, and destined, as Waters predicts, for suicide. All of his actions, to paraphrase Sartre, are equivalent in that they are all doomed to failure.[11]

Bergen, on the other hand, begins the play uncommitted except to an abstraction he calls belonging, which in his case really just means avoiding conflict. He has divested himself of his tribal, political and familial identities in favor of the cozy anonymity provided by the masses and the Army. More and more frustrated by the ineffectuality that comes with invisibility, however, he gradually re-asserts his identity. By play's end, he has re-upped as a Jew, declared a cause, boarded a train and gone off to fulfill his own prophecy: "You're gonna go to war, and you're gonna die, and everybody knows it but you."

Though each man goes to his death, only Bergen's is meaningful. His is the story of regeneration in the play, while Henry's is simply a spiral into the abyss. There is in Martin Heidegger[12] another way of stating the difference: Bergen grows toward his own "authenticity," and Henry does not. By "authenticity," Heidegger meant an awareness of the existential structure of one's life and of one's own finitude, and of the resultant freedom to re-invent or commit oneself, which is, I think, precisely what Bergen does before he goes rather triumphantly to his death. Henry, on the other hand, defines himself only in relation to each moment and what others in it want him to be; he is unable to project himself beyond each moment, and so is unable to "be" anything. Even his most important and potentially authentic decision—not to return Cetnik to the prison camp—he reverses while in jail for the fleeting illusion of belonging. Ultimately, he learns only that he is lost, although not why, nor how, nor that he always been, and so achieves the condition that both Heidegger and Sartre called Nothingness.

IV

My favorite writerly quotations are ones that indemnify me from the responsibility of thinking about my own choices, like the following from Wallace Shawn:

> I don't have an idea for a play until after I've finished writing it. I write first, and come up with what it's about later. My technique could be compared to having a large canvas and coming in every day and putting a dot on it somewhere, and after several years—literally—I begin to say, "that reminds me of an elephant, so I think I'll make it one."[13]

As a recipe for committing any creative act, one could do a lot worse than that. The difficult thing about writing is that you never really know what you're doing, and the better you get, the harder it is. The only wisdom that experience confers is not to think too much about it—until one day you're writing your own Introduction.

As Jim points out in his preface, this book is a chronicle of my association with Trustus Theatre, about which I have so very much to say that I'll say only this: to belong to such a gifted theatre family and to see my plays given such excellent productions exceeds the dreams I once allowed myself. Certainly our relationship has been the most important and most utterly frightening component of my creative life. Important because being allowed to contribute to such a vital and vibrant institution has given my own life very real meaning. Frightening because, as Herb Gardner wrote, "The fear that no one will put your plays on is quickly replaced by the fear that someone *will*."[14]

Certainly this book would not exist without the contributions of the cast and crew members listed herein and the enthusiasm of the whole Trustus staff; without the warmth and intelligence of the wonderful Trustus audience (you know who you are); without my friend Dewey Scott-Wiley, whose many gifts to me include an essay included herein; without the generosity and support of the administration at Francis Marion University, where it is my privilege to teach; without the confidence and hard work of Roberta Mock and May Yao at Intellect; and most certainly without Jim and Kay Thigpen, who have made so many things possible for so many for so long, and to whom this book is fondly and gratefully dedicated.

I am thankful also for the constant support of such friends and colleagues as Ken Autrey, Thorne Compton, Phillip Gardner, Christopher Johnson and Ken Kitts, and finally for the love of my wife Cheryl and our wonderful children Staci, Jill and Josh.

– Jon Tuttle
June 2008

References

1. Soren Kierkegaard, *Either/Or*, ed. and trans. Howard V. Hong and Edna H. Hong, vol. 2 (Princeton, NJ: Princeton University Press, 1987), 159.

2. Luigi Pirandello, *Six Characters in Search of an Author*, in *Three Plays*, trans. Edward Storer (New York: EP Dutton & Co., 1922), 64.

2. Soren Kierkegaard, *Fear and Trembling, and The Sickness Unto Death*, trans. Walter Lourie (Garden City, NY: Doubleday, 1941).

4. Virginia Woolf, *To the Lighthouse* (New York: Harcourt Brace & Co., 1927), 194.

5. Albert Camus, "An Absurd Reasoning," in *The Myth of Sisyphus* (New York: Vintage Books, 1955), 3.

6. Albert Camus, "The Myth of Sisyphus," in *The Myth of Sisyphus* (New York: Vintage Books, 1955), 91.

7. Oscar Browstein, *Strategies of Drama: The Experience of Form* (New York: Greenwood Press, 1991), 117-118.

8. Jean Paul Sartre, "The Origin of Negation," in *Being and Nothingness*, trans. Hazel Barnes, 7th ed. (New York: The Citadel Press, 1971), 3-45.

9. See Ron Robin, *The Barbed Wire College*, (Princeton, NJ: Princeton University Press, 1995).

10. Nick Olcott, e-mail message to the author, 23 May, 2005.

11. Jean Paul Sartre, "Conclusion," in *Being and Nothingness*, trans. Hazel Barnes, 7th ed. (New York: The Citadel Press, 1971), 545.

12. Martin Heidegger, *Being and Time*, trans. John Macquarrie and Edward Robinson (New York: Harper and Rowe, 1962), 230-234.

13. Wallace Shawn, qtd. in "The Quotes Archive," *The Playwriting Seminars*, ed. Richard Tocsan, http://www.vcu.edu/arts/playwriting/seminar/html.

14. Herb Gardner, "Introduction," in *Herb Gardner: The Collected Plays* (New York: Applause, 2000), 9-10.

THE HAMMERSTONE

*When we grew up and went to school
there were certain teachers who would
hurt the children any way they could.*
                                    – Roger Waters

SETTING: Somewhere in the American southwest is a public liberal arts college with virtually no admission requirements. Its buildings are for the most part adobe and are worn down enough after many years in the sun and wind to suggest a ruin.

This college is represented on stage by two offices, one in the Humanities Building (Murray's), and the other in the Social Sciences building (Victor's). Though the offices are adjacent on stage, it should be established that they are not actually next door to one another. Perhaps a crumbling wall separates the two; perhaps they face different directions.

In Victor's office there's an old wooden desk and bookcase, upon which will sit (when he puts it there) an ancient human skull and a jar of coins. There's a plaque on the wall, but otherwise not much that would qualify as decoration. A door is upstage or to one side, as is a window. The office is neat enough, although like its occupant, some dust has settled on it.

Murray's office is much more lively and bright. He's got a metal desk and bookcase and probably some colorful prints or posters on the wall, plus some miscellaneous junk. His window is on the implied downstage wall, looking out upon the audience.

There is also a Teaching Area, down center, between the offices, where Victor, Murray and later Dotty will stand to address their classes. Ideally, it will be approached from up center (as opposed to from the wings). When Victor or Dotty is teaching, it will be from behind a lectern. Murray doesn't need a lectern, but perhaps he uses a stool.

The action takes place in the present, over the course of several days. References to sports or popular culture figures can be updated in production, at the director's discretion.

CHARACTERS

VICTOR RANSOME	About sixty-two, a professor of anthropology. A conservative and dapper dresser, if a decade or two behind the times.
MURRAY STONE	Maybe fifty-six, a professor of English. He's in good shape and is reasonably good-looking. He doesn't take himself too seriously, and neither do his students.
WOODY DRUMM	Nineteen or so. He's on the baseball team.
GRACE BERGER	Mid-seventies. Loopy, but not without dignity.
KRISTI	Twenty or thereabouts. A great-looking girl.
DOTTY DUNBAR	Late twenties. A graduate at one of the flagship universities up the road. She's very earthy and sort of granola and maybe a little overweight and tries very hard to be liked.

A NOTE ON INDIAN POKER

At two points in the play, Victor and Murray play a variation of an elementary poker game commonly called "Indian," which calls for each player to take a card and, without looking at it, hold it up to his forehead where the other players can see it. Betting proceeds blindly, each player hoping he has a better card than the others. It's a good game for good bluffers.

The game Victor and Murray play follows the same fundamental logic, except that it is played with five cards per player. Each player takes a card and places it in a headset (a "war bonnet"), and a round of betting follows. The next card is then placed, and another round of betting follows, and so on until all five cards are placed and played, or until someone folds.

A "war bonnet" can be any contraption which can fit snugly around a person's cranium and securely hold five cards. The cards might be slipped into a cloth bandanna, stuck onto a plastic headband or secured with paperclips or clothespins. In any case, it should look pretty stupid. Fake Indian braids attached to the sides would not be inappropriate.

Instead of playing with poker chips, Murray and Victor play with coins. Murray may have a cloth bag or something that he keeps his in, while Victor uses a small jar, which should be made somewhat conspicuous in the first act. Their betting should be gracefully and unobtrusively woven into their conversations.

ACKNOWLEDGEMENTS: This play owes much to the research of Dr. Christy G. Turner, II, and to the wit of Dr. Tom Dabbs. Thanks also to Jayce Tromsness, Melissa Swick, David Avin, Lisa Davis, and everyone at the 1994 South Carolina Playwrights Conference.

"Leda and the Swan" by W. B. Yeats is reprinted with permission of Simon and Schuster, Inc., from *The Poems of W. B. Yeats*, edited by Richard J. Finneran, copyright © 1928, McMillan Publishing Co. Copyright © renewed 1954 by Georgie Yeats.

"The Song of Wandering Aengus" by W. B. Yeats is in the Public Domain.

THE HAMMERSTONE premiered at the Trustus Theatre in Columbia, South Carolina, on August 12, 1994, as the winner of the Trustus Playwrights' Festival. It was produced by Kay Thigpen and directed by Jim Thigpen. The set design was by Brian Riley and the production stage manager was Dorcas Bean. The cast was as follows:

VICTOR	Larry McMullen
MURRAY	Bob Hungerford
WOODY	Steve Harley
GRACE	Barbara Seabrook
KRISTI	Mindi Blackburn
DOTTY	Melissa Swick

Melissa Swick (Dotty) meets her class for the first time in Act I.
Photo: Jocelyn Sanders.

THE HAMMERSTONE

ACT ONE
Prologue

(With house lights still up, perhaps even while members of the audience are still finding their seats, VICTOR Ransome enters and approaches his lectern in the Teaching Area. He looks rather dour and fails in his attempts to contain his contempt for his students—the audience.)

VICTOR Everyone shut up, please. …Everyone shut up, please.

(He waits until his students settle down, perhaps exhorting them once or twice more to:)

VICTOR Shut up, please. Take your seats.

(House lights come down as a special comes up on VICTOR. He holds up a brown, jawless, ancient human skull; in its cranium is a gaping hole.)

VICTOR I am holding in my hand the skull of a young Anasazi male, excavated from the Mancos Valley, where he died about 1250 A.D., a date which coincides with the I said shut *up back there.*

(He waits, calmly, then continues.)

VICTOR …with the collapse of the civilization to which he belonged, which, though it is long dead, may nonetheless teach those among you who actually do the *reading* a thing or two about human nature. I will now hold the skull thus, ask you what we might ascertain, based on the physical evidence, about his death, and thereby about his people, and pause to entertain your learned speculations.

(He turns the skull and waits. And waits.)

VICTOR …That having been done, I will draw your attention to the gaping *hole* in the side of his *head,* which, while it may be a phenomenon occurring naturally in members of *your* generation, was not, in fact, in *his.* …That having been done, I will tell you that his body was completely disarticulated and bore evidence of hammerstone abrasions, which are terms familiar only to those among you who have actually done the *reading,* if in fact any of where are you going?

(He is answered.)

VICTOR   Well sit back down. Nobody's walking out on me today, or I'll hunt
                    you down like wild pigs and kill you. How many of you have read
                    the assignment?

(He surveys the classroom.)

VICTOR   ...I am reminded, as I stand here looking at you all, of the great stone
                    heads perched on the shores of Easter Island, gazing vacantly out to
                    sea. *How did this man die?!*

(He waits.)

VICTOR   ...You're like Helen Keller at the pump, waiting for the miracle.
                    ...Very well. Take out a piece of paper and a Crayola. I see that it's
                    time for a quiz.

(Lights to black. Music comes up: the play begins.)

Scene 1

*(Lights up on Victor's office as music comes down. It is mid-morning. VICTOR is sitting
at his desk, pouring some coins from a jar onto his desk. He will begin shuffling
a deck of cards. MURRAY Stone is standing or walking around the office, deeply
engaged in a diatribe on a topic close to his heart:)*

MURRAY   Sexual *desire*, Victor. Healthy, normal physical attraction. Is a basic,
                    biological *instinct*, it's a fundamental life *force*. It's not a, a, an *idiot*
                    light on your dashboard, it's not a *smoke alarm*, it's not a, a, a—

(He mimes it.)

VICTOR   —spigot—

MURRAY   —a *spigot* you can turn on and off. I *refuse* to, to, to *apologize* for
                    my most, my most *natural*. Normal.

VICTOR   Primal.

MURRAY   *Primal*...impulses. Birds do it. *Bees* do it.

VICTOR	Birds, Murray, do not crash sorority Halloween mixers dressed as Caligula.
MURRAY	I was *invited*.
VICTOR	Bees, Murray, do not go to tanning parlors or splash on Hai Karate.
MURRAY	My point—
VICTOR	If you've come seeking my permission to defile one of your students—
MURRAY	I don't need *anybody's* permission. That's my point.
VICTOR	Then why are you feeling so guilty?
MURRAY	I *don't* feel guilty. I haven't *done* anything. But what if I could, see. What if I *did*.
VICTOR	Meriwether would have you fired in a heartbeat. It's unethical, *and,* I might add, it's undignified. Can't you hear yourself?
MURRAY	It is not *undignified,* it is not *exploiting* my position as an English professor…to be a *male*. And you tell me Meriwether, you tell me the dean *himself,* every time some, some sprightly young thing bends over his desk, begging for a *late withdrawal,* you tell me the same, the same *urges* don't…
VICTOR	…riddle his loins?
MURRAY	It's hypocrisy. Is what it is. It's *oppression*.
VICTOR	It's *obsession*. Cut these. You do this every spring semester. Every time we have one of these talks I feel like going outside and hosing off.

(MURRAY cuts the cards and situates himself across the desk. VICTOR deals the cards, five apiece.)

MURRAY	I'm not an old man. I'm not ready to give up sex. When I am, I'll get married.
VICTOR	And what if *she* heard you, this what's-her-name.

MURRAY   Kristi.

VICTOR   Kristi. What would *she* think of this?

MURRAY   *(Optimistically)* That's the *thing*, see. You never know.

VICTOR   What does she look like?

MURRAY   Ooooo-ho. I can't even. I mean, it's—her skin is like *silk*. Her body, it's a perfect Coke bottle. She sits next to the window and she just, she just—

VICTOR   —fizzes.

MURRAY   Yeah. And her *cheekbones*—

VICTOR   War bonnets.

(They put on their war bonnets, which should look very stupid.)

MURRAY   And her lip does this, this little pouty thing.

VICTOR   Put your glasses on.

(MURRAY puts on his glasses, and the first game of Indian Poker begins. They will place a card in their war bonnets, then another, and so on, silently placing bets after each card by sliding coins to the center of the desk while they talk.)

MURRAY   I can't get her out of my mind! I sit in my office, I'm grading papers, whatever, and she just…walks into my head. And then I'm talking to her, and before you know it—

VICTOR   You're joking.

MURRAY   She's an armed *warhead*. She's a walking estrogen bomb, and she doesn't even *know* it.

VICTOR   Well it's not your job to detonate her.

MURRAY   I can't help it! It's like my imagination just…*takes over*. I can't get anything done anymore. You've had students like that.

(VICTOR takes the three or four cards played thus far from his war bonnet, and then from MURRAY's—in effect folding.)

VICTOR   No, Murray, I haven't, and frankly, I find the whole thing disgusting.

MURRAY   Are you folding?

VICTOR   I'm talking about sex, not just you, though you disgust me too.

MURRAY   Why did you fold?

(VICTOR shuffles the cards as he speaks, and MURRAY rakes in the pot.)

VICTOR   When you think about it, how the hell did mankind stumble over sex in the first place? What in God's name, what in God's *name* inspired the first troglodyte to *plunge* the most repulsive member of his deformed anatomy *into* the person of another troglodyte. *Murder?* Did he think it was a, an *arrowhead?* And how many creatures had he tried to kill that way before deciding to assassinate *her?* Man could just as easily have descended from the musk ox. And whatever happened to racquetball?

(VICTOR has dealt a new game: five cards apiece.)

MURRAY   My back couldn't take it.

VICTOR   Then *how*, Murray, how in God's name could it take a *twenty-year-old girl?* For that matter, is there any part of your body that *could?*

MURRAY   You never know.

VICTOR   …Do you know what the difference is between you and I, Murray?

MURRAY   It's you and *me,* and yes.

VICTOR   I am a clear-headed man.

MURRAY   *(Simultaneously)* —"a clear-headed man." Raise a nickel.

VICTOR   I do not delude myself with sad menopausal fantasies about women younger than the food stuck in my teeth. I have come to terms with later life; I've made my peace with it. And how have I done this? Very simple. I don't think about sex. Ever. In the sixteen years since I booted my worthless shank of a wife out the door, the number of erections I've had you could count on the fingers of one fairly badly mangled hand. This isn't funny. The last one I had, I *slammed* in the shower door.

(MURRAY laughs out loud, and VICTOR allows himself a smile. This is what they do.)

VICTOR   And have you ever met a more clear-headed man? I ask myself.

(By now they have placed all five cards in their war bonnets.)

MURRAY   *(Still chuckling)* Raise a dollar.

VICTOR   You can't raise a dollar.

MURRAY   Why not?

VICTOR   It's a quarter limit.

MURRAY   You raise a dollar sometimes.

VICTOR   When?

MURRAY   I don't know, sometimes! The bet's a dollar. Are you in or what?

(Pause.)

VICTOR   …You're trying to bluff me, Murray.

MURRAY   Maybe.

VICTOR   I've met banana slugs with more cunning. I've met Chihuahuas with more subtlety.

MURRAY   So call.

VICTOR   Look me in the eyes and tell me you're not bluffing.

(MURRAY leans forward confidently; VICTOR peers carefully into his eyes.)

MURRAY   …I'm. Not. Bluffing.

(VICTOR immediately throws a dollar in.)

VICTOR   Call. You've got queen high.

MURRAY   *Dammit!*

(VICTOR looks at his own cards.)

VICTOR   Ha! Two fours!

MURRAY   Dammit, dammit, son-of-a-bitch! How the hell—you know when to fold, you know when I, every time I—

(VICTOR rakes in the coins.)

VICTOR   I'm a clear-headed man.

MURRAY   You've got some system going. No wonder you always want to play this stupid—

VICTOR   My system is I do not distract myself with visions of carbonated nymphets exploding on my lap.

MURRAY   She's not a *nymphet*. This isn't just about sex.

VICTOR   What do you fantasize about, decorating your office?

(MURRAY takes off his glasses, stands, and paces.)

MURRAY   No, this is… I don't know how to say it. She, the way she *smiles* at me, when she talks to me, the things she—I know how this sounds. I'm fifty-four years old, and I'm—

VICTOR   You're fifty-six.

MURRAY   I'm fifty-five, and I swear to God I feel like an idiot schoolboy again.

VICTOR   As well you should.

MURRAY   What do you want, Vic, you want me to live like *you?* You're a *troll*. When was the last time you, you went out in the sunshine or did something frivolous or, or, or had a good hard *laugh* even? You don't even laugh anymore, you know that?

VICTOR   Yes I do.

MURRAY   No you don't. You don't laugh.

VICTOR   Of course I *laugh*.

MURRAY   When?

VICTOR   I don't know! What the hell kind of—

MURRAY   What *happened* to you? You didn't used to be like this. Don't you ever sit here, don't you ever…look. Okay.

(MURRAY goes to the window.)

MURRAY   Look out there. Don't you ever look out there, at all of them, and say…what if?

VICTOR   What if what?

MURRAY   Just what *if*. You know? That's what's so great about this job! Every year, school starts, it's like *life* starts all over again. New people, new energy, like a total transfusion of, of hope or…possibility or, or—it's like you never have to graduate—you don't even have to grow old! —if you just…breathe it in!

VICTOR   You're fifty-*six*.

MURRAY   Well I'll tell you what I don't want. I don't want to end up like Dunaway, over in my department a few years ago? Remember? Before he retired, you know what he had on his office door?

VICTOR   Dunaway did not retire.

MURRAY   He had a little card taped to his door and on the card it said, "I do not think they will sing to *me*."

VICTOR   He didn't retire. He drank himself into oblivion and cried in class about once a week, so Meriwether ran him off.

MURRAY   The *point*, Vic—

VICTOR   He forced him out. He'll come after you too, if you're not careful. He's *looking* for reasons to weed out the senior faculty.

MURRAY   Oh, God.

VICTOR   I'm telling you, he wants to replace us with cheap new assistant professors.

MURRAY   How do you know this?

(Having sat and shuffled, VICTOR calmly deals the cards.)

VICTOR   Because now he's coming after me.

MURRAY   You're paranoid.

VICTOR   Dunaway. Whelan. Autrey. Where are they?

MURRAY   Autrey's gone?

VICTOR   Why haven't I been allowed to teach an upper division course in three years? And why do you think I'm teaching only one course now?

MURRAY   I thought it was release time.

VICTOR   I didn't ask for release time!

(There is a knocking at the door. Pause.)

MURRAY   …Why you?

VICTOR   Put your glasses on.

MURRAY   Why would he come af—

VICTOR   Put your glasses on!

(Pause. MURRAY puts his glasses on, and they begin playing.)

MURRAY   …Somebody knocked on your door.

VICTOR   I heard.

(Another knocking.)

MURRAY   …Want me to get it?

VICTOR   Keep your voice down.

MURRAY   What, are you *hiding*?

(VICTOR does not answer. Another knocking: three times, ominously.)

MURRAY   This feels like "The Monkey's Paw."

VICTOR   Be. Quiet.

(WOODY calls from outside the door.)

WOODY   *(Off)* Anybody in there?

MURRAY   I know that voice. That's Woody Drumm. That you, Woody?

WOODY   *(Off)* ...Uh-huh.

MURRAY   That's only Woody. He's in my lit survey. Have you got him too?

VICTOR   Yes. It's your bet.

MURRAY   Dime.

(Knocking.)

WOODY   *(Off)* Mr. Ransome? You in there?

MURRAY   Nobody's in here, Woody!

VICTOR   Oh, for God's sake, just open the door.

(MURRAY gets up and opens the door, still wearing his war bonnet. WOODY enters.)

WOODY   Hey, Murray. What's that on your head?

MURRAY   This is a war bonnet, Woody.

WOODY   Hey, Mr. Ransome. You got one a' them things too.

(VICTOR hastily removes his.)

MURRAY   Dr. Ransome is an Indian chieftain.

WOODY   Cool. What are you?

MURRAY   I am just a brave.

VICTOR   What do you want, Mr. Drumm?

WOODY   Oh, uh, I heard there was this quiz thing this morning.

VICTOR   Which you were not there for.

WOODY   Well, yeah. But I got a good excuse.

VICTOR   As far as I'm concerned, Mr. Drumm, every excuse I hear, and I hear them all, is excellent.

WOODY   Cool.

VICTOR   It is my policy, however, to accept none of them.

WOODY   …Uhhh.

VICTOR   Since I adopted that policy, I have found that grandmothers miraculously stopped dying, alarm clocks amazingly started functioning, tires never blew out, dogs quit eating homework, in short, the world operated much more smoothly than when I tried to distinguish who was full of shit from who was not.

WOODY   …So I don't…I don't get to take it?

VICTOR   No. Goodbye.

WOODY   Well, I got—wait a minute.

(WOODY searches through his pockets, where he has folded/wadded up pieces of paper.)

WOODY   I got another question, on—that ain't it. On the last one? When you gave it back? I got this—here it is. I got this F.

VICTOR   And?

WOODY   And I don't know why.

VICTOR   Did you read my comments?

WOODY   There wasn't any. There was just this F. I figure that's kinda low, you know?

(He gives the quiz to VICTOR.)

MURRAY   Lowest grade we've got, Woody. Baseball season start yet?

WOODY   Yup. Played Trinidad A & M yesterday. They had a pitcher with one eye.

MURRAY   Any good?

WOODY   Kinda wild. Hit me in the neck once. We play Mesa State next week, y'oughta come out.

VICTOR   *(Looking at the quiz)* Ah yes. I remember this one. One of my personal favorites. In item two, you define "nomads" as "what my dad used to call my balls."

WOODY   ...Well, he did.

VICTOR   In number five, you define "foragers" as "people who sign other people's names."

WOODY   Is that wrong?

VICTOR   And in number nine you claim a "homo erectus" is—well, I can't even bring myself to read it.

(VICTOR tosses the quiz on his desk; MURRAY picks it up to look at it, and winces.)

WOODY   Well, the thing is, Mr. Ransome, I need a B.

VICTOR   ...You need a B.

WOODY   Yeah. On accounta baseball.

VICTOR   This is not the mall, Mr. Drumm. This is not the customer service desk. I don't make exchanges here. You break it, you bought it. The customer is never right. That's what the *thing* is.

WOODY   ...But. If I don't get like a two-oh? The coach, he said there's—

VICTOR   Mr. Drumm, do you know what a gene pool is?

WOODY   ...Uh, no.

VICTOR   Well, I'd say yours was about ankle deep and had scum floating in it.

MURRAY   Vic—

WOODY   Mr. Ransome, if I don't play baseball—

VICTOR   Would you like me to change it?

WOODY   …Would ya?

VICTOR   Certainly.

WOODY   *(To MURRAY)* Whoa, what a guy.

(VICTOR marks the paper and hands it back to WOODY.)

WOODY   …A "G"?

VICTOR   For "gonad."

WOODY   …Oh man. Oh *man*! This sucks! You can't *do* this!

MURRAY   Easy, Woody.

WOODY   You can't do this, you asshole! I got *rights*!

(He pounds his fist on the desk and looms over VICTOR.)

VICTOR   Let me explain something to you, Mr. Drumm.

(VICTOR calmly removes a revolver from a desk drawer and places it on the desk. WOODY freezes.)

VICTOR   I am the professor here. All power flows toward *me*. Academically speaking, I have complete and unbridled dominion, and as long as you are in my class, you are hostage to my will. You have no more rights here than if you were in a Turkish prison.

MURRAY   Jesus, Vic!

VICTOR   I can even *kill* you if I want. I *got* tenure!

WOODY   …But…Mr. Ransome—

VICTOR   It's *Dr.* Ransome. And I'm not an asshole. I'm anal retentive. Nobody bothers to make that distinction anymore.

(WOODY looks at MURRAY, who shrugs and shakes his head. WOODY then runs out of the room, leaving the door open. Pause.)

MURRAY   …You know, I'm pretty sure the administration frowns on our packing firearms.

VICTOR   Well then the administration should stop admitting lower primates.

MURRAY   It's not loaded, is it?

VICTOR   Hell yes it's loaded. Last year one of them came in here with a *brick*.

MURRAY   Perhaps if you quit *abusing* them.

VICTOR   What was I supposed to do, *reason* with him? He couldn't butter toast without courting a cerebral hemorrhage.

MURRAY   He's having a hard time, and he's a little high-strung.

VICTOR   He's an evolutionary U-turn.

MURRAY   Has he told you his story? His father died last year; it's the worst thing I've ever heard.

VICTOR   I'm devastated for him, but I'm not his therapist.

MURRAY   It wouldn't kill you to cut him some slack. He hasn't got much to look forward to. This place is his one chance to have something good in his life.

VICTOR   I have standards, Murray. I am a *professor*.

MURRAY   That doesn't give you the right to demoralize him.

(Pause. VICTOR puffs himself up.)

VICTOR   …*Don't* you presume to read me my *rights*!

MURRAY   I'm not, I'm just saying—

VICTOR   Don't you sit there and tell me how to run *my life* while you look up *skirts* and throw yourself *prostate* to your deluded adolescent pipe-dreams! *I've* been teaching for almost forty years!

MURRAY	*(Smiling)* I know.

VICTOR   I was a Fulbright Fellow!   Dr. Kum-bay-yah, professor of Fuzzy Studies! *I* have been an officer in *three* honor societies! And here, what is this? Do you see this?

(He means a plaque on the wall.)

MURRAY   Professor of the Year.

VICTOR   Professor of the Year, 1985. And in 1978, what is this?

(He takes a book from his shelf.)

MURRAY   That's your book, yes.

VICTOR   That's my book, yes. One of the best books ever written on ancient southwest culture! *This* is who I am, Murray. This is my vindication, my foothold!

(MURRAY begins chuckling, which makes VICTOR even angrier.)

VICTOR   Is this funny? No. No. In the ocean of knowledge, Murray, I am a gill net and you are a Popeil Pocket Fisherman!

MURRAY   *(Chuckling)* It's "prostrate."

VICTOR   …What?

MURRAY   "Prostrate." You said "prostate." That's a gland.

VICTOR   I did not say prostate.

MURRAY   You get there through your butt.

VICTOR   I did not say prostate! I know the difference between prostrate and prostate and I did not say prostate!

MURRAY   *(Chuckling harder)* Okay! Okay! …Jeez, I'm sorry!

VICTOR   …No you're not. You don't understand me anymore than these… savages do… God. God, I hate this place.

MURRAY   Eh, c'mon. It's not so bad.

VICTOR   Most of our students have S.A.T. scores lower than their cholesterol counts. They come here from dirt farms and oil fields and dying little towns with quaint little names like...*Armadillo.* They don't want knowledge. They don't even want information. All they want is to find something to *hump,* preferably one of their own cousins, so they can all go back to Armadillo and perpetuate their septic bloodline.

MURRAY   So it's not Harvard.

VICTOR   Harvard? It's not even *UTEP.* Our mascot is the *Aggie,* Murray. An Aggie is a hunch-backed, toothless, water-headed agrarian boy with both eyes on the same side of his face, holding a hoe. It's a granite quarry. Schools of tuna have higher admission standards.

MURRAY   It's a typical, small, under-funded public college. And I happen to enjoy our students. What they lack in preparation, they make up for in—

VICTOR   —in bewilderment! I spend the first day of every semester checking for opposable *thumbs.* This morning, my alleged students, you should have seen them. A whole classroom: stricken with rigor mortis. My words... filled the air like nerve gas. I killed them Murray, killed them all.

MURRAY   So you had a bad day.

VICTOR   No, that was *good* day. *Bad* days they escape before I can kill them... This can't go on, Murray. I can't do this much longer.

MURRAY   So what does that mean?

VICTOR   I don't know. I've got to do something. And I've got to do it before Meriwether does.

MURRAY   It's your imagination, Vic.

VICTOR   No. He's coming for me. I can feel it.

MURRAY   Well, you've got tenure. Shoot him.

(GRACE Berger appears in the door. She carries a paper plate full of bite-sized fried eggplant. MURRAY collects his coins from the desk.)

GRACE   Yoo hooooo! It's meeeee!

VICTOR   *(Grim, trapped)* Ah. Grace Berger. What a surprise.

GRACE   I brought you some eggplant!

VICTOR   How very nice. Miss Berger, this is Dr. Stone; he's in our English department. Miss Berger is in my Anthropology class.

GRACE   Beannacht libh! That's Irish!

MURRAY   Really? What does it mean?

GRACE   I have no idea. Care for some eggplant?

MURRAY   Uh, no, actually, I've got to—

VICTOR   Stay, Murray… Is there something I can do for you, Miss Berger? I was just about to, uh—

(He shuffles papers, tries to look occupied.)

GRACE   I won't keep you, Victor. I just had a question. There was something I was going to ask you. I can come back later, though, if—

VICTOR   No, later's, uh, bad for me, actually. Ask your question, Miss Berger. Murray, *stay.*

(MURRAY stays.)

GRACE   Well, let me see. —I'm not an actual student, you see. I'm not working on a degree. I just like to keep my mind occupied. I don't want to be one of those women who loses her mind in her declining years. Especially now that…now that I'm all alone.

MURRAY   Very admirable.

GRACE   *(Sadly)* My son left, you know. He went to Los Angeles. Would you like to see a picture?

(GRACE rummages in her purse for a packet of pictures.)

MURRAY   Actually, I've got class in fifteen—

VICTOR   *No,* you want to *see* this.

GRACE   Here, here he is. He wants to be a movie actor.

MURRAY   Mmmm. Very dashing. That's a handsome mustache.

GRACE   Oh, that isn't a mustache. He has a cleft palate. His name is Fergus. That's Irish!

MURRAY   *(Contemplating)* "…Fergus…Berger."

(He and VICTOR exchange a look.)

GRACE   Isn't he wonderful! Do you have children, Dr. Stone?

MURRAY   No, I uh, never married, actually.

GRACE   Oh, neither did I. Fergus is a bastard. His father was a wounded naval officer I met at the VA hospital. We had a fling.

VICTOR   Miss Berger was a nurse.

GRACE   I've always had a tremendous weakness for anyone in pain, you know. And Wallace, that was his name, he was in *tremendous* pain.

(She turns to another picture.)

GRACE   This is him, the day I met him. That's a Purple Heart on his gown.

MURRAY   Uh-huh. And did he play football?

GRACE   Oh, no, that's a colostomy bag. Poor thing, his body was like a salmon run. And here's what killed him.

MURRAY   A…flounder?

GRACE   *(Looking carefully)* …It does look like one, doesn't it. Actually it's his liver. I'll never forget the last words he spoke, before he slipped into repose. He looked up, out of his good eye, and he said, "Leo, Leo, take good care of our Angel of Mercy."

MURRAY   And who was Leo?

GRACE   I have no idea. Wallace had a series of strokes. He would speak to all kinds of people I couldn't see. That doesn't mean they weren't *there*, of course. I'm a firm believer in the other side, you know. I once had an out-of-body experience. I saw my own naked body from across the bathroom, as if through a haze.

MURRAY   ...Perhaps it was the mirror.

GRACE   *(Struck by this)* ...Hmmm!

VICTOR   Miss Berger—

GRACE   I *was* on a prescription at the time. How very strange!

VICTOR   Miss Berger, I recall you had a question about the class.

GRACE   You may call me Grace. —He always calls me Miss Berger.

MURRAY   He treats all his students with the same dignity and respect.

GRACE   He's a good professor.

VICTOR   So your question, then?

GRACE   Oh, yes. Well. Actually, it's not about the class.

VICTOR   It's not.

GRACE   No, it's...of a more...personal nature.

(Pause. She looks uncomfortable.)

MURRAY   *Yup.* Gotta go teach that class.

VICTOR   Murray!

MURRAY   Lovely meeting you, Grace. Hope we'll be seeing more of you around here.

GRACE   Thank you!

MURRAY   I'll bet she'd like to see your arrowhead, Vic.

(And he exits. Pause.)

GRACE   ...You have an arrowhead, Victor?

VICTOR   ...Nnnnot anymore. I broke it.

(Pause.)

GRACE   Oh... Well. Here we are again.

VICTOR   Yyyyes.

GRACE   You know, I was going to tell you. My cat, Muffy. She died.

VICTOR   I am deeply sorry.

GRACE   She was seventeen. That's very, very old, for a cat. And she was never fixed. I never had her fixed.

(She lets the news hang in the air. VICTOR nods stupidly.)

GRACE   But now she's dead. She'd been having seizures, you know, and foaming at the mouth, for quite some time. The veterinarian said it had something to do with a blow to the head. I think it's because she was blind. She'd just *bash* into things. I put all the furniture in the garage, but she still just *bashed* into the walls. She had scabs on her scalp, where all the fur had rubbed off. They would *seep,* you know, all over the carpeting.

VICTOR   *(Helpfully)* There but for the grace of God.

GRACE   But I don't blame her. No, no. She was all the company I had, since...since my son ran off.

VICTOR   Again, I weep for you, Miss Berger.

GRACE   I have my plants, of course. I talk to them, and give them names, but—

VICTOR   Probably just isn't the same.

GRACE   No. No, it just isn't. But they are all I have. My plants, my books, my pictures...and one dead Muffy. ...Victor?

VICTOR   ...Yes, Miss Berger.

(Pause. GRACE sighs.)

GRACE   ...Thank you for seeing me, Victor. I hope you have a nice day.

(*She stands, goes to the door, looks sadly over her shoulder, and exits, leaving the door open.*

VICTOR sits silently, then picks up the plate bearing the eggplant, stands, and drops it in the trash can. Then, as he closes the door, the lights fade to black. Musical bridge to next scene —perhaps something heroic, like Wagner.)

Scene 2

(*Special up on the Teaching Area, sans lectern, as music reaches a crescendo and then is silent. MURRAY is addressing his class—the audience—perhaps while standing on a stool. He is truly an engaging speaker, a storyteller at heart, which makes up for his tendency to sensationalize.*)

MURRAY So here he is, the great god Jupiter, standing on a cloud, high up over the Roman countryside, when suddenly, he hears…the voice of a young girl—singing! So he looks down, and, *damn*, there she *is*. Bathing in the river. Totally…*naked*. Her name is Leda and she's, she's *incredible*! He wants her! He's got to *have* her! Are you with me so far? …Okay! So! He calls Venus over, the goddess of love, and he says, "Venus, sistah, I *need* this girl." And Venus says, "Gangsta, you got eight wives already!" But he's tearing his hair out—"I *got* to have this girl! I got to!" So Venus, this is her job, she comes up with a plan. She changes Jupiter into a swan. She changes herself into an eagle. And she pretends to chase him around the sky.

(*If MURRAY was standing on the stool, he now jumps down.*)

MURRAY So here's Leda, standing there in the river like Miss September, and she hears this squawking, and she looks up! And there's this swan! Terrified out of his mind! Heading straight for her! She sees the eagle chasing him, so she holds out her hands like this, and *yoowww*! He flies straight into her arms! And while she's holding the poor, trembling creature against her bosom, his eyes kinda go—

(*He leers.*)

MURRAY —and *vooom*!

(He segues seamlessly into the Yeats' "Leda and the Swan," which he recites dramatically and engagingly from memory.)

MURRAY   "A sudden blow: the great wings beating still
                  Above the staggering girl, her thighs caressed
                  By the dark webs, her nape caught in his bill,
                  He holds her helpless breast upon his breast.

                  How can those terrified vague fingers push
                  The feathered glory from her loosening thighs?
                  …And how can body, laid in that white rush,
                  But feel…the strange heart…beating…where it lies?"

(Blackout. End scene.)

Scene 3

(Warm lights up on Murray's office. MURRAY has just stood up from his desk chair. In his open doorway stands a beautiful girl: it is, of course, KRISTI. She wears sexy clothes. Oddly, there becomes evident in her voice just a touch of Blanche Dubois.)

MURRAY   "…Drop my class? What do you mean, drop my class?"

KRISTI   "Yes, sir. I'm sorry."

MURRAY   "But—but—but… Kristi! *Why?* Aren't you…*enjoying* it? Is it—"

KRISTI   "Oh yes, I am sir. I'm enjoying it *very* much. I'm just…I can't tell you, I'm—please, it's—"

(MURRAY moves around her to close the door, and she moves into the center of the office. Romantic music will gradually insinuate itself beneath their conversation.)

MURRAY   "I don't understand! Has something happened? Did—"

KRISTI   "Oh, no sir. It's…I don't know if I understand it myself. I'm not, I shouldn't even be…"

MURRAY   "Please, Kristi, I, I want to know. What is it?"

KRISTI	"...Well. Today, for instance. That poem, by William Butler Yeats."
MURRAY	"Didn't you enjoy it?"
KRISTI	"*Enjoy* it? That poor, young girl, being taken, being *ravished* by that, that—"
MURRAY	"Did it...offend you or sca—"
KRISTI	"No, no, it, it...I don't know how to—"
MURRAY	"Please, you can tell me."
KRISTI	"It suddenly seemed as if she was...she was..."
MURRAY	"She was, she was what?"
KRISTI	"It made me so confused, so uncomfortable, the conflicting passions, the swan—"
MURRAY	"What about it? Did it—"
KRISTI	"At first it was like a, a bird of prey, Dr. Stone, at once so brutal and—"
MURRAY	"Call me Murray."
KRISTI	"And then it was a swan, a beautiful, majestic thing! And the union, the union between them, it, it..."
MURRAY	"Yes, it, go on, it—"
KRISTI	"It was as if *she* were, it suddenly *struck* me that...she was—"
MURRAY	"*What*! She *what*?"
KRISTI	"—she was *enjoying* it! As if—"
MURRAY	"Good! Yes!"
KRISTI	"—as if *she* were the predator, taken suddenly by the power beating in her own breast! And the swan was just, was just a...a *symbol* of her own unbridled sensuality!"

MURRAY   "Really?"

KRISTI   "Her own primal passions, yearning to breathe free! Oh, Murray, I...I think I understand the poem!"

MURRAY   "Yes! Yes, you *do!*"

KRISTI   "And it was all so, so natural—"

(They begin drawing nearer one another.)

MURRAY   "So natural, yes, so pure—"

KRISTI   "—yes! That they should be lovers! Passionate—"

MURRAY   "—desperate—"

KRISTI   "—lovers! And it's not sinful or wrong—"

MURRAY   "—no, no, it's—"

KRISTI   "—it's a secret love, a love she dared not speak nor dream of!"

(They are nearly upon one another. The music is up full, and climaxing.)

KRISTI   "My God, Murray! I am afraid I can no longer keep separate my feelings for you as my professuh—and my feelings for you as a, as a *may-un!*"

MURRAY   ...Nnnnnnno. No. That's just, this is stupid.

(And so MURRAY breaks the spell: the music suddenly crashes and the lights change to signify that this has been his fantasy in action. Quotation marks indicate when they fall back into it.)

MURRAY   Go, uh, go back a little.

KRISTI   *(Backtracking, adjusting her pose)* "And it was all so natural!"

MURRAY   Farther.

KRISTI   *(Again)* "Enjoy it? That poor young girl—"

MURRAY   Good. Okay. Undo your button.

KRISTI   "—being taken, being simply ravished by that—it made me so confused, Murray!"

(Abruptly, there comes a knock at the door.)

KRISTI   "The conflicting passions! The swan, at first, a bird of prey, and then just a, just a—"

MURRAY   "—a swan," keep going, do another one.

(She undoes another, and keeps going.)

KRISTI   *(Pouring it on)* "—a beautiful, majestic thing, and the, the, the union between them—"

(Another knock.)

KRISTI   "—it was as if she were *enjoying* it, as if" are you gonna get that?

(She breaks the mood completely.)

MURRAY   They'll go away. Keep—

KRISTI   I lost my place.

MURRAY   The union, the whatever, she was—

(WOODY calls from outside.)

WOODY   *(Off)* Anybody in there?

MURRAY   Shit.

(More knocking.)

WOODY   *(Off)* Hello? Murray?

MURRAY   Just. *Dammit.* This'll just.

(Putting her, as it were, on hold, MURRAY goes to the door and opens it. WOODY enters.)

MURRAY   Yes, Woody.

WOODY   Hey, Murray. You talkin' to someone?

MURRAY   No, Woody. Come in.

WOODY   I thought I heard you talkin' to someone.

MURRAY   There isn't anyone here, is there?

(WOODY looks around. KRISTI stands or sits somewhere out of the way.)

WOODY   …Uh, no.

MURRAY   What can I do for you?

WOODY   Well, it's like, I'm not doin' so hot in your class, what is it.

MURRAY   Literature.

WOODY   Yeah. Like on the last essay? I didn't do so hot on it. I was gonna ask you what—wait a minute.

(He is digging through his pockets for his essay.)

MURRAY   The essay about A *Streetcar Named Desire?*

WOODY   Here it—no, wait a—

MURRAY   I remember that one, Woody. I gave you a D+. You turned it in late, and you didn't follow directions again.

WOODY   Here it is. D+.

(He presents MURRAY with a crumpled essay.)

MURRAY   You wrote about your father again, didn't you.

WOODY   That Stanley guy reminded me of my dad.

MURRAY   Yes, and so did Richard III, which is really very disturbing.

WOODY   But you gave me a C+ on that one.

MURRAY   I cut you some slack on that one Woody. Because I *like* you. But look: as painful as your father's death was for you, and I know it was very painful, don't you think it would help you to, to *heal* if you quit writing every assignment about *him?*

WOODY   ...I ain't thought about it that way.

MURRAY   They're also becoming very painful for me to *read*.

WOODY   Well, the thing is, though, I gotta get a B, on accounta baseball—

MURRAY   *(Overlapping)* —baseball, I know, and I sympathize but...well, look. Do you remember the day we sat right here, and we talked about right words and wrong words? How you, you can't go around pounding square pegs into round holes?

WOODY   Yeah. That was important.

MURRAY   Yes, it was. All right. Here, in your essay, after your father has been shot...you say you tried to perform "VCR" on him.

WOODY   It didn't work.

MURRAY   I know. He went into what you refer to as "kodiak arrest."

WOODY   His heart stopped.

MURRAY   I know, and I'm sorry. And here, after he died, you refer to "the *urine* in which we put his ashes."

WOODY   Is that wrong?

MURRAY   It's *urn*, Woody. *Cardiac.* These are square pegs, they're the wrong words.

WOODY   ...I'm sorry, Murray.

MURRAY   You don't have to apologize. These are, these are simple listening errors.

WOODY   No, I'm a idiot.

MURRAY   No, you're not.

WOODY   Yeah I am. I gotta call and tell my mom.

MURRAY   No you don't.

WOODY   I'm failin' all my classes—'cept Bio. I gotta tell her I'm comin' back to the farm.

MURRAY   Now, come on, you're—

WOODY   *(Getting worked up)* I hate that place, Murray! Ain't nothin' there, nothin' but *beans*! You know how many bean farms there are in Clyburn County? Far as the eye can see, *beans*! You know what we ate? Bean stew, bean casserole, bean sandwiches, spaghetti with beans, three-bean-salad, 'cept we only had two!

MURRAY   Woody—

WOODY   Tried growin' artichokes. Tried cabbage, barley, corn, rutabagas. Hell, we even tried *ostrich* farming! Kept steppin' in the rabbit holes and breakin' their legs. So we had ostrich burgers, *with beans*!

MURRAY   Woody—

WOODY   *(Very worked up)* I can't go back there, Murray! Not after what happened! I promised my mom I'd take her and the dogs and that jar we got my daddy in away from there, 'cept I can't, 'cause I ain't ever gonna play pro ball, 'cause I ain't gonna get a B, 'cause I'm—

MURRAY   *Woody!*

WOODY   —a idiot!

MURRAY   You're getting carried away again.

WOODY   I'm sorry, Murray.

MURRAY   No, no, ummm…look. Uhh. Okay. Here.

(MURRAY picks up the essay, marks something on it, and hands it to WOODY.)

WOODY   *(Reading)* …"B–"?

MURRAY   Yes.

WOODY   …Thanks, Murray!

MURRAY   Quite all right. Thanks for popping by.

(WOODY heads out the door, and MURRAY turns to KRISTI, but wheels back around when:)

WOODY   Oh, uh, look, 'long as I'm here, I gotta question about this next assignment, on the poems and stuff? It says I gotta—wait a minute.

(He starts digging through his pockets for the assignment; MURRAY picks up a paper from his desk and hands it to him. WOODY reads it.)

WOODY   Thanks. Okay. It says, "Describe your impressions of the poetry of William Butler Yeast."

MURRAY   *Yeats.* What is your question.

WOODY   My question is…like, what do you mean, *impressions?* I mean, like, what do you *mean?*

MURRAY   Uh, well, your…*reactions,* Woody. Your *responses,* how do the poems *strike* you, how do they *affect* you?

WOODY   …That's what "impressions" means, huh?

MURRAY   Yes.

WOODY   Oh. Well. I ain't got any.

MURRAY   Not a one?

WOODY   Damndest stuff I ever read.

MURRAY   Uh-huh. And our discussions in class haven't helped any?

WOODY   Well, I kinda missed a few days in there, on accounta baseball.

MURRAY   *(Overlapping)* —baseball, I know.

WOODY   And there's this guy, on the team? He's got this other perfessor? And he said they could write about their favorite sports hero.

MURRAY   Uh-huh.

WOODY   So it'd be okay if I wrote about Alex Rodriguez?

MURRAY   No, Woody. Just this once, you have to follow my instructions. You have to look at the poems and write about your impressions.

WOODY   But I don't *have* any.

MURRAY   Yes you *do*! How can you *not*?

WOODY   I don't *know*! I *tried*, but I *don't*!

(Pause. MURRAY is befuddled, but then comes up with a plan.)

MURRAY   ...Listen, Woody. If you went out to play baseball. If you went onto the field without, say...your *head*, could you play your position?

WOODY   ...Probably not.

MURRAY   This is what I'm talking about. This is what you're telling me when you say you have no impressions: "I don't have a head." Do you see?

WOODY   Uh, no.

MURRAY   I have, in effect, just hit a long fly ball to you in deep right. You're standing there, got your glove on, all the best intentions, but no head. What are you going to do?

WOODY   ...I don't know.

MURRAY   Are you going to catch it?

WOODY   Probably not.

MURRAY   Why not?

WOODY   *(Piecing it together)* ...Because I...I don't have a head.

MURRAY   A run will score, Woody. The coach will pull you from the game. That's like an F, Woody, the coach is giving you an F.

WOODY   Oh, man.

MURRAY   He doesn't want any headless outfielders on his team. It's bad strategy, and it freaks out the fans.

WOODY   This is wild.

MURRAY   Your batting average will *plummet*, Woody. You'll get struck out by twelve-year-old girls. You won't be able to run the bases without a specially-trained dog!

WOODY   Oh *man*!

MURRAY   You'll frighten the batboy, Woody. Your teammates will call you Ichabod and go to Pizza Hut without you, and you won't even know it! You'll have to *staple* your hat to your *shirt*, Woody!

WOODY   But—

MURRAY   *(Big finale)* And what about the cheerleaders? Are they going to want to go *out* with you? Are they going to want to *neck* with you when you haven't even *got* one? You're going to have to give 'em up, Woody! You're going to have to give up cheerleaders and baseball and school and *everything else,* because there's just no future for you *anywhere* if you *have no head*!

WOODY   *(Horrified)* But I have a head! I do!

MURRAY   Where? Where is it?

WOODY   It's *here*! It's here, on my *body*!

(WOODY grabs his head and pulls it toward MURRAY. Pause. MURRAY reconsiders.)

MURRAY   …My God. So it is. You have a very fine head, Woody. It's like a Rottweiler.

(It gradually dawns on WOODY: he chuckles.)

WOODY   …Huh. Huh huh huh.

MURRAY   See there? How about that.

WOODY   Huh huh. You were playin' a joke on me.

MURRAY   Yes I was. You're even getting a bald spot.

WOODY   I am?

MURRAY   Yes you are. And I think that clears up the whole thing, don't you? You were right, and I was wrong.

WOODY   Huh huh huh. *Whoa.*

MURRAY   All right then. Good man. Is there anything else?

(WOODY thinks hard.)

WOODY   …I don't think so.

MURRAY   Okay. Then go write that paper!

WOODY   Okay!

MURRAY   And keep your head on straight!

WOODY   Okay! Thanks Murray!

(And WOODY exits. Pause.)

MURRAY   *(To himself)* …I should make much more money than I do.

(He rubs his hands, looks at KRISTI, and re-groups.)

MURRAY   Okay. Once more, from the top!

KRISTI   All the way back?

MURRAY   From the top! A soft rapping at the door…

(She sighs, raps on the open door, and falls into her character. Different music comes up.)

KRISTI   "Dr. Stone?"

MURRAY   "Kristi, what a surprise! Come in! What can I do for you?"

KRISTI   "Dr. Stone, I'm afraid I'm going to have to drop your class."

MURRAY   "Drop my class? What do you mean, drop my class?"

(Blackout. End scene. Music continues as bridge to next scene.)

Larry McMullen (Victor) insults his students at the top of Act I.
Photo: Jocelyn Sanders.

Scene 4

(Lights up on Victor's office. It is a day or two later. VICTOR is at his window, looking out. When that picture is established, someone knocks at his door, and the music comes down. He doesn't move. More knocking. He doesn't move. Then there is a jangling of keys in the lock, and the door opens to reveal DOTTY Dunbar, casually dressed and in fact rather earthy. She's wearing glasses and has an armful of books and keys in her hand. VICTOR has not turned.)

DOTTY   Oh, I'm sorry, I didn't think anybody was—

VICTOR   I've already emptied my wastebasket.

DOTTY   Oh, no, I'm not the custodian. Are you Dr. Ransome?

(VICTOR turns.)

VICTOR   …I am.

DOTTY   Hi! Excellent to meet you! Dotty Dunbar! Dorothy, actually, but I thought that sounded too geeky.

(She puts her books down on the floor or somewhere, and shakes his hand enthusiastically. He is baffled.)

DOTTY   At school they call me Dee Dee, but that's too unprofessional, so I'm going with Dotty. Or Dot. I haven't decided. What do *you* think?

VICTOR   Who are you, and how is it you have a key to my office?

DOTTY   Oh, uh, Dean Meriwether gave it to me, so I could bring th—

VICTOR   *Meriwether…gave…?*

DOTTY   Yes sir… I'm *Dotty Dunbar.*

(VICTOR is still baffled.)

DOTTY   …You know. Your new TA?

VICTOR   …My…TA.

(DOTTY makes one or two trips into the hall as she speaks, and comes back with more books or boxes.)

DOTTY   Yes, sir. I'm really looking forward to working with you! It's going to be an excellent semester! I won't take up much room. All I need is a desk, a bookcase, and maybe a little wall space. I just bought a *great* Georgia O'Keeffe, and a Navajo rug to go with it, and I've got this little stereo thingy, if that's okay? I read an article in the *Chronicle,* about how music helps, you know, *soothe* students who perceive the academic environment as hostile?

VICTOR   What do you mean, my...*TA*?

DOTTY   ...Your...Teaching Assistant.

VICTOR   Yes, I know what TA means. I don't have one.

(DOTTY digs in her pocket or somewhere for a letter, unfolds it, and checks it.)

DOTTY   ...Are you the same Dr. Ransome who teaches Anthro 150?

VICTOR   What is that?

DOTTY   It's the letter from the dean. He said I'm supposed—

(VICTOR snatches it from her and reads it.)

DOTTY   ...I'm supposed to help you teach it. Starting next week... And like I said, I'm really looking forward to it. This is an excellent break for me. I've been doing a lot of thinking recently about heuristics and epistemology, and whether teachers are, like, gatekeepers or housekeepers—

VICTOR   *(Reading)* "—*share* an *office*"?

DOTTY   Yes, sir. I *did* think it was a little odd, coming in the middle of the semester like this, but the dean said—

VICTOR   This is how it begins, isn't it.

DOTTY   ...Sir?

VICTOR   ...Just...just a minute.

(He picks up the phone and punches four numbers.)

VICTOR   How old are you?

DOTTY　　　　Twenty-seven.

VICTOR　　　You're still just a graduate student.

DOTTY　　　　Yyyyes, sir. I'm starting my disserta—

VICTOR　　　And you've never even taught before, have you.

DOTTY　　　　Nnnnot exactly *taught*, as in, to a *class*, but I was hoping you could—

(VICTOR waves for silence as the phone rings in Murray's office, and the lights come up there. MURRAY is further engaged in his fantasy with KRISTI.)

KRISTI　　　　"A secret love, a love she dared not speak nor dream of! Sweet mother of God, Murray, tell me you feel the way I do!"

(The phone rings.)

MURRAY　　　"But Kristi, I—"

KRISTI　　　　"I know it's wrong, but I can contain my feelin's no longer!"

(The phone rings.)

KRISTI　　　　"Tell me Murray! Tell me or answer the phone!"

(And so the spell is broken.)

MURRAY　　　Mmmmrrraaaaaagh! Dammit!

(MURRAY answers the phone; he and VICTOR speak to one another.)

MURRAY　　　*Hallo!*

VICTOR　　　Murray, come to my office. I need you to see something.

MURRAY　　　Kinda busy here, Vic.

VICTOR　　　It's important, Murray. The eagle has landed.

MURRAY　　　What eagle?

VICTOR　　　Listen. The train is leaving. Ahead of schedule.

MURRAY	…The dog howls at midnight.
VICTOR	*Murray.*
MURRAY	Kinda busy here, Vic.
VICTOR	This is not my imagination, Murray. Do the letters "TA" mean anything to you?
MURRAY	Tits and ass. What, the Angel of Mercy show up braless or something?
VICTOR	Murray, for—
MURRAY	Kind of busy here, Vic, but if you want my permission, I say go for it.
VICTOR	…Thank you. You've been very helpful.

(VICTOR hangs up, then MURRAY. For a moment, lights stay up on both offices. VICTOR rubs his face, and sighs.)

MURRAY	Okay! Where were we?
KRISTI	*(Bored)* "Tell me, or send me away forever."
MURRAY	Back up a bit.

(KRISTI groans. Lights out on MURRAY's office. Pause. DOTTY breaks the silence in VICTOR's office.)

DOTTY	…Dr. Ransome, if you have any questions about my qualifications, I'd be happy to—
VICTOR	Your qualifications.
DOTTY	Yes, sir. I mean, I haven't taught before, and I'm still working on my people skills, but my grades are—
VICTOR	Pick up that skull.
DOTTY	…Pick it up?
VICTOR	Pick it up. Is it Anasazi or Mesoamerican?

DOTTY ...I don't know, I—

VICTOR It's Anasazi. How did he die?

DOTTY ...It's hard to say, he—

VICTOR Tell me how he died!

DOTTY From a blow to the head!

VICTOR How do you know?!

DOTTY There's a big hole in it!

(DOTTY is getting anxious. When DOTTY gets anxious, she twirls her hair or fidgets.)

VICTOR That could have happened after.

DOTTY I don't know! I need more—

VICTOR Then *look* at it!

DOTTY Dr. Ransome, please, I don't—

VICTOR See that book? Pick it up. That's my book.

(Without putting down the skull, DOTTY picks up the book.)

DOTTY (Reverential) I know, sir.

VICTOR As far as ancient southwest culture is concerned, Miss *Qualifications*, that's the *Bible*. I suggest you read it.

DOTTY I have, sir, twice.

VICTOR One of the best books ever written on the subject. I put eleven *years* into it. Miss *Graduate Student*. And look: do you know what this scar is from?

(He lifts his pant leg; he's got a scar on his calf.)

DOTTY A rattlesnake.

VICTOR A rattlesnake, that's right.

DOTTY   You were—

(She opens the book to the first few pages, juggling the skull as she does so, and reads anxiously.)

DOTTY   —you were "sifting carefully through some collapsed vigas at Pueblo Bonito, when out from beneath one emerged a—"

VICTOR   —six-foot western—

DOTTY   *(Reading, overlapping)* "—five-foot western diamond-back rattlesnake, which plunged its fangs into my lower-right leg."

VICTOR   Twice!

DOTTY   "Twice."

VICTOR   I nearly gave my life for that book.

DOTTY   "I nearly gave my life for this book." …It's in your preface, sir.

VICTOR   I *know* that. I'll tell you something else, something that's not in my goddamn preface. I gave up my *marriage* for that book.

DOTTY   Your marriage?

VICTOR   She thought it was…*boring.* Retrieving forgotten civilizations from oblivion, unwinding the death shroud of *time* from lost humanity—I was…boring!

DOTTY   That's amazing, sir.

VICTOR   And what was *her* contribution to mankind? How did she leave her mark? …As a, as a *hair* model. What is that, a *hair* model! Selling *shampoo* and *hair* color in those idiot *women's* magazines. In our haste to get married, we hadn't realized how shallow she was.

DOTTY   I'm sorry.

VICTOR.   *This* is what I'm up against. Still. Every single *day.* These students, they're no goddamn different. They don't care about anything but getting theirs, getting off and getting *out.*

DOTTY   Agreed, sir. And that's why teaching, I think that's the challenge, to—

VICTOR   They're not interested in anything that happened before this morning, unless you make it into some TV movie with car chases and gunfights and enormous naked breasts!

DOTTY   Understood. And that's why we—

VICTOR   If you want to get their attention, Miss *People Skills,* you'll have to drive through a wall, rip off your shirt, and *shoot* yourself in the *head!*

DOTTY   *(Aghast)* …I appreciate the advice, sir.

(VICTOR moves to the window again, and darkens. Pause.)

VICTOR   …And sometimes…it will occur to you…that you have spent your life…fooling yourself. You've made no difference, you were…*wrong.* And you will ask yourself…why you ever got into it…at all.

(Pause. He stands looking out the window, desolate. DOTTY notices something about the skull in her arms, and examines it.)

DOTTY   …There's a cut along the anterior cranium. Discoloration above the temporal line.

VICTOR   *(Without turning)* …Yes.

DOTTY   Signs of…pot polish. Hammerstone abrasions.

VICTOR   …Go on.

DOTTY   What condition was the body in?

VICTOR   Disarticulated, almost completely.

DOTTY   And the long bones?

VICTOR   Broken and burned.

DOTTY   So it probably wasn't buried.

VICTOR   We found it in a trash midden.

DOTTY   Then it could only be one thing.

(VICTOR turns.)

VICTOR   Namely?

DOTTY   Somebody cooked him up and ate him.

VICTOR   Yes! Exactly!

DOTTY   This is from Mancos! You wrote about him in your book.

VICTOR   Yes! Nicely done, very nicely done, Miss… I'm sorry, I've—

DOTTY   Dunbar. Call me Dotty, sir. Or Dot.

VICTOR   Dot. I…I haven't met anyone like you in years. This is…you'll have to
                forgive me. I didn't know such people even existed anymore.

DOTTY   That's very gratifying, sir. I mean, I've always admired you, too.

VICTOR   (Delighted) …Have you?

DOTTY   Oh, yes sir. For your book, I mean. I wouldn't have made it through
                my comps without it.

VICTOR   That's very kind. Dot. And please…call me Victor.

DOTTY   (Blushing) Thank you, Victor. Are you having your class read it?

VICTOR   Them? Are you kidding? They're still struggling through *Horton
                Hears a Who*.

(DOTTY giggles.)

DOTTY   You're very funny, Victor.

VICTOR   (Blushing, gushing) …Ohhh. Huh-huh!

DOTTY   But you should really consider it. It's still a seminal work in many
                ways.

VICTOR   It is, yes, isn't it.

DOTTY   In fact, with some updating, it could be as relevant as ever. Have you
                thought about putting out another edition?

VICTOR   (Struck by the notion) …Another edition?

DOTTY   I could help you. I mean, if that's—

VICTOR   Would you…would you like to?

DOTTY   Like to? Oh, *yes*, I'd *love* to!

VICTOR   …Do you mean it?

DOTTY   Are you kidding? It would be so *fun!* We could, we could bring the bibliography up to date, and of course we'd have to reconcile the discrepancies with Sanborn's work, his Chaco Canyon stuff especially, which would mean gutting some of the later chapters, but the *rest* of it, all it would take is—

VICTOR   What do you mean, what…what do you mean…*discrepancies?*

DOTTY   Oh, you know.

(VICTOR is dumbfounded.)

DOTTY   …You *know*. About the cannibalism.

VICTOR   …There *was* cannibalism.

DOTTY   Well, yes, but not—

VICTOR   I found *proof.* You said so yourself, he was—

DOTTY   But he was one of very few. And not for the reasons you said.

(Pause.)

VICTOR   …I was…*wrong?*

DOTTY   Well, not…well, *yes,* on a minor, on a kind of—

VICTOR   What did this…this Sandberg—

DOTTY   Well, he developed a new violence taphonomy to test for anthropophagy. It was supposed to mitigate ethnologic prejudice and account for—

VICTOR   What did he *say?*

DOTTY   They weren't just savages! It was desperation! …They were starving. …And it's Sanborn. Sir.

(VICTOR looks at her for a few long moments. Then he averts his eyes, and sits at his desk or turns away, humiliated.)

VICTOR   …Sanborn.

DOTTY   Uh, look. *Wow.* I hope I haven't—

VICTOR   No, no, that's quite, you're…yes, I've…I've forgotten what I was going to say.

DOTTY   *(Regrouping)* …Well, anyway, there's *that*, but that won't, I could do that, and you could, you know, *add* what, or we could work on it *together*! Have you had lunch? I'll take you to lunch, we could have a toast or something, get things off—

VICTOR   *(Calmly)* You pretentious, overbearing little bitch.

DOTTY   …Ummm.

VICTOR   *(Not calmly)* How dare you come in here and, and, and *presume* to tell me—

DOTTY   Victor, please, I didn't—

VICTOR   I am *Dr.* Ransome. And if you think I'm going to let some, some, do you think I'm just going to roll over? Do you think I'd let you just *waltz* into my classroom and—

DOTTY   No, that's not, that's—

VICTOR   You wouldn't stand a chance, you obnoxious little disaster! They'd see right through you and they'd tear you *apart*!

(Pause. DOTTY is shaken. She twirls her hair.)

DOTTY   I'm sorry. I didn't mean to—

VICTOR   Please just…leave. I have a…I have to prepare now.

DOTTY   Dr. Ransome, I—

VICTOR   Get. *Out.*

(Pause. Then she moves to the door.)

VICTOR   …And close the door.

(She exits, closing the door behind her. Pause. VICTOR sits at his desk, and puts his head in his hands. Lights to black on VICTOR's office.

Lights up on Murray's office. MURRAY and KRISTI are locked in a passionate kiss. Finally, she pushes herself away.)

KRISTI   "Oh, Murray! You must have such a low opinion of me now!"

MURRAY   "And you of me!"

KRISTI   "If we allow this to continue, I'm afraid I will no longer be responsible for my actions!"

MURRAY   "Nor I, mine!"

KRISTI   "Oh, Murray!"

MURRAY   "Oh, Kristi!"

(He starts to lay her back on the desktop, but then she breaks out:)

KRISTI   You know, you should really have a couch in here.

MURRAY   …That's not a bad idea.

KRISTI   A lot of other professors do.

MURRAY   …How do you know?

KRISTI   How do *I* know?

MURRAY   Yeah. How do you know?

KRISTI   I don't know, *you* know. You thought of it.

MURRAY   …Have you ever…done this before with, you know, with—

KRISTI   What, like my psych professor?

MURRAY   Yeah.

KRISTI   Or my music professor, or my speech professor?

MURRAY   Yeah.

KRISTI   *(Deliciously)* Or my math tutor?

MURRAY   *Have* you?

KRISTI   I don't know, have I?

(MURRAY thinks about it.)

MURRAY   ...Naaaaah. Okay. "Oh, Kristi!"

(He tries to pick up where he left off, but she breaks out again.)

KRISTI   Speaking of which, do you have any protection?

MURRAY   What?

KRISTI   Protection. Rubbers, condoms.

MURRAY   ...Uhhhh, no, no, I—

KRISTI   Don't you think you ought to get some? I mean, what if I get pregnant?

MURRAY   *Pregnant*?

KRISTI   With child? Knocked up? Talk about a scandal! It could cost you your job.

MURRAY   ...Just, you're getting off the—

KRISTI   I'm not the one who's worried about it. If I were you, I'd stash a few Trojans around here.

MURRAY   Okay, okay! Skip all that. We'll just...we'll keep it simple. Uhh, rip your shirt off.

KRISTI   Rip my shirt off?

MURRAY　　　Yes, just...rip it right off.

KRISTI　　　But...I'd have to walk out of here in broad daylight. I can't just walk around with my shirt all torn up.

MURRAY　　　*Look—*

KRISTI　　　And besides, you want more than just a cheap fling here.

MURRAY　　　No, I don't! Rip it, rip it, rip it!

KRISTI　　　C'mon. You're falling in love with me.

MURRAY　　　I'm...?

KRISTI　　　You *are*, Murray, you just *are*, which in itself is idiotic.

MURRAY　　　I've got to get my head straight.

KRISTI　　　I mean, what are you going to do, introduce me to your colleagues? Take me to faculty brunches? Can you *imagine*?

MURRAY　　　Stop *talking*.

KRISTI　　　Are you going to carry my books to class? Or *kiss* me in the *hall*, for God's sake? Am I supposed to sneak you into the *dorms*?

MURRAY　　　*Would you shut up!*

(Pause.)

KRISTI　　　...Boy, is this weird.

MURRAY　　　I know.

(The phone rings. Pause. KRISTI will straighten herself out and head for the door. The phone rings again, and MURRAY answers it.)

MURRAY　　　...Hello.

(Lights up on Victor's office. VICTOR is on the other end.)

VICTOR　　　Murray? ...I'm having a crisis.

MURRAY	Is something wrong?
VICTOR	No, Murray, this is a *happy* crisis. This is the kind of crisis where nothing is wrong.

(KRISTI opens the door, waves goodbye to MURRAY, and exits, closing the door behind her.)

MURRAY	*(Sighs)* ...What is it?
VICTOR	It's happening. I'm out. Meriwether's hired someone to take my place.
MURRAY	...You're serious.
VICTOR	Yes.
MURRAY	Well, you know, we can, we can fight it, Vic. We can take it to the faculty senate.
VICTOR	He won't *fire* me, Murray, he isn't stupid. He's trying to humiliate me away. The next step is leave time or early retirement or—
MURRAY	Then say no, just—
VICTOR	I don't *want* to say no. I hate this place, you know that.

(Pause.)

MURRAY	...What's the crisis, Vic?
VICTOR	What do you mean, what's the crisis?
MURRAY	I mean, *he* wants you out, *you* want you out, your students *must* want you out—
VICTOR	My point, Murray, my point—
MURRAY	*Everybody* wants you out.
VICTOR	Yes! Yes! Everybody wants me out!
MURRAY	...And that bothers you?
VICTOR	What do you think?

MURRAY	Then why are you such an *asshole* all the time? I'm your best friend in the world, and you treat me like shit!
VICTOR	You are not my best friend.
MURRAY	All right, then I'm your *only* friend. I'm the only person you call when you think you have a *crisis*. I'm the only person who can stand to be around you for more than a few minutes. I'm the only—
VICTOR	You've made your point.
MURRAY	No, I haven't. I'm the only person who remembers when you *weren't* an asshole, back before you tried very, very hard to *become* an asshole.
VICTOR	I am not an—
MURRAY	You're a miserable teacher, and you keep finding ways to get worse. You abuse everyone who gets *close* to you, you abuse them when they *don't*, you delight in others' misfortunes, you hate the weather, small animals, food, music, women, children, little baby *ducks*, you're a paranoid hypochondriac, and I *know* you're cheating at cards! That's what *I'd* call an *asshole*, Vic! But that doesn't mean I don't *like* you! That doesn't mean I'm not *disturbed* by this. I am! I'm *very* disturbed! I just *don't see what the damned crisis is!*

(Long pause. Then VICTOR begins to laugh, at first so slowly and softly that it sounds like weeping. Then he laughs harder, louder. MURRAY smiles, and VICTOR laughs harder still.

The laughter is infectious—MURRAY begins laughing, too. It reaches a crescendo, and then tapers off, the tension finding its catharsis. Pause, as they gather themselves. Then:)

MURRAY	…You all right, Vic?
VICTOR	Yes. I'm fine now. Thank you, Murray.
MURRAY	You want me to come down?
VICTOR	No, no, I'm…Murray?
MURRAY	Yeah?
VICTOR	…Goodbye, Murray.

MURRAY   I'll see you around, Vic.

VICTOR   …Goodbye.

(MURRAY hangs up his phone, and lights fade to black in his office. VICTOR hangs up his, and smiles—strangely, sadly.

Special comes up on Victor's lectern in the Teaching Area. It is the next day. DOTTY approaches the lectern and stands ready to address a classroom for the first time. Despite the fact that she's tried to spiff herself up a bit, she is petrified. She clears her throat a few times. Then:)

DOTTY   Good morning. May I have your attention please?

(She doesn't get their attention. Behind her, in his office, VICTOR sits at his desk, opens some drawers and begins emptying papers into a wastebasket.)

DOTTY   Hello? I have an announcement to make. If everyone would, hello?

(As the class settles, the lights in VICTOR's office fade to black.)

DOTTY   Thank you. Good morning. As you may have heard, your professor, Dr. Ransome, is, uh, well…he's *dead.* I've been asked to take over the class. My name—

(She is interrupted by a question.)

DOTTY   …I am not at liberty to discuss the details. But I know this comes as a terrible sh—hmm?

(Questions keep coming from the class; she will direct her attention to different parts of the room each time, and become more frazzled.)

DOTTY   …Yes. Three times. In the head. …I don't know *how.* He, uh, he missed or something. I'm really not supposed to— …Yes, but they cleaned it all up. …I'm trying to tell you. Dotty Dunbar. Dot. Dee Dee, Dotty, or Dot. The dean has advised me to give you the rest of the day off, so we can all get over the terrible sh—what? …Twenty-seven. Have a nice day. Class dismissed.

(And she exits to the wings. Special to black as music comes up. End Act One.)

ACT TWO
Scene 1

(Lights up on Victor's office; it's a few days later. Victor's office is now Dotty's office, and she's doing her best to make it look homey. There are some new knick-knacks dressing up the bookcase, a plant or two, maybe some stuffed animals, and a Navajo rug on the floor. Perhaps the furniture has been rearranged a little, too. There are still a few books and things lying around on chairs and so on, but on the whole the place certainly looks very accommodating. There's also a new CD player on the desk or bookcase, playing something sickeningly New Agey.

DOTTY, dressed up and no longer wearing her glasses, is straightening up the place, putting this here and that there, but she seems a tad on edge. She takes off her shoe and pounds a nail into the wall with the heel, then hangs her new O'Keeffe print. She steps back to look, then suddenly and spasmodically blinks one eye and pounds the side of her head.

While she is thus occupied, MURRAY appears in the open door. He looks a little detached and perhaps a little weary, but is outwardly neither happy nor sad. He waits to be noticed. Failing in that:)

MURRAY   …Ahem.

DOTTY   *(Screams)* Aaaahh!

MURRAY   Sorry.

DOTTY   Hi! Whew! Come uh, come in, come in! I'm, I'm just—

(She hops around, putting her shoe on.)

MURRAY   I didn't mean to startle you. I'm here to pick up the…personal effects.

DOTTY   *(Still rattled)* The? Oh, the, uh, *right*. Right.

(She hurries to the CD player and turns it off.)

DOTTY   I was just, that was, that was *music*.

MURRAY   Yes.

DOTTY   It's soothing, it's supposed to, for students, when they, it's supposed to *soothe* them, if, I take it you're, uh, family, or—

MURRAY   Oh, no, I'm sorry. Murray Stone, English department.

DOTTY   *(Committing to a name)* Hi! I'm, uh, Dotty Dunbar. Dotty. Dot-ty.

(A cordial handshake. She is blinking her eye, in obvious discomfort. From time to time, she'll pound the side of her head again.)

MURRAY   Is something wrong with your eye?

DOTTY   My, uh, my contact, I'm trying out some new contacts, I read somewhere that glasses, uh, *intimidate* students, they create an unapproachable teaching persona that students, I think it's stuck in the corner, or—

MURRAY   Ah. Is this the, uh—

(He indicates a box full of stuff.)

DOTTY   Oh, right. It's all, I put it all in there. There wasn't very much really. Mostly some things from his desk. *This.*

(She means the skull.)

DOTTY   And do you know what these are?

(She holds up the war bonnets.)

MURRAY   *(Smiling)* I have no idea.

DOTTY   Somebody from the library came for his books this morning. I was going to keep *his,* the one he wrote, if you think that's—

MURRAY   I'm sure he'd be flattered. And I hope somebody has…apologized for the circumstances that—

DOTTY   Oh yes! No, I'm, it's, yes. Thank you! I'm still, it's still a little, I just feel *awful.*

MURRAY   No, no.

DOTTY   I mean, I feel like I—

MURRAY   If Victor Ransome hadn't shot himself, somebody else would have. Like what you've done with the place, by the way.

DOTTY   Oh, thanks. I'm trying to...soften things up in here, warm things up a
               bit. I believe an office is a vital part of the total learning environment.

MURRAY   Well, it's certainly much nicer.

DOTTY   I'm excited to be here. This is my first teaching position, and I'm very
               excited about it. I think a good teacher can make a real difference. I
               want to make a real contribution.

MURRAY   Are you nervous?

DOTTY   Nervous? No, no! I'm *excited* to be here... Except I can't find his
               grade book, actually. Or any of his notes, or what I'm supposed—
               when I go in there—I'm fine, though.

MURRAY   I was petrified when I first started. But I found that, if I rehearsed my
               lectures, in my office, just to, you know, get the bugs out, it—

DOTTY   Oh! Yes, that's—

MURRAY   I had note cards and everything, too.

(He hoists the box.)

DOTTY   Thank you! But I'm fine! No problem! Do you need any help?

MURRAY   I'll manage.

DOTTY   I take it you and...you and he were...close.

(Pause. MURRAY ponders that.)

MURRAY   ...Actually...no. In fact, we were...no. We weren't.

*(He smiles a bit sadly and exits. DOTTY hammers her head again, blinks hard, and
squints: the contact has popped out somewhere. She mutters something and gets down
on all fours to look for it. She spots it beside the desk or chair, and, still on her knees,
puts it back in. While she's on the floor—and possibly out of our view—WOODY
walks in. He looks around, sees her on the floor, and waits. Finally:)*

WOODY   Hey.

*(She bangs her head on the chair or desk, pokes herself in the eye and staggers to
her feet.)*

WOODY   Sorry.

DOTTY   *(Squinting, blinking)* Uh, hi! Hi! Come in!

WOODY   Mizz Dunbar, right?

DOTTY   Right! Right! Dotty, actually. Or Dee Dee! Dee Dee or Dotty.

WOODY   I'm in your class, what is it, uh—

DOTTY   Excellent!

WOODY   —Anthro.

(He stares up at the ceiling.)

DOTTY   Excellent! Excellent! My very first student! This is wonderful! It's going to be an exciting semester!

WOODY   Those the bullet holes?

DOTTY   ...Uh, yes, those are, that's...them.

(Pause. They both stare up at the ceiling.)

WOODY   ...How could he shoot himself three times?

DOTTY   ...I don't know.

(Pause. They keep staring until DOTTY breaks the spell.)

DOTTY   ...So!

WOODY   *(Still staring)* My dad got shot.

DOTTY   Did he? That's...that's terrible.

WOODY   Is that blood?

DOTTY   Where?

WOODY   There.

DOTTY   I don't know.

(Pause. They look. Then:)

DOTTY   So! Listen! Why don't we, we clear off a spot here, I'm sorry about the mess, I'm still—

(She clears a place for him to sit, but he's still looking around.)

WOODY   That's a nice picture.

DOTTY   Thank you! It's an O'Keeffe.

WOODY   Looks like a flower.

DOTTY   Yes, it's uh, I'm trying to make everything in here as comfortable, I want to avoid the old presumptions about power dialogics and present a, uh, mutually accommodating, uh, uh, ambiance.

WOODY   I'm gettin' a bald spot.

(He points to his head.)

DOTTY   Really?

WOODY   On accounta baseball. You gotta wear a hat. I'm on the baseball team.

DOTTY   A student athlete! Excellent! Excellent!

WOODY   Lotta ballplayers got bald spots. Wade Boggs, he had a bald spot. Cal Ripken. Kirk Gibson. They all had bald spots.

DOTTY   I don't believe I—

WOODY   Dave Winfield, he's had a bald spot. Will Clark. My mom's got a bald spot.

DOTTY   Your...?

WOODY   She started drinkin', after my dad died? And she couldn't sleep, had 'somnia? And her hair fell out. It's a pretty sad story.

DOTTY   Umm, well, would you, would you like to tell me about it?

WOODY   I kinda don't like to talk about it. They get the bullets out, or they still in there?

(He looks up again, she doesn't.)

DOTTY   I don't believe I caught your *name.*

WOODY   Oh. Woody.

DOTTY   Woody? Excellent to meet you. Dee Dee Dunbar.

(They shake hands.)

WOODY   Woody.

DOTTY   Is there…something I can do for you, Woody? Is there something on your mind, anything, uh, troubling you? Anything…you'd…?

WOODY   …Kinda, yeah.

DOTTY   Good! Okay! Excellent. I'm glad you've come.

(She hurries over and starts the CD player; the music should provide a suitable soundtrack for the tragedy WOODY is about to narrate. Before he begins, DOTTY situates herself at her desk, brushes back her hair, and makes ready to help her first student.)

DOTTY   Okay. Now—

WOODY   *(Grave, distant)* It was at the rabbit roundup.

DOTTY   …Whh, ummm.

WOODY   It's a regular thing in Clyburn County. On accounta the beans. Far as the eye can see, beans. Rabbits, they hit 'em pretty hard, so every year, guys from all over'd come to help chase 'em outta the field, until you get 'em surrounded. Then you're supposed to club 'em to death. But Jimmy Sisson, he says, hell, that takes forever, why don't we just *shoot* 'em. …So we all stood around the rabbits in a great big circle, and started…firin' away.

(Pause. It dawns on DOTTY.)

DOTTY   …Oh my God.

WOODY   That was when we figgered out why you was supposed to club 'em.

DOTTY   I'm…I'm very sorry, Woody.

WOODY   That ain't the bad thing, though.

DOTTY   ...What's...what's the *bad* thing?

WOODY   ...It ain't the kinda thing I like to talk about.

DOTTY   *(Deeply moved)* ...I see. I'm...yes. Thank you, Woody, thank you for sharing this with me.

(She can't take the music anymore, and turns it off.)

DOTTY   This is...this is very nice. And I want you to know. If there's anything I can do for you, I want you to, to...feel free to—

WOODY   You mean that?

DOTTY   Absolutely. This is crucial. I want you to think of me as a person you can trust.

WOODY   Well. The thing is...

DOTTY   What? What is it? You can tell me.

WOODY   ...I...I gotta get a B.

DOTTY   ...Are you having trouble with the class?

WOODY   Oh *yeah*. I'm havin' trouble with *all* my classes. 'Cept Bio.

DOTTY   I see. Okay. This is terrific. The thing is, though, I don't know where he, I can't seem to find a uh, a gradebook or a, do you have something you were assigned, perhaps? Is there something you're working on *now*, that I could...?

WOODY   *(Thinking)* Uhhhh.

DOTTY   Anything at all, that we could—

WOODY   I'm supposed...to write an essay.

DOTTY   An essay. Excellent!

(She turns the CD player on again and re-situates herself.)

DOTTY   Okay. Now. Can you tell me what it was on?

WOODY   …I'm supposed…to write…about my *impressions.*

DOTTY   Your impressions of…?

WOODY   Well, I *wanted* to write about Alex Rodriguez.

DOTTY   Uh-huh, uh-huh. And who is Alex Rodriguez?

WOODY   You don't know Alex Rodriguez?

DOTTY   Uhhh, wwwwell, is he, he's in the field?

WOODY   The in-field, uh-huh.

DOTTY   Well, his, his *name* rings a bell. Did Dr. Ransome approve this project?

WOODY   Ransome? He probably never even *heard* of Alex Rodriguez.

DOTTY   Well, he *was* a bit out of touch.

WOODY   He was *mean.*

DOTTY   Well, he was probably just unfamiliar with collaborative educational techniques. Some professors feel threatened by their students, you know.

WOODY   I know. I threatened him a few days ago.

DOTTY   Well, there you are. So this paper, this Rodriguez fellow, refresh my memory, tell me about him.

WOODY   Well, he used to be at Texas.

DOTTY   Ah, good school!

WOODY   But now he's at New York.

DOTTY   City College? Columbia? NYU?

WOODY   Uh, Yankees.

DOTTY   …Yankees?

WOODY   Won the MVP coupla years ago, got a buncha gold gloves.

DOTTY   Alex Rodriguez…is a baseball player.

WOODY   I know.

DOTTY   I see. And what is the…what is the relationship, can you tell me the, uh, *connection,* between Alex Rodriguez…and anthropology?

WOODY   …Boy, that's a tough one.

DOTTY   Woody, you see, this is—

WOODY   Is this a quiz?

DOTTY   No, this is a bad, you can't write about him.

WOODY   Oh, I know. Murray told me. He's my English professor.

DOTTY   Oh yes! He was just here!

WOODY   He says I got a good head on my shoulders.

DOTTY   He seemed very nice, yes.

WOODY   He's been *real* nice to me, especially since…since I…I told him the *bad* thing.

(WOODY looks up at the bullet holes again. Pause.)

DOTTY   …Wh, what was that?

WOODY   …I think…I think it was me what shot him.

DOTTY   …Your father?

WOODY   My mom says I didn't. The sheriff, he said he could figure it out, but it didn't make no difference. It was a accident.

DOTTY   Yes, I'm sure it, it—

WOODY   That ain't the bad thing, though.

DOTTY   It *isn't?*

WOODY   The bad thing is...I ran over to where he was. And I kneeled down and...and I picked up his head in my hands—

DOTTY   *(Welling up)* Oh God.

WOODY   —and he looked up at me, and he looked up at me and he said—

DOTTY   Oh boy!

WOODY   —he said..."You *idiot.*" And then his eyes kinda rolled back and—

DOTTY   *(Grief stricken)* Oh my God! Oh my God! No, no! That's...I'm sorry, I'm sorry. Excuse me!

(She fumbles for the CD player and turns it off, trembling. Pause, while they struggle separately with the tragedy. Then she gathers herself with heroic resolve.)

DOTTY   Woody? You're...you're going to do *fine!* You're going to do just fine! We'll...we'll get you through, I promise!

WOODY   Really?

DOTTY   Absolutely. We're going...we'll find a way. We're going to fix you up with a new essay topic. It'll be extra credit, okay?

WOODY   What's it gonna be about?

DOTTY   Uhhh...

(She thinks, and her eyes fall upon Victor's book. She picks it up.)

DOTTY   ...Okay. Okay. This is perfect. This is excellent. Take this book. This is Dr. Ransome's book.

WOODY   Ransome wrote a book?

DOTTY   Yes. It's an excellent book. It's all about indigenous pre-Columbian civilizations. You pick one, and—

WOODY   I don't know what that means.

DOTTY   The, uh, the Anasazi, the Mogollon, Hohokam, Patayan—

WOODY   I don't know what them things are.

DOTTY   Local aboriginals.

WOODY   I don't know what—

DOTTY   Indians.

WOODY   Those guys are Indians?

DOTTY   Yes. Long, long ago.

WOODY   I never heard of 'em.

DOTTY   Well, this will help you learn, you see? This is what—

WOODY   But I don't—I mean, you think that'll be okay?

DOTTY   I think it would be perfect. You pick one, I want you to write a paper about your favorite Indians of antiquity.

WOODY   You're *sure*.

DOTTY   I *insist*.

WOODY   *(After careful thought)* ...Okay! Cool! You sure are a good teacher, Mizz Dunbar.

DOTTY   Thank you, Woody. You can call me, uh, Dee Dee. And I prefer the term "co-learner."

WOODY   "Co-learner."

DOTTY   It's a way of de-centering myself and creating a more centripetal, as opposed to centrifugal classroom dynamic.

WOODY   Cool.

DOTTY   It's part of the new pedagogy.

WOODY   Excellent.

DOTTY   Okay! So there we are! I'm glad you came to see me, Woody. This was very helpful! I want you to come by whenever something's troubling you. I am here to help you, okay?

WOODY   Okay!

DOTTY   Okay! Cool! See you in class!

WOODY   Okay!

DOTTY   Okay!

(And WOODY exits, leaving the book behind. DOTTY feels wonderful about everything.)

DOTTY   ...Okay. Cool. I can do this. I can do this!

(End scene.)

Scene 2

(Lights up on Murray's office. MURRAY has just entered with the box of Victor's personal effects. He places it on the desk and begins to sift through it. First he removes the skull, and places it on his desk. An idea strikes him, and he pops a pencil into the hole in it. Next come the war bonnets: with a smile, he drapes one of them over the skull. Then he removes a stapler.)

MURRAY   One stapler. Jammed. Throw.

(He throws it away and picks up a pack of Odor Eaters.)

MURRAY   One pack, Odor Eaters. Unopened. Keep.

(He puts it on his desk, picks up a plaque, and reads.)

MURRAY   "Professor of the Year, 1985."

(He stands, removes one of his own pictures, hangs the plaque in its place, and stands back.)

MURRAY   Keep.

(He returns to the box, removes a jar of coins.)

MURRAY   Poker money. Mostly mine.

(He puts it out of the way somewhere as GRACE appears in his open door, looking troubled. She raps softly on it.)

GRACE   Dr. Stone?

MURRAY   Yes?

GRACE   I don't know if you remember me. I'm Grace Berger. I was auditing Dr. Ra—Dr. Rans—oooohh!

(And she bursts into tears.)

MURRAY   ...Would you like to come in?

GRACE   *(Shrieking)* It's all so horrible!

MURRAY   Easy does it, Grace. Here you go.

GRACE   How could he do it? How could he just— *(A gunshot sound:)* poooougsssh! Grown men simply do not go around blowing their heads off!

MURRAY   There, there.

GRACE   And in the *middle* of the *day*!

MURRAY   I know, I know.

(She takes his face in her hands and squishes it.)

GRACE   You poor, poor man! What *pain* you must be in!

MURRAY   *(His face scrunched)* Try to relax, Grace.

GRACE   The desolation, Dr. Stone! The betrayal! The emptiness and heartbreak and horror of it all! Many a good man has wept on my bosom!

(She hugs him tightly to her bosom.)

MURRAY   I'm *fine*, Grace. *Really.*

(She releases him, pats his cheek, smoothes his shirt and composes herself.)

GRACE   …I'm terribly sorry, Murray. I didn't intend to come in and cause a riot. May I call you, Murray?

MURRAY   Uh, yes, and that's quite alr—

GRACE   You have my deepest, *deepest* sympathies, Murray.

MURRAY   I appreciate that, Grace, but the fact is, I haven't really given it much thought, and I don't intend to.

GRACE   It's unhealthy to suppress your anguish, Murray. Crying is a healthy, normal, physical reaction. *I* know.

MURRAY   *(Overlapping)* I *know*. But Victor and I, we really had very little in common. To tell you the truth, I'm not even sure why we were friends.

GRACE   …Oh.

(From offstage, through Murray's open door, we hear VICTOR's voice.)

VICTOR   *(Off)* Good morning, Murray.

(At this point, or soon hereafter, VICTOR will enter and make himself at home. He is, of course, a projection of Murray's imagination. MURRAY will react to VICTOR's presence by rubbing his temples or blinking his eyes, trying to filter out his voice.)

GRACE   Well, in that case, there was something I needed to ask you.

VICTOR   I see the Angel of Death has wasted no time.

GRACE   As you know, I was auditing Victor's class.

VICTOR   Now she's coming for you.

MURRAY   Yes, I know.

GRACE   I think it's important for a woman to keep herself vital in her declining years. And I *am* declining, you know.

VICTOR   Declining? She's *plummeting*.

MURRAY   If you don't mind my saying so, Grace, you don't look a day over sixty.

GRACE   *(Horrified)* …Sixty?

VICTOR	Way to go, Murray.
MURRAY	Or, fifty-five. *Fifty*, really, with a good, strong light behind you.
GRACE	*(Touched)* Really?
VICTOR	And so it begins.
GRACE	You know, in my salad days, I was considered quite a hot tamale, especially for a big-boned girl.
VICTOR	I see you wasted no time plundering my office.
MURRAY	No, I, I mean *yes*, I can—
GRACE	You said you weren't married, is that right?
VICTOR	You hung my plaque on your wall!
MURRAY	Yes, that's, that is I'm—

(The voices form a fugue in MURRAY's head; he struggles to focus his attention.)

VICTOR	What's this doing on your wall?
GRACE	I have a son, you know.
VICTOR	Why don't you just knock my fillings out, Murray!
GRACE	Life must be *awfully* empty without children.
MURRAY	I'm, I don't, it's—
VICTOR	Is this supposed to fool anybody?
GRACE	It's not too late for *you*, you know.
MURRAY	*(Under siege.)* You had a *question*, as I recall, Grace.
GRACE	Oh, oh yes. There is a woman, taking over for Dr. Ransome.
MURRAY	Yes, I know.
VICTOR	*(Simultaneously, dour)* Yes, I know.

GRACE   She seems awfully young, you know. I don't think she knows what
               she's getting herself into.

VICTOR   She doesn't.

MURRAY   Well, thank you for bringing this to my attention, Grace, I'll see what—

(MURRAY tries to show her the door.)

GRACE   My question, though, is—

VICTOR   She will want to audit your class.

GRACE   I see you teach an Introduction to Literature, I was looking in the
               schedule, is that right?

MURRAY   Uh, yes, that's—

VICTOR   Let us now pause to savor this moment.

GRACE   I was wondering, then, if I might—

VICTOR   Let us relish the irony.

GRACE   —if I might sit in on your class.

VICTOR   Murray Stone and Grace Berger!

GRACE   I have the form right here. All it needs is your signature.

(She produces a form.)

VICTOR   It's like Icarus flying over the Bermuda Triangle.

MURRAY   Well, I, uh, I guess that—

VICTOR   On a hot summer day.

MURRAY   I suppose…that would be all right.

(He signs the form, and hands it to her.)

VICTOR   Sp-lash.

GRACE   Thank you, Murray! God bless you!

MURRAY   Quite all right.

(He takes a sheet of paper from his desk.)

MURRAY   And, uh, here's a, uh, syllabus. We're reading Yeats for the rest of the week.

GRACE   Yeats? He's Irish! I love Yeats! "Things fall apart, the center cannot hold!" That's Yeats!

MURRAY   That's Yeats, very good. I'll see you in class, then.

(He starts her toward the door again.)

GRACE   Thank you, yes, thank you, Murray. "A terrible beauty is born!'

MURRAY   Yeats again. Bye-bye.

(He's got her out the door.)

GRACE   "This is the way the world ends! Not with a bang, but a whimper!"

(And he pushes the door closed.)

MURRAY   …That's *Eliot.*

(Pause. MURRAY sighs and goes back to the box.)

VICTOR   …One day, she asked me to feel a lump in her breast. She thought she had some sort of tumor. I told her it was probably a corn.

MURRAY   One old copy of…*Cosmo.* Pause briefly to wonder. Throw.

(He throws it away, keeps rummaging.)

VICTOR   Ah. You're *ignoring* me. You are…"not giving it much *thought.*"

MURRAY   One deck of cards. Keep.

VICTOR   If it's a souvenir you're looking for, here's an interesting one.

(VICTOR picks up the skull.)

VICTOR   "Alas, poor Victor! I knew him well!" Now I am *truly* a clear-headed man.

MURRAY   One copy of *Vogue*. What the hell is this?

VICTOR   Who are you asking? Me? I'm just a shadow.

(VICTOR picks up the cards and shuffles them.)

VICTOR   Speaking of which, what happened to what's-her-name, your phantom concubine. Bambi. Candy. Lolita.

MURRAY   Kristi.

VICTOR   Kristi. I thought she hung out here in your twisted psyche.

(VICTOR places a war bonnet on himself and will play a game of Indian Poker with the skull, occasionally calling out the bet as he goes.)

MURRAY   Another pack of Odor Eaters. We've discovered a motif.

VICTOR   Why isn't she here? I thought I might get to meet her now.

MURRAY   It got...complicated.

VICTOR   "Complicated"? Dime to open. What do you mean "complicated"?

MURRAY   One bottle of Preparation H. Suspicions confirmed.

(MURRAY throws it away. He then removes a few odds and ends, like tape and paper clips, and puts them on his desk.)

VICTOR   What happened, did you meet her imaginary parents? Did you dream her father beat you up? How could it get *complicated*?

(MURRAY retrieves a photograph from the box. VICTOR keeps playing.)

MURRAY   One...photograph of you, me and...Dunaway at—

VICTOR   At the faculty softball game. Quarter. You're wearing sideburns and sandals.

MURRAY   Look how thin I was. And look at your hair!

VICTOR   Don't you feel a bit like a *ghoul* rifling through my life that way?

MURRAY   A bit.

VICTOR   Is there something you're looking for?

MURRAY   …I don't know.

(Pause. MURRAY takes out another magazine and throws it away.)

MURRAY   …I want…I want to know why.

VICTOR   Why what?

MURRAY   *Why*! Why you—

VICTOR   It's all right there, isn't it? My feet stunk, my ass was swollen, and I couldn't staple anything.

(VICTOR places the fifth card, and keeps playing.)

MURRAY   …You didn't want to do it.

VICTOR   Obviously I did.

MURRAY   Then tell me why you missed.

VICTOR   Last card. Your bet.

MURRAY   The first bullet went straight into the ceiling. Clean miss.

VICTOR   *(To the skull)* A dollar?

MURRAY   The second just grazed your scalp.

VICTOR   You can't bet a *dollar*.

MURRAY   The last one ripped straight through your skull.

VICTOR   You're trying to *bluff* me.

MURRAY   I want to know why you *missed*! You were shooting at the easiest target in the world! You could have *stopped*! Why didn't you?

(Pause. They look at each other.)

VICTOR   …I don't know, Murray. Why didn't I?

(Pause. MURRAY grows angry.)

MURRAY   You son-of-a-bitch. You spineless, selfish son-of-a-bitch! It's not my fault you sat in your office feeling sorry for yourself! It's not my fault your life—a box of shit, a box of worthless *shit!*

VICTOR   Then why are you—

MURRAY   I don't feel guilty!

(Pause. He steels himself, continues:)

MURRAY   Living. Just, just *living.* It's all just an act of *will.* Happiness, it isn't something you, you *get,* it isn't a reward, there are no rewards! You are happy, your life is happy, by the *force* of your *will.* Over time, over, over *pain,* that's *living,* you get the life, the *happiness,* that you create. And you *keep* creating it!

VICTOR   And you're happy, huh?

MURRAY   *(Angrily)* Yes, I'm happy! I *choose* to be happy!

(Pause. VICTOR looks him right in the eyes.)

VICTOR   …Call.

(He removes his war bonnet and looks at his cards.)

VICTOR   Ha! Pair of fours! It's pretty pathetic, Murray, when a man cannot beat his own imagination in a game of cards.

MURRAY   That's enough.

VICTOR   I mean, you'd think that being dead would leave me at a disadvantage.

MURRAY   Shut up, Vic!

VICTOR   What are you going to do, hit me? Are we going to wrestle? I'd probably win.

MURRAY   I said that's *enough*!

(Pause.)

VICTOR   …Yes. That's exactly what I said.

(VICTOR goes to the door, and opens it.)

VICTOR   …I'll uh…see you *around*, Murray.

(And he exits, leaving the door open. End scene.)

Bob Hungerford (Murray) and Mindi Blackburn (Christie) mid-fantasy, Act I.
Photo: Jocelyn Sanders.

Scene 3

(Lights up on Dotty's office. It is later that morning. DOTTY is standing in the center of her office, rehearsing her first lecture. She reminds herself of Effective Teaching Techniques as she goes, refers to note cards, and makes notations on them as things occur to her. Quotation marks indicate the lecture itself. She begins with a rousing wail.)

DOTTY   *(Wailing)* "Aaaaa-ooooooo! Aaaaa-oooooo! In Brunei-Malay, that means 'Hello across the river!' A pleasant, reaffirming greeting which I would like for *us* to use at the start of each class meeting. Let's all try it, shall we? Aaaaa-oooooo!"

(She waves.)

DOTTY   "Hello across the river! Very good! I am Dee Dee Dunbar. It's going to be a wonderful semester!"

(She refers to the next note card.)

DOTTY   "Now, despite the tragedy which has brought us together, I would like you to think of today as an exciting new beginning in the exciting field of," pause, breathe, "anthropology! When life gives us lemons, what do we do?" Pause. "Yes?" Gesture, palm up, don't point. "That's right. We make lemonade. With that in mind, then, I have in fact *brought* some—"

(She produces a pitcher of lemonade and some plastic name tags.)

DOTTY   "—and some name tags, because I thought it would be fun to spend this time getting to know each other, and discussing those—" *(Shirley Temple grimace)* "—Practical Classroom Matters that I know are on your mind." Eye contact, enthusiasm, smile.

(She makes a note of it on a card.)

DOTTY   Smile. "So. Why don't we all come up and get one, 'kay?"

(Lights down on Dotty's office as lights come up on the Teaching Area, where MURRAY sits on his stool with an open book on his knee. He recites, mostly from memory, Yeats' "Song of Wandering Aengus" for his class. Again, he recites gracefully and naturally, as if narrating an incident that happened to him.)

MURRAY   "...I went out to the hazel wood,
                Because a fire was in my head,
                And cut and peeled a hazel wand,
                And hooked a berry to a thread;
                And when white moths were on the wing,
                And moth like stars were flickering out,
                ...I dropped the berry in a stream
                And caught a little silver trout.

                When I laid it on the floor
                I went to blow the fire aflame,
                But something rustled on the floor,
                And some one called me by my name:
                It had become a glimmering girl
                With apple blossom in her hair
                Who called me by my name and ran
                And...faded through the brightening air."

(He pauses briefly to signify a transition, and becomes more circumspect:)

MURRAY   "Though I am old with wandering
                Through hollow lands and hilly lands
                I will find where she has gone,
                And kiss her lips and take her hands;
                And walk among long dappled grass,
                And pluck till time and times are done
                ...The silver apples of the moon,
                ...The golden apples...of the sun."

(He lets the poem settle in, and then asks:)

MURRAY   Now. Who can tell me. What sort of man is speaking, and what is
                his...situation?

(Lights down on MURRAY as lights come up on Dotty's office, where DOTTY continues:)

DOTTY   "When something is important, I will write it on the board in white
                chalk. If something is *very* important, I will write it in *blue* chalk. But
                if something is *extremely* important, if it's absolutely *essential* that
                you understand it, I will write it in *red* chalk. Again, that's white
                chalk, blue chalk, red chalk. If it helps you to remember, think of the
                ultraviolet spectrum, or the American flag." Smile.

(She refers to the next card.)

DOTTY   "If at any time something is unclear or you do not hear me, you may raise your hand like this. If you feel you have something helpful you'd like to add, raise your fist. And if you suddenly have to leave the room for some emergency, raise your fist and wave it around. In this way I can better prioritize whom to call on, when, and why. Questions?"

(Lights out on Dotty's office, up on the Teaching Area, where MURRAY is trying to get some cooperation.)

MURRAY   What were your impr—. What is the poem *about*.

(Pause; no response.)

MURRAY   ...Did you, did you *like* it? Or, or what?

(Still nothing; he tries sarcasm.)

MURRAY   ...Was it a *happy* poem or a *sad* poem? ...All right. Then riddle me this: why is it, why is it, today is the day your papers are due, and I'm holding *four*, count 'em, *four* papers here. I realize that in the past, my due dates have been...I've been *flexible*, I've been *generous* enough to give you extensions. But I do not recall, when was it I gave you permission to, to *exploit* me? To take *advantage* of me? When did I do that?

(Pause.)

MURRAY   What is happening here? Is there a *problem* here? The poems were assigned, I *know* you read them, I read them *to* you! How could you, what are you *thinking*?

(Lights up on Dotty's office, where DOTTY continues her presentation. The speeches will briefly alternate.)

DOTTY   "Now let me ask you this."

MURRAY   What have I got to do, god-dammit, set myself on *fire*?

DOTTY   "How many of you feel intimidated by the college environment?"

MURRAY   What the hell is *wrong* with you people?

DOTTY   "How many of you associate education with humiliation?"

MURRAY   Why are you even *here*?

DOTTY   "How many of you feel stifled by the traditional A-B-C grading scale?"

MURRAY   Why am *I* even here?

DOTTY   "Everybody?"

MURRAY   Just…

DOTTY   "Yes?"

MURRAY   …forget it.

(He waves them off in disgust and exits as the lights fade to black on the Teaching Area. Meanwhile, DOTTY continues happily and confidently:)

DOTTY   "*Good!* Then look now at the handout titled—"

(She holds up a poster bearing a brightly-colored graph.)

DOTTY   "'Fulfillment Graph.' You'll notice that it asks you to measure 'Effort Invested' along the bottom, against 'Understanding Gained' up the side. This is how we will *mutually* determine your grades from now on, and I think you'll find that, the *farther* out you go on one line, the *higher* up you'll go on the other, and *that* way, you can measure your progress according to the *diagonal* line, which I call the 'Empowerment Quotient.'" Pause. Breathe. "And if you'll look on the other side—"

(She turns it over, where a triangle is drawn.)

DOTTY   "—you will see a diagram demonstrating the triangular relationship between *Investment*, *Understanding*, and *Power*, and how each one leads to more of the other and thereby a more fulfilling, pleasant, and useful learning experience." Gesture, smile, pause, and: "Thank you. Have a wonderful day!"

(She beams triumphantly. Lights to black. End scene.)

Scene 4

(Lights up on Murray's office. It is the following day. MURRAY is standing at his window, looking with weary, empty eyes out upon the campus. A knock on the door. He doesn't acknowledge it. Another; he says nothing. Then, WOODY calls through the door.)

WOODY   *(Off)* …Hey Murray?

(MURRAY groans. More knocking.)

WOODY   *(Off)* Hey Murray, you in there? …Murray?

MURRAY   It's unlocked, Woody.

(The door opens, and WOODY sticks his head in.)

WOODY   Hey, Murray. I didn't think you was in here.

MURRAY   Is that why you kept pounding on my door?

WOODY   Uh-huh. I brung that paper.

(He enters, and digs through his pockets.)

MURRAY   Which paper?

WOODY   You know. The paper.

MURRAY   You're not referring to the paper I assigned to our class.

(WOODY has found it in his back pocket.)

WOODY   Uh, yup. Here ya go.

MURRAY   The one that was due yesterday.

WOODY   Oh, uh, I know I was supposed to turn it in already, but I got a good excuse.

MURRAY   And what would that be?

WOODY   I was absent.

MURRAY   …And what is your excuse.

WOODY   That's it.

MURRAY   That you weren't in class.

WOODY   Yup. Here ya go.

(MURRAY will not take the paper.)

MURRAY   Woody. This is not a correspondence course. You can't just drop things by when you feel like it.

WOODY   Well, I got a good reason for not being in class though, Murray.

MURRAY   Because your paper wasn't done yet.

WOODY   Yup. Here ya go.

MURRAY   ...Woody. Do you detect any *absurdity* in our conversation? Do you sense the, the slightest tremors of *irony* in my voice?

WOODY   ...Are you mad at me, Murray?

MURRAY   Do you understand that the kindest thing I could do for you right now is to tear up that paper and give you an F?

WOODY   ...Uh, no.

MURRAY   Can you give me one good reason why I should accept it? One that, just this *once*, has nothing to do with baseball?

WOODY   ...Aren't you gonna?

MURRAY   I don't know. You tell me. Why should I?

WOODY   (Dumbfounded) ...Well.

(GRACE appears in the door, carrying a plate.)

GRACE   Yooooo-hooooo! Murray!

MURRAY.   (Grim, trapped) Ah. Grace Berger. Here you are again.

GRACE   Is this a bad time?

(WOODY has started slinking for the door.)

MURRAY   Where are you going, Woody?

WOODY   I better oughta go.

MURRAY   No! Uh, Woody, this is Grace. She's new in class.

(WOODY shakes her hand, glumly.)

WOODY   Woody.

GRACE   Nice to meet you, Woody. Care for a latka?

WOODY   Thanks.

(He takes one, and heads for the door.)

MURRAY   Woody! You haven't given me your reason yet.

WOODY   I ain't got one. I'm sorry, Murray.

MURRAY   You can th—*Woody!* You sit right down there, and you don't *move* until you think of one.

WOODY   But—

MURRAY   Just sit there, and *think.* Think very, very hard. And when you have one, you tell me.

WOODY   ...Oookay.

(He will sit and think. GRACE extends the plate to MURRAY.)

GRACE   Latka, Murray?

MURRAY   Uh, what?

GRACE   Latka. Potato cakes. I made them just for you.

MURRAY   Uhh, no thank you, Grace. I'mmmm...allergic to potatoes.

GRACE   Oh, my. How horrible, Murray. Well, what about truffles? I could bring you a plate of those.

MURRAY	Truffles too, I'm afraid. The whole…tuber family.
GRACE	How very odd.
MURRAY	Yes. I swell up like a horse.
WOODY	*(Matter-of-fact)* The truffle is a fungus.

(Long pause.)

MURRAY	…What?
WOODY	A tuber is a swollen, bud-bearing underground stem. A fungus is a plant that lacks chlorophyll.

(MURRAY looks at him, baffled and astounded. WOODY continues.)

WOODY	…Beans are legumes, artichokes are thistles, cabbages are coleworts and the truffle is a fungus.

(Another astounded pause. WOODY concludes confidently:)

WOODY	…I *got* Bio.
GRACE	Are you allergic to fungi, Murray?
MURRAY	Well, I, uh—
GRACE	I could bring you some truffles, some, some—
WOODY	—mushrooms—
GRACE	—some mushrooms, and some yeast rolls. How does that sound?
MURRAY	As lovely as that sounds, Grace, I'm afraid I can't have any of that. I'm…getting an ulcer.
GRACE	Oh. Worse and worse! Duodenal, hiatal, or peptic?
MURRAY	Oooooral. I have a canker. Can't eat a damned thing without screaming in pain.
GRACE	My God, Murray, you're a wreck!

MURRAY	Yes, I am.
GRACE	Wallace used to have the same problem, you know. He had some condition that made his mucous membranes crust over like a rock. Looking in his mouth, you'd swear you were in Carlsbad Caverns. I'd give him a sprig of aloe vera to suck on. It tasted terrible, of course, but it numbed his whole head.
MURRAY	Grace, you had a, a question or something, didn't you?
GRACE	No, no. Frankly, Murray, I came by to cheer you up.
MURRAY	Uh-huh.
GRACE	In class yesterday, you didn't seem very…*chipper.*
MURRAY	No, I, I wasn't.
GRACE	Not that I would blame you, of course. Trying so hard up there, to, to *stimulate* them, to *convince* them. It must be very frustrating.
MURRAY	I felt like I was conducting a *seance.*
GRACE	Not to mention the, the indignity and humiliation of it. Sometimes you must feel like a clown.
MURRAY	Sometimes I do.
GRACE	Or a buffoon. A booby. A stooge!
MURRAY	Yes.
GRACE	A stripper, a—
MURRAY	*Okay.*
GRACE	—a sideshow, a freak!
MURRAY	It's not my job to *convince* them.
GRACE	No, it certainly isn't.
MURRAY	I don't have to be *stimulating.* I don't even have to be *interesting.*

GRACE	I couldn't agree more.
MURRAY	I have the right, I am owed *respect*…to be *listened* to. I am a professor!
GRACE	Yes, you are. Sometimes I look at these young people and think: *what* the *fuck* is *wrong* with all of you? They don't seem to realize the opportunity they're squandering—as if they think they'll be young forever.
MURRAY	Exactly, yes. Thank you.
GRACE	And yet, Murray, when we were their age, we were probably much the same way.
MURRAY	…*I* wasn't.
GRACE	Oh, I was. I suppose I struck my teachers as being just as—
MURRAY	They're ignorant.
GRACE	They're learning.
MURRAY	They're hollow.
GRACE	They have not yet been filled up.

(Pause. MURRAY looks at her, sees what he's walked into.)

GRACE	…They should be dealt with *gently*, Murray. Don't you agree?
MURRAY	…It's not my job to be gentle.
GRACE	*(Gently, gracefully)* No… But it's your nature.

(An uncomfortable pause. MURRAY is trapped. He looks over at WOODY, who has by now assumed the posture of Rodin's "The Thinker.")

MURRAY	…How's it goin' over there, Woody?
WOODY	Oh, uh, I ain't got one yet.
MURRAY	Ah. …Was there anything else, Grace?
GRACE	Oh. No. I suppose I should be going. It was a lovely visit, wasn't it.
MURRAY	Always an unexpected surprise.

(She offers WOODY a latka.)

GRACE   Care for another, Woody?

WOODY   Thanks.

(He takes one.)

GRACE   I'll be by to cheer you up tomorrow, Murray.

MURRAY   Won't that be nice.

GRACE   And now, "Good night, sweet prince!"

MURRAY   Yes, yes.

GRACE   "And flights of angels sing thee to thy rest!" *Romeo and Juliet*!

(MURRAY closes the door as she exits.)

MURRAY   It's *Hamlet*. Hamlet! …You pretentious old dishtowel.

WOODY   *(Of the latka)* These are terrible.

(He throws it away.)

MURRAY   All right, Woody. Let's have it.

(WOODY reaches for the latka in the trash can.)

WOODY   You want it?

MURRAY   No, Woody, your—

WOODY   You gonna take my paper?

MURRAY   Yes.

WOODY   Whoa. Excellent. What a guy.

(He gives MURRAY the paper.)

MURRAY   Okay.

WOODY   Thanks, Murray! This is excellent. I'll see you later!

(WOODY starts to go.)

MURRAY   *Woody...* Wait. Come back here.

WOODY   ...Somethin' wrong?

MURRAY   ...Woody. Woody. I distinctly remember. Telling you. *Imploring* you.
             To stay on topic on this paper. Do you remember that?

WOODY   Sorta.

MURRAY   And yet, I have here...an essay titled: "My Impressions of Albert Belle
             and Pedro Alomar." Who are Albert Belle and Pedro Alomar?

WOODY   Indians.

MURRAY   ...Indians.

WOODY   *Cleveland* Indians. Long, long ago.

MURRAY   ...What...series of miscalculations could possibly have led to this?

WOODY   Well...it's sorta hard to explain.

MURRAY   Try.

WOODY   Dee Dee said it would be okay.

MURRAY   And who is Dee Dee.

WOODY   She's my co-learner.

(Pause.)

MURRAY   ...Wh...what kind of an idiot *are* you, Woody?

WOODY   I don't know.

MURRAY   For God's sake!

WOODY   Is it bad?

(And here the levee breaks. MURRAY purges his accumulated frustration and grief in an increasingly loud and vicious assault.)

MURRAY Bad? *Bad?* This is, this is *biblical,* Woody! This is the fucking *apocalypse!* Do you know how *bad* this is? The whole inheritance of, of Western culture, Woody, it's all about to fall into your hands, and you can't even find your *ass* with them! Does that sound *bad?* The total collapse of civilization?

WOODY Ummm.

MURRAY Eons, Woody, *eons* of accumulated knowledge are about to hit your generation, and it'll be like, like...*Hoover Dam!* You'll all be scavenging in dried-up river beds, while the whole blue ocean is welled up against the *back of your head!* Does that sound *bad?*

WOODY But—

MURRAY *Machines* will stop running. Satellites—plummeting to the earth! Lightbulbs blinking out, shoes on the wrong feet! Total cultural *meltdown,* Woody! Critical mass! Educational holocaust! Physics 101 will be an extended discussion of the *Lego!*

WOODY Oh, man.

MURRAY Chemistry classes will explore the mysteries of, of Jell-O pudding! English will die, Woody, you'll all be banging on garbage cans! Tenderfoot will be an advanced degree!

WOODY Oh, man!

MURRAY *(Thundering)* The national anthem will rhyme with *Nantucket!* The national bird will be the, the, the *aardvark!* And the motto, Woody, the national motto, printed on the seashells you use for money, will be: *"It's sorta hard to explain!"*

(Pause. He's thoroughly winded.)

MURRAY ...Now you tell me. Is that bad?

(A long pause. WOODY is shell-shocked. Then slowly, he starts to chuckle.)

WOODY ...Huh. Huh huh. Huh huh huh huh huh.

MURRAY   Is this funny?

WOODY   *(Harder)* Huh huh huh huh huh huh huh huh huh huh.

MURRAY   Woody?

WOODY   Huh huh. The back of my head! Whoa.

(WOODY keeps chuckling as the magnitude of the joke reveals itself to him. MURRAY just stands there, stupefied.)

WOODY   Huh huh huh huh huh. Aardvark! Huh huh huh!

(MURRAY sighs and shakes his head, picks up Woody's essay, and as WOODY watches, slowly tears it in half. WOODY stops laughing. MURRAY tears it again, in quarters.)

WOODY   …Wh…what're you doin', Murray?

(MURRAY throws the paper away, sits down at his desk, and puts his face in his hands.)

MURRAY   *(Muffled, into his hands)* I think you'd better go.

WOODY   But—

MURRAY   Please. Just…go.

(Long pause. Finally, WOODY exits, stunned. MURRAY remains seated at his desk. Behind his hands, he gasps suddenly, choking back tears. Again. He raises his head, shakes it, breathing heavily, struggling to suppress his anger, his grief, but failing.

These moments are given their dignity, until finally KRISTI appears in the door. This is the "real" KRISTI, dressed in a sweatshirt or some other non-descript clothing, and much more youthfully naive than the one he imagined. He does not see her, so she raps softly on the open door.)

KRISTI   …Dr. Stone?

(MURRAY looks up, bleary eyed, and wipes his hand across his face.)

MURRAY   …Kristi?

KRISTI   …Are you okay?

MURRAY   Uh, I'm… Yes, I'm, come in, I'm uh—

KRISTI   I needed to ask you something? About my paper? I can come back later, though, if—

MURRAY   No, no. Come in, please. I was, I was just. This is a surprise.

(She enters; he will run his hands through his hair, pull himself together.)

KRISTI   I was going to turn it in yesterday, but my roommate? She forgot to set the alarm? And when I got in my car, it had a flat tire.

MURRAY   Mm-*hmm.*

KRISTI   But I was wondering? I mean, I heard you got all pissed off in class and everything, and—

MURRAY   Would you like to sit down?

(She sits, nervously.)

KRISTI   —and I know you don't have to accept it? But I'm kinda worried about, like, my grades.

MURRAY   That's very conscientious.

KRISTI   Yes, sir. I'm pledging a sorority, the Zetas? And if I don't get like a two-oh?

MURRAY   Yes, I, uh, I see. Do you…have it with you?

KRISTI   Yes, sir.

(She digs it out of her backpack.)

MURRAY   Please, call me Murray. Are you uh, are you enjoying the class?

KRISTI   Oh. Yeah. Sorta.

MURRAY   Sorta?

KRISTI   I don't know. I don't see why they make us take it. I mean, I don't know why we need stories and poems and stuff.

MURRAY   We all need stories and poems and stuff, Kristi. It's what separates us from the animal kingdom and the baseball team.

KRISTI   I know. I just think it should be an elective, like PE. I'm a business major. Are you sure you're okay?

MURRAY   …Yes. Thank you.

(He smiles at her as he takes the paper she holds out for him. While they both hold it, their eyes linger for a moment; then she becomes uncomfortable, smiles awkwardly, and looks away.)

MURRAY   …Well. I see you've written about "Leda and the Swan."

KRISTI   Yes, sir.

MURRAY   You may call me Murray.

KRISTI   Okay.

MURRAY   This is an interesting choice. Did you…*enjoy* it?

KRISTI   …It was okay. Actually it sorta…bugged me.

MURRAY   *Really.*

KRISTI   Do you think you're gonna accept it?

MURRAY   Well, why don't we, we haven't had a chance to, to *talk,* to, you know, get uh, why did it, why did it, what *bugged* you about it?

KRISTI   The whole thing. Like, the guy changing himself into a swan.

MURRAY   Jupiter. He can do that. He's a god.

KRISTI   Yeah, but, like…*why?*

MURRAY   …Well. Because…because he's trying to *seduce* her. It's a symbol.

KRISTI   It is?

MURRAY   Yes, it's a symbol of, of, of *romance.* That's what the poem's about. Passion, and romance.

KRISTI   Well then, how come he doesn't just turn himself into a *hunk*?

(Pause. MURRAY is stumped.)

MURRAY   …Wwwwwellll.

KRISTI   Like…Johnny Depp or Justin Timberlake or somebody, or like a stud or something with great buns and long black hair and big pecs and a suntan?

MURRAY   …But she, she's very young, you see, she is *pure*, and he doesn't want to, to *frighten* her.

KRISTI   But, wouldn't you be afraid if a big white duck was trying to screw *you*?

MURRAY   …I, you're not—

KRISTI   Wouldn't that frighten you? I mean, if you were young?

MURRAY   But he's not just trying to *screw* her! He…he's in *love* with her.

KRISTI   *(Almost laughing at the idea)* No he isn't!

MURRAY   He might, yes, it might be a—

KRISTI   That's not what I thought.

MURRAY   What did you think?

KRISTI   I don't know. Maybe he just loves himself.

(Pause.)

MURRAY   …Oh.

KRISTI   …Are you gonna accept it?

MURRAY   …Accept it?

(He looks at her for a moment, sadly. She looks at him hopefully.)

MURRAY   …I suppose I…I suppose I probably have to…don't I.

KRISTI   Cool. I really appreciate it, sir.

(She stands to leave.)

MURRAY   …Please. Murray.

KRISTI   Thanks, Murray. I'll see you around!

(On her way out, she runs into WOODY, who enters looking very hangdog.)

KRISTI   Oh! Hi, Woody!

WOODY   Hey Kristi.

KRISTI   *(Obviously smitten)* There's a party at the Sig house Saturday. You
                coming?

WOODY   I dunno.

KRISTI   Come on out. I'll look for ya! See ya!

(And she's gone. Pause. WOODY stands in the door.)

WOODY   I'm sorry to bother you again, Murray. I need you to sign somethin'.

(He hands MURRAY a form; MURRAY looks briefly at it.)

MURRAY   …You're…dropping my class.

WOODY   I'm droppin' all of 'em. You gotta sign where it says.

(Pause. MURRAY looks at him.)

WOODY   I'm sorry about what happened, but I figure it'd be best if I just went
                ahead and…went on home… I just ain't cut out for this, I guess. I'm
                sorry, Murray.

*(Pause. MURRAY sighs, picks up a pen, and holds it poised over the drop form. He thinks
for a few moments. Then a few more. Then, he puts the pen down, stands, picks up a
book from his desk, opens it to a particular page, and places it in front of WOODY.)*

MURRAY   Sit down.

WOODY   How come?

MURRAY   *(Gently)* Sit. …Read this.

(WOODY sits, and MURRAY puts his glasses on.)

WOODY   How come?

MURRAY   Read it to me.

(Pause. WOODY is puzzled, but reads, laboriously.)

WOODY   "I went out to the hazel wood
             Because a fire was in my head,
             And cut and peeled a ... hazel wand,
             And hooked a berry to a thread..."

             ...He's gonna go fishin', huh.

MURRAY   ...Yes, he is. He's gonna go fishing.

WOODY   *(Reading)* "And when white moths were on the wing,
             And moth-like stars were fli—, flick—"

MURRAY   "Flickering."

(The lights begin to fade on MURRAY's office, and with them, WOODY's voice:)

WOODY   "—moth-like stars were flickering out,
             I dropped the berry in the stream
             And caught a little silver trout..."

(Special up on the lectern in the Teaching Area, as DOTTY enters and prepares to address her class. She is very agitated and is soaking wet in places. Lights to half on Murray's office, as MURRAY leans over the desk, silently helping WOODY.)

DOTTY   I am Dorothy Dunbar. On the way here, some idiot ran into me and
             spilled lemonade all over the place, and my note cards got all mixed
             up and now they're all stuck together.

(She shuffles through them briefly.)

DOTTY   It's going to be a wonderful semester. I think we should all get to
             know each other, 'kay?

(She consults the next card, squints at it painfully.)

DOTTY   I got some in my eye and now my contact is stuck to the inside of my
             eyelid or something so I can't see a thing.

(She shuffles through them quickly.)

DOTTY   Despite this tragedy, I'd like to think this is only the beginning.

(She squints at the next one, looks up, smiles a big grim smile at her class, and looks through the cards again.)

DOTTY   Just a…just a minute.

(She puts them aside, tries to wing it:)

DOTTY   Okay. Let's, uh, let me ask you this. How many of you, how many of you feel, uh, intimidated?

(She raises her hand. From offstage, through the open doorway of her office, we hear VICTOR's voice.)

VICTOR   *(Off)* You pretentious, overbearing little bitch.

(VICTOR—her memory of him—enters her office as the lights come up there. She becomes more frazzled.)

DOTTY   How many of you feel, uh, humiliated?

VICTOR   How old are you?

DOTTY   How many of you want good grades?

VICTOR   You've never even *taught* before.

DOTTY   …Nobody? Good. Okay. Then, everybody repeat after me!

VICTOR   You're still just a graduate student!

DOTTY   *(Meekly wailing)* Aa-ooo.

VICTOR   You obnoxious little disaster!

DOTTY   Hello across the river, aa-ooo.

VICTOR   They see right through you!

DOTTY   This is how I'd like to begin every—

VICTOR   You don't stand a chance!

DOTTY   Does anyone have any ques—?

VICTOR   They're going to tear you apart!

(Utterly petrified, she grips the lectern tightly. Meanwhile, lights return to full in Murray's office. WOODY is looking up at MURRAY, who is standing over him.)

WOODY   ...Hey, Murray. That's cool.

MURRAY   Hmm?

WOODY   ...I can see myself in your glasses.

MURRAY   ...Can you?

WOODY   Uh-huh.

(MURRAY takes his glasses off, turns them around, and looks into them. DOTTY, now looking down at her hands, tries to steel herself.)

DOTTY   ...I want you to think of me as someone you can trust.

(MURRAY suddenly smiles broadly, picks up a playing card, holds it to his forehead and, seeing it clearly in his reflection, begins to chuckle heartily. VICTOR, in his old office, begins to laugh also. WOODY doesn't get it, of course, but smiles anyway. DOTTY continues, still looking down.)

DOTTY   ...I want to be someone you can turn to for help.

(MURRAY and VICTOR laugh harder still. The laughter is merry but, surrounding DOTTY as it does, sounds eerily derisive. The lights begin to come down everywhere but on her.)

DOTTY   ...I want to make a real contribution.

(She looks up, determined, resolute. The laughter abruptly stops.)

DOTTY   I want to be a good teacher.

(Immediate and total blackout. End play.)

Drift

All this buttoning and unbuttoning.

> – anonymous 18th century suicide note
> *The Oxford Dictionary of Quotations.*

There is only one serious question. And that is:
Who knows how to make love stay?

Answer me that and I will tell you whether or not to kill yourself.

> – Tom Robbins
> *Still Life with Woodpecker.*

SETTING: In a city, all minimally suggested: a sports bar; a table at a fine restaurant; a small living room; a bedroom; the exterior of a motel room; the front seat of a car; an airport terminal; a burger joint; the bedroom of a small apartment; a city sidewalk; a backyard bench.

The time is the present, several days in May.

ACKNOWLEDGEMENTS: To Keith Hollin, P.I., and Melissa Johnson, J.D., for their invaluable professional advice; to the South Carolina Arts Commission and the South Carolina Academy of Authors, for their financial and moral support; to friends and artists like Bob Parham, Ken Autrey, David Avin, J. Lee Bryant, Phil Gardner, Barbara Lowrance Hughes, Houston McMillion, Bob and Fannie Hungerford, Melissa Swick,

Gene Aimone, Alex Smith, Bruce Jacoby, Adam Kraar, Kim Stafford and many others, for their encouragement and counsel; to Jim Yost and Barebones, for all the risks they take; and most particularly to Cheryl, for being my wonderful, beautiful wife—I am deeply and eternally grateful.

CHARACTERS:

BARBARA	Middle-aged.
ARTHUR	Barbara's husband; late middle-aged.
LEE	Middle-aged.
GRADY	Thirties.
JOEL	Early twenties.
WAITRESS/MARIE	Joel's wife; early twenties.
WOMAN/LOUISE	Thirties; attractive.

DRIFT premiered at the Trustus Theatre in Columbia, South Carolina, on August 7, 1998, as the winner of the 10th Annual South Carolina Playwrights' Festival. It was directed by Jim Thigpen. The cast was as follows:

BARBARA	Barbara Lowrance Hughes
ARTHUR	Houston McMillion
LEE	Bob Hungerford
GRADY	Gene Aimone
JOEL	Alex Smith
WAITRESS/MARIE	Fannie Hungerford
WOMAN/LOUISE	Melissa Swick

Interim Artistic Director:	Dewey Scott-Wiley
Artistic Director:	Jim Thigpen
Producing Director:	Kay Thigpen
Technical Director:	Brian Riley
Sound and Design:	Ed Breland
Master Electrician:	Teddy Palmer
Production Manager:	Greg Leevy
Stage Managers:	Sarah Hammond and Tim Semon
Props:	Katie Robbins

DRIFT

ACT ONE
Scene 1

(Evening: lights up half on a sports bar. We hear a baseball game on an overhead TV.

LEE, middle-aged, sits at the bar. By his elbow is an ornate gift box no larger than a shoebox. JOEL, in his early twenties, sits nearby working on a beer and watching the game. The bartender, GRADY, in his thirties, watches also.

Elsewhere: lights up full on ARTHUR and BARBARA, a well-to-do, middle-aged couple sitting at a table in an upscale restaurant. A candle is on the table; strings play in the background. BARBARA is perusing the wine list while a WAITRESS, in her early twenties, awaits her order.)

BARBARA   …I believe. I think I would like… No, never mind.

ARTHUR   What, darling.

BARBARA   No, nothing. You decide.

ARTHUR   Chardonnay?

BARBARA   I don't know. That's fine.

ARTHUR   *(To the WAITRESS)* The…Mer Soleil, please.

BARBARA   No. I'm sorry. I'd like…I'd like some cognac.

ARTHUR   Cognac?

BARBARA   No, no. Never mind.

ARTHUR   Would you like some cognac, darling?

BARBARA   No, I'm sorry. That's all.

ARTHUR   *(To the WAITRESS)* The Remy, please.

BARBARA   Arthur, no.

ARTHUR   Thank you.

BARBARA   Arthur, it's—

(She waits for the WAITRESS to leave:)

BARBARA   —it's *ten dollars* a glass.

ARTHUR   Fourteen.

BARBARA   I couldn't help myself. I'm sorry.

ARTHUR   I didn't know you liked cognac.

BARBARA   I don't know what's gotten into me.

ARTHUR   When have you had cognac?

BARBARA   When have I had it? …We had it at, at, the, the uh—you know who I. You were dancing with that—at the Newmans, Newburgs—

ARTHUR   That was benedictine.

BARBARA   …It was?

ARTHUR   The Newsomes. Benedictine.

BARBARA   …Oh. Then…what is cognac?

ARTHUR   It's brandy.

BARBARA   Isn't benedictine brandy?

ARTHUR   Less expensive.

BARBARA   I'm sorry.

ARTHUR   Quite alright.

(They look over their menus. Meanwhile, lights up full at the bar: LEE sits, staring at nothing in particular.)

GRADY   …Ready?

LEE   …Huh? …Yeah. No.

(He checks his watch, taps it, grumbles.)

LEE   What time you got.

GRADY   Quarter till.

LEE   Shhheeees.

(LEE pushes his beer toward GRADY, who refills or replaces it. LEE glances at the TV and turns to JOEL:)

LEE   ...'sa score there, ace?

JOEL   One–nothin'.

(Pause. LEE stares blankly at the TV.)

LEE   ...Tell you what: baseball is one boring-ass game, boys and girls. Look at 'em. Not a care in the world.

(Pause. They all stare blankly at the TV.)

LEE   ...Grown fuckin' men.

(Pause. Back at the restaurant:)

BARBARA   ...Camille?

ARTHUR   Hm?

BARBARA   Camille. The woman. At the party.

ARTHUR   ...The woman at the party.

BARBARA   With the long hair. You *danced* with her, Arthur. I don't know, she came with one of your friends. The one named after the opera.

ARTHUR   I don't have any friends named after an opera.

BARBARA   You don't need to be embarrassed, darling. She was very attractive.

ARTHUR   ...Carmen?

BARBARA   Nnnoooo.

ARTHUR   …Medea?

BARBARA   Actually, you danced with her tits. You and everyone else.

ARTHUR   …Giselle!

BARBARA   Giselle! That's it.

ARTHUR   *Giselle* is a ballet, darling.

(The WAITRESS enters and places one glass each of cognac and wine on the table.)

WAITRESS   Here you are. Are you ready?

BARBARA   I'm sorry, I haven't even—

ARTHUR   We'll need a few more minutes. Thank you.

(The WAITRESS nods politely and exits. ARTHUR and BARBARA consult their menus.)

ARTHUR   "…Tits"?

BARBARA   Well they weren't breasts. Breasts are *glands*. These were *tits*.

ARTHUR   I didn't realize there was a difference.

BARBARA   Thank you for the cognac, Arthur.

ARTHUR   My pleasure.

(BARBARA downs her cognac in one gulp.)

BARBARA   I used to have tits. I had tits in high school. Now I have breasts. *That's* the difference.

ARTHUR   …Is something wrong, darling?

BARBARA   Not a thing! —Excuse me!

(This last to the WAITRESS, then back to ARTHUR:)

BARBARA   Would you mind if I had another?

ARTHUR   …Uhh.

(The WAITRESS returns.)

BARBARA   If it's too expensive, I'll have someth—

ARTHUR   No, no, no, you—

BARBARA   *(To the WAITRESS)* This was delicious. I'd like another, please.

WAITRESS   ...Um. Okay.

(The WAITRESS takes the glass and exits. Pause. BARBARA smiles sweetly at ARTHUR and returns to her menu. ARTHUR stares at her for a moment, then returns to his.)

ARTHUR   ...I saw Tom this morning. He told me to give you his best.

BARBARA   I'm trying to remember. Which one of your friends was she with? It wasn't Barry, his wife was there. Was it Morris?

ARTHUR   I really don't know.

BARBARA   Would you rather not talk about it?

ARTHUR   We can talk about anything you'd like.

BARBARA   Well then let's talk about Tom. How is ol' Tom?

ARTHUR   Doing very well.

BARBARA   It was sweet of him to give me his best. I always just love it when Tom gives me his best. Please tell Tom hello.

ARTHUR   I'll do that.

BARBARA   I haven't seen him in ages. I wonder if he'd like to have lunch sometime.

ARTHUR   I'm sure he would.

BARBARA   With me, I mean.

ARTHUR   I know what you mean.

BARBARA   You're going out of town Thursday, aren't you? Maybe we could—

ARTHUR   I'm sure he'd enjoy that.

BARBARA   ...Hm!

(Pause—still consulting their menus.)

BARBARA   ...And how is Beverly?

ARTHUR   He didn't say.

BARBARA   *(Knowingly)* Mm-hmm. ...And you wouldn't mind?

ARTHUR   Why would I mind?

(The WAITRESS enters with another cognac.)

WAITRESS   Here you are.

BARBARA   Thank you very much. —Thank you, Arthur.

ARTHUR   My pleasure.

(The WAITRESS glances briefly at ARTHUR, then exits.)

BARBARA   ...Well. That was certainly a look.

ARTHUR   I'm sorry?

BARBARA   The look she just gave you.

ARTHUR   I didn't notice.

BARBARA   What did it mean, I wonder.

(Again, she downs her cognac in one gulp.)

BARBARA   She probably thinks you're attractive. You *are* attractive, I can't blame her. And you keep saying "my pleasure." —Yoo hoo!

(She waves to the WAITRESS, who returns.)

BARBARA   You're *too* fucking attractive, if you ask me. And it keeps compounding daily.

ARTHUR   ...What are you doing?

BARBARA   *(To the WAITRESS:)* I'd like another, please.

ARTHUR   Barbara.

BARBARA   What was that look you two exchanged just now?

WAITRESS   Ma'am?

BARBARA   Let me ask you another question. How attractive would you estimate
                my husband to be, in round numbers?

ARTHUR   Bring it. I'm sorry. Just...bring her whatever she'd like.

BARBARA   I would like two, actually. I've always wanted to have two. I've always
                wondered what that would be like. —May I have two, Arthur?

ARTHUR   ...Of course you may.

BARBARA   I'm being so selfish.

ARTHUR   No, you—

BARBARA   I've changed my mind. I'll just—

ARTHUR   She'll have two.

BARBARA   *(Sweetly, to the WAITRESS)* ...Two.

(The WAITRESS glances at ARTHUR, then exits.)

BARBARA   ...There it was again. She's *ashamed* of me. Isn't that charming?
                She's ashamed of me for you.

ARTHUR   Would you like to leave?

BARBARA   Nooooo! I'm having such a lovely evening. Aren't you?

(Pause. No answer.)

BARBARA   ...Arthur? Aren't you having a lovely evening?

ARTHUR   ...Yes. I am.

BARBARA   Isn't this dress attractive?

ARTHUR   Yes, it is.

BARBARA   Did I thank you for it? I thanked you for the earrings, didn't I?

ARTHUR   Yes, you did.

BARBARA   Between the dress, the earrings, and all the other things you buy for
            me, I must be the most attractive woman in the room.

ARTHUR   You are by far the most attractive woman in the room.

BARBARA   In fact, I must be the most attractive woman you know.

(Pause.)

BARBARA   ...Am I? ...Am I the most attractive woman you *know*, Arthur?

ARTHUR   ...Of course you are.

Bob Hungerfrod (Lee) and Melissa Swick (Woman/Louise) at the restaurant.
Photo: Jocelyn Sanders.

BARBARA   Ooooh, I think you're lying to me. I think you're lying to spare my feelings.

ARTHUR   I wouldn't do that.

BARBARA   Say it, then. …Say it.

(The WAITRESS enters, with two cognacs.)

WAITRESS   Here you are: *two* cognacs. …Are you ready?

(Pause. ARTHUR looks again at his menu; BARBARA keeps looking straight at him.)

ARTHUR   Yes, I think so. Barbara? …Darling?

(He looks up from his menu: she is looking at him. He looks straight back:)

ARTHUR   …I'm ready when you are.

(Pause. End scene.)

Scene 2

(Lights up on the bar: LEE, JOEL and GRADY as before, watching TV.)

LEE   *(Yelling at the TV)* Ah, fer—*the hell're you swingin' at?*

JOEL   Inside curve.

LEE   *It's a curve ball!*

JOEL   Guy lays down for anything off-speed.

LEE   *You're a disgrace!*

JOEL   Like he's hypnotized.

LEE   *Snap out of it!*

JOEL   Second in the league in strikeouts.

LEE   Pathetic. Paaaa-thetic. —Time you got now.

GRADY   Little after.

LEE   Fffff.

GRADY   ...Gettin' stood up?

LEE   What, like five after or.

GRADY   Eight...oh-nine.

LEE   Fffffuck. Pull this shit every time. Aura of *mystique*, know what I mean?

GRADY   Oh yeah.

LEE   Ten bucks she shows at *eleven*. Come glidin' in here— "Waitin' long, baby?" Body like a racing yacht. Kinda woman—you take off her bra? Her boobs actually rise *up*.

JOEL   *(To LEE)* Hey.

LEE   "Nah, baby. Come over here and grind your heel in my *eye*."

GRADY   She'll do it too.

LEE   Yes she will. And I'll *let* her.

JOEL   Hey.

LEE   Because men. Because men.

GRADY   Are idiots.

LEE   Yes we are. We are *slaves*.

JOEL   *Hey.*

LEE   Hey! Men are talking.

JOEL   Your guy struck out.

LEE   I know that. I know my guy struck out. He's an idiot. —What's that say?

(He means GRADY'S nametag.)

GRADY   ·   Grady.

LEE   Grady. Lee Valeo. Gimme another one.

(GRADY gets him another beer.)

LEE   ...*Oooor:* okay: she won't show at all. She'll stand me *up*. Know what I'll do?

GRADY   Ask her out again.

LEE   *That'll* show her. Keeps it up, I'll ask her to *marry* me, I'll *have* to, I'll *beg* her to marry me.

GRADY   Yuh. Yuh.

LEE   Six months later, eh? Right? Her nipples are at her *knees*. She weighs two hundred pounds, her butt looks like a *catcher's* mitt. The lessons of history. I don't care how beautiful she is: putting a ring on a woman's finger is like pulling a ripcord on an inflatable raft.

(GRADY laughs.)

LEE   I been there, buddy. Laugh it up.

GRADY   I been there. I am there.

LEE   Hey: hey: three fuckin' times.

GRADY   I ain't been *there*.

LEE   To very, very different women.

GRADY   It's a bitch.

LEE   Yes it is. It is a bitch. ...And her name...was *Lillian*.

GRADY   ...You married the same woman—

LEE   —three fuckin' *times*.

GRADY   Damn!

LEE   I'm an optimist.

GRADY   You're an idiot.

LEE   Yes I am. I'm a *disgrace*, I'm a *slave*. ...Ffff—

(Pause. LEE broods.)

GRADY   ...Hey. She's probably just late.

LEE   Hey: it don't even matter.

GRADY   My wife, she's late all the time. Says she gets *lost*. Sits there daydreaming, looks up, doesn't even know where she is. "What're you *thinking* about?"

LEE   Who *knows*.

GRADY   "I don't know." She's got all these books and goes to these "groups" and puts this stuff in her bath.

LEE   Eh, they all get lost.

GRADY   She's got, like, *emotional* problems.

LEE   They *all* got like emo—

GRADY   She cries all the time.

LEE   They *talk* all the time. They *talk*, they *talk*—

GRADY   I mean about nothing.

LEE   —blah blah blah—

GRADY   "What'sa *matter* with you?"

LEE   —and they never *say* anything.

GRADY   "I don't know." And it's like—

LEE   You just sit there—

GRADY   —what am I supposed to do?

LEE   —slack-jawed, eyes rolled back in your.

GRADY   What about *me*?

LEE   The Silence of the Husbands.

GRADY   I don't understand why they can't just be, you know—

LEE   *Stable.*

GRADY   Stable, just, just—

LEE   *(Pounding the bar for emphasis)* Stable, stable! Just stable! Jesus!

(Pause. GRADY nods his agreement. LEE turns to JOEL:)

LEE   What'sa fuckin' score?

JOEL   Three–nothin'.

LEE   Fuckin' retards. Fuckin *loser retards*! Looka that guy—look at him. Throws like a faggot ordering a spritzer.

JOEL   It's a knuckle ball.

LEE   It's a butterfly. I could kill that. I could do all that—

(His gesture means "—stuff they're doing." JOEL scoffs.)

LEE   Oh—what.

(LEE scoffs back.)

LEE   What is *that.*

JOEL   You couldn't hit that.

LEE   And you could.

JOEL   I didn't say that.

LEE   What're you, some sorta talent scout? Some…all-pro base-coach washed-up fuckin'—what're you, *twelve*?

JOEL   *(Overlapping)* No. No. I played.

LEE	You *played?*
JOEL	I played.
LEE	Oh. Lemme guess, lemme guess, high school.
JOEL	So?
LEE	I'm so depressed.
JOEL	Who is this guy?
LEE	You're torturing yourself. You're—he's watching to see if he's up there, he's waitin' to—what's your name?
JOEL	Forget it.
LEE	How come I never heard of you?
JOEL	Forget it.
LEE	You're a big muscly kid. Why aren't you up there? Why aren't you fuckin' up there fuckin' wailin' on—
JOEL	I had to quit.
LEE	—every guy's *dream*—
JOEL	I had to *quit.*
LEE	What for, you get wounded, you get, what—
JOEL	*(Overlapping)* I had to. No. I got married. …I got married.
LEE	…Now you're torturing *us.*
JOEL	I had to get a job.
LEE	Well. …Okay. Then it's worth it. —Right?
GRADY	Right. Marriage is.
LEE	Marriage is *good.*

JOEL   It *is* good.

LEE   Get him a beer.

JOEL   I'm okay.

LEE   Shut up. —Get him a beer.

JOEL   I gotta drive.

LEE   Have a mint. What's your name.

JOEL   Joel.

LEE   How long you married, Joe.

JOE   …'Bout, two years.

LEE   Two years. Alright. …You happy?

JOEL   Sure. You know.

LEE   Then okay. Marriage is…it separates us from the reptiles.

GRADY   More power to you.

LEE   She treat you okay?

JOEL   Yeah.

LEE   A good wife.

JOEL   *(Shrugging)* She's…

GRADY   You count yourself lucky.

LEE   That's all you can ask.

GRADY   That's right.

LEE   That's exactly right. That's admirable. I respect that. Cheers, hey.

(They raise their glasses and take a sip. Long pause. JOEL sits nodding.)

LEE	...You uh...you still have sex?
JOEL	...What, with my wife?
LEE	No, your dog.
JOEL	...Well...*yeah*. You know. We have.
LEE	Not so much though.
JOEL	No, no, we're...we *have* sex.
LEE	It's boring, though.
JOEL	Nooooo—
LEE	Like beatin' a dead horse.
JOEL	We don't see each other, we—
GRADY	"I'm tiiiired."
JOEL	She works at night, she goes to college.
GRADY	"I don't feeeeel like it."
LEE	Wait'll she stops shaving.
GRADY	"Yeeeeast infection."
LEE	The honeymoon is over.
JOEL	No, we—
LEE	The gild is off the lily.
GRADY	Why God invented cable.
JOEL	It's not like that.
LEE	It's okay.
JOEL	It *is* okay, it's—

LEE   Perfectly natural.   Listen to this, this is something I read: average
             male, *married*, produces less sperm *aaaaaand* less testosterone…
             than a single guy.

(A stunned pause.)

GRADY/JOEL *(Simultaneously)* …No fuckin' way./No way.

LEE   Very scary.

JOEL   It's not my fault.

LEE   It's *not* your fault.   Don't worry about it.   …It'll change.

JOEL   …It will?

LEE   Sure. Wait. Wait'll she wants *kids*.

GRADY   Oh man.

JOEL   She does want kids.

LEE   I mean *wants* kids.

GRADY   Man, my wife got pregnant—

LEE   I mean right *now*.

GRADY   She decided it was *time*—

LEE   We tried for years.

GRADY   She went on this, like this *mission*, this—

LEE   We plowed that field.

GRADY   —this surge, this machine, she was like—

LEE   's like a rodeo.

GRADY   Which, frankly, I never saw in her before.

LEE   Or *since*.

GRADY   Or since.

LEE   Am I right?

GRADY   That's exactly right.

JOEL   You *guys*.

GRADY   It was like, after that, it was like—

LEE   Your job is done.

GRADY   —I'm a paycheck, I'm a—

LEE   You're a sperm donor.

JOEL   Hey.

LEE   You didn't sign up for that.

GRADY   I *didn't* sign up for that.

LEE   When women have children—

JOEL   Hey.

LEE   —it *changes* them. And when women *don't* have children—

JOEL   Hey!

LEE   —it *changes* them.

JOEL   She's not like that.

GRADY   She *is* like that, she *is*, you *wait*. You—I mean—don't get me wrong. I *love* my kids. I love bein' a dad. But sometimes…it's like I don't even *exist*. It's *her*, and *them*, and I'm just…this *guy*, this other *guy*… And what am I gonna do, I'm—

LEE   You're stuck, chief.

GRADY   I'm stuck. I'm trapped, I'm—I *am*.

(Pause. They all think about it.)

LEE	...Well, I'll tell ya. You know who's got this figured out? Know who doesn't have this conversation?
GRADY	...Who?
LEE	Know what a soft-shell crab is?
JOEL	...Yeah.
LEE	What is it.
JOEL	...It's...it's a crab with—
LEE	It's a female crab when she's molting. When a female crab is molting, she sheds her shell, so she's soft. Right? When she's soft, that's when she's vulnerable for like octopuses or fish or whatever to eat her. Obviously.
GRADY	Right.
LEE	It's *also* the only time she can get laid. This is a beautiful story. The male crab comes around, he gets on her, they have, you know.
GRADY	Sure.
LEE	And then what. What does the male crab *do* after he has sex.
GRADY/JOEL	*(Simultaneously)* He leaves.
LEE	He *stays*. He *stays* right on top of her, for like...days. He *holds* her, I'm saying, until her shell grows back, until she's *safe*.
GRADY	I didn't know that.
LEE	It's a love story. Makes you ashamed almost.
GRADY	It's a beautiful story.
LEE	*Wrong*, boneheads, *wrong*. Worst fuckin' story you ever heard. He doesn't give a shit about *her*. He's protecting his *eggs*. Soon's she's crusty, he's *outta* there... Now, what does that *tell* us.
GRADY	...Well.

LEE   Rhinos, hippos, same thing. Whole animal kingdom practically. Know who hangs around to be *husbands*? Wolves. Whales. And they're *endangered*. Life's rich pageant. Let me tell both you something. Listen to this. Marriage. Okay? *Marriage*. Is an institution. That benefits the male. In no way, shape or form whatsoever. Financially, cost of living: you tell me.

GRADY   Sssshees–

LEE   You produce, she consumes. You create, she destroys. She's a *liability*. You're better off alone, okay? Yes? But no. You exchange that, this is what you are *told*, for, for, for what: "quality of life." What does that *mean*?

GRADY   That, I'll tell you what th—

LEE   That means you're *saddled* with this great...bloated black *hole* of emotional *need*, hopelessly in *debt*, dick in your fist, praying for prostate cancer.

GRADY   *(Interspersed)* Mmm. That's. Yup. Yup.

LEE   It's a fairy tale. It's a unicorn, it's a two-headed coin. Marriage is the death of hope, is what it is.

GRADY   *(Echoing, agitated)* —fairy tale—unicorn—it is—it is, yup.

LEE   And you wanna know what else? ...She feels the *same*. *Way*.

(Long pause. GRADY and JOEL process that.)

GRADY   ...Huh.

LEE   ...So let me ask you this. You ever cheat on her?

GRADY   ...My wife?

LEE   Your dog.

GRADY   *(Waffling)* ...Uhhh. Huh!

LEE   I mean, I don't mean to pry. You're among friends, right?

JOEL   Yeah.

LEE   Male code. Guys in a bar.

GRADY   Hey: no.

LEE   I cheated on Lil, makes you feel any better. Only, I didn't think of it as cheating.

GRADY   ...What'd you think of it as?

LEE   I don't know. Being married. It's like...it's like chewing the same damn gum over and over for the rest of your life. Sometimes you need some new gum.

GRADY   Some Juicy Fruit.

LEE   Some Juicy Fruit. Huh? Some *Bazooka*! Boom, pow! Fidelity, hey, for my money, I'm all for it. But it's not the same thing as *monogamy*. This is a common mistake. Monogamy—is *demeaning*, it's an imposition on *nature*. Nature abhors a wedding. It's *blackmail*, the whole thing. And they work it so the only fuckin' thing worse'n bein' married is gettin' divorced. Know how easy it is to get a divorce in Egypt? You walk up to her, you say, "I divorce thee, I divorce thee, I divorce thee." Three times: boom.

JOEL   Wow.

LEE   That was like, in olden times. Tijuana, you get a divorce for what, fifty bucks. Here? Christ. It's easier to fake your own *death*. My wife, we litigated like *wolverines*. You think you know somebody? You say you're *married* to her, you *live* with her? So *what*. You divorce somebody, you see shit you never seen before.

(Pause. LEE drinks, remembers:)

LEE   ...People are vicious fucks. You know? People are savage, flesh-eating vicious fucks. ...And I have a high opinion of people.

(Pause. End scene.)

Scene 3

(ARTHUR and BARBARA at the restaurant. ARTHUR is finishing his dinner; BARBARA has already finished and is by now politely drunk. She is holding the WAITRESS hostage to a story.)

BARBARA   You remember it, dear! —It was this, this incredible restaurant right on the water with these incredible aquariums full of angelfish and lionfish and...tigerfish and I was wearing this slinky black strapless number with heels and pearls and he couldn't take his filthy eyes off me a minute—could you, Arthur.

ARTHUR   *(Perfectly agreeable)* Not for a moment.

BARBARA   It wasn't even mine, the dress wasn't, and the pearls were fake, but the dinner was fabulous and the view was spectacular—wasn't it, Arthur.

ARTHUR   As was the ocean.

BARBARA   Isn't he sweet? On our second date, we went to somebody's wedding and I wore a skirt that was entirely too short, but he walked around with his old fraternity brothers sticking his chest out all night—didn't you, darling.

ARTHUR   As did you, darling.

BARBARA   We ended up in one of those—what do you call it—a pagoda—

ARTHUR   Gazebo.

BARBARA   —a gazebo, under a perfect crescent moon listening to the orchestra and drinking a bottle of bordello.

ARTHUR   Bordeaux.

BARBARA   Bordeaux. —I've only recently started drinking.

WAITRESS   Would you like some dessert?

BARBARA   I'm just getting to the best part. It was on our...I don't know, we were drinking—what was it—at Nico's, that awful Greek stuff. Uzi?

ARTHUR   ...Yes.

BARBARA   We were drinking Uzi, after dinner, and he said the most wonderful, wonderful thing. He was gazing at me almost…sadly almost, so I asked him, "What are you thinking about?" And he touched—

(BARBARA takes ARTHUR's hand and holds his fingers to her cheek:)

BARBARA   —he touched the tips of his fingers to my cheek. And he said, "Eternity…is on your lips and your eyes." —That's Shakespeare or something, isn't it darling.

ARTHUR   Would you like some dessert?

(ARTHUR gracefully withdraws his hand.)

BARBARA   Oh, no, no thank you, I couldn't.

ARTHUR   Another drink, perhaps.

BARBARA   May I?

ARTHUR   I insist.

BARBARA   *(To the WAITRESS)* Just one more.

(The WAITRESS exits, relieved. Pause.)

ARTHUR   …Did you enjoy your snapper?

BARBARA   My snapper was a little gamey. How is your flounder?

ARTHUR   It's haddock. It's what they call scrod.

BARBARA   Sounds delicious.

ARTHUR   It is. I can't remember ever having scrod so tender.

(Beat. They smile.)

ARTHUR   Would you excuse me?

(He folds his napkin and stands.)

BARBARA   Where are you going?

(He stops to answer, decides not to, and exits. Pause. BARBARA sits alone. End scene.)

Scene 4

(Back at the bar: LEE, GRADY and JOEL, as before. The game is still on TV.)

GRADY Back of the head with a toilet seat. I mean—*wham.*

LEE Ehhh.

GRADY Four stitches. Plates, ashtrays, potted plants. Curtain rod, magazine rack. I'm not saying she's a bitch. I'm just saying she has six nipples.

LEE This is nothing.

GRADY She told me she hates me. I mean, "Hate you, I hate you." And she meant it.

LEE Aaah, they get bored.

GRADY I don't think she's very happy.

LEE I still got that beat. —Whatta *you* got?

(This last to JOEL, who shrugs.)

GRADY She was happy *before* we got married. I mean, *I'm* the same guy. She didn't hate me *then.*

LEE *(Coaxing JOEL)* What.

GRADY It's like I live alone sometimes. And maybe she feels the same way, but that doesn't—

LEE *(To JOEL)* 's her name?

GRADY Sylvia. But then sometimes it's okay again. You know? …Sometimes, sometimes you think maybe you oughta just stick it out because maybe maybe *maybe* someday it's gonna be great again. …I don't know.

LEE *(To JOEL)* …Go ahead.

JOEL Nah, man.

LEE Hey.

(But JOEL gestures it away.)

LEE — Brady, set him up.

JOEL No, hey.

(But GRADY gets JOEL a beer.)

LEE Listen to this: my wife? Stabbed me in the *back*.

GRADY How.

LEE With a letter opener. I mean actually *stabbed* me in my *back*. In my *sleep*. This was divorce number one.

GRADY And you married her again?

LEE It's sorta hard to explain.

JOEL What'd she stab you for?

LEE For screwin' around on her.

GRADY And she married *you* again?

LEE It's really very hard to explain.

JOEL Hey.

(JOEL gestures toward the door. They all turn toward it as an attractive WOMAN in her mid-thirties enters.)

LEE …Whoa.

JOEL That her?

LEE …I wish.

GRADY *(To the WOMAN)* How ya doin'?

WOMAN Hello.

(THE WOMAN finds a seat at a table or at the bar away from the others. GRADY pours her a drink. LEE takes a notepad out of his pocket, glances at his watch, and makes a quick notation. Then he reaches into the gift box beside him for a moment, closes it, repositions it, and turns to JOEL.)

LEE   ...So where is she, this...what'd you—?

JOEL   Marie. Work.

LEE   Where work.

JOEL   Waitress, coupla blocks over. I gotta pick her up.

LEE   *(Nodding)* ...I knew a Marie once.

(Pause. LEE returns to the game.)

JOEL   How'd...how did she—?

LEE   *(Loudly, to the TV)* Alright now, Senor...Qui-no-nez-whoever-you-are, let's...get a hit here, something.

JOEL   ...How'd she catch you?

LEE   Who, Lil?

JOEL   Yeah. How'd she?

LEE   *(Knowingly, not defensive)* ...Why you wanna know?

JOEL   Hey, I'm—

LEE   I'll tell you. It's okay, no. You listen to this: I experienced *lapses*. I did not respect my craft. In the manner of my forefathers. It's like the Ten Commandments, you know your Ten Commandments?

JOEL   "...Thou shalt not commit adul—"

LEE   One—shut up and be saved. One: She's a blonde, the other woman, got blonde hair, wears Chanel #5: never wear a blue shirt, blue suit, blue anything. Two: any wife, anywhere, can pick up Chanel #5 from a hunnerd feet. You stop off at the gas station, you spill gas all over yourself, you go home, wife says, "Boy, do you *stink*, go take a shower." You follow me?

JOEL   …Aaaah.

LEE   Never give her your cell number. They record everybody who calls in. You buy *her* pearls for Christmas, whatever, you buy the *wife* the same thing. See what I'm saying?

JOEL   Yeah.

LEE   Cover: always have a cover. Some guy, "I was out with the guys," Brady over there, *me*, whoever, we'll back you up. You go out: no credit cards. Never undertip, never overtip. Always keep an extra pair of shorts under the driver's seat, never *tell* anybody, and never, *never* shit where you eat. Oh, and one more thing: here is wisdom: *lllllie*. Always always always *lie*. This was my undoing. *…Let's go there, Lllllouis, put 'er inna parkin' lot, here we go, here we go.*

(This last to the TV.)

JOEL   …You told her?

LEE   She asked. Honesty, I'm sorry, is a very flimsy policy. They're like, they hang *on* to it, the *details*, they're *haunted* by details. "Let's get *past* it, baby." They can't get past it. This was divorce number two. Years later, *great* husband, good husband, doesn't matter, you're still that *asshole*, they're like *obsessed*: "How many times? What did she *do*?" You love this wife of yours? You got respect for her? You hang your head high and you *lie*.

(Pause. GRADY has engaged the WOMAN in small talk that we can't hear. LEE glances at them, then turns back to JOEL:)

LEE   …Gonna bring her back here?

JOEL   …Nah. Go home, probably.

LEE   …She's okay, you say?

JOEL   Yeah. She's—

LEE   Well that's good. That's okay. You deserve it. Hard to…hard to find a—*wrong parkin' lot there, Lllouis,* Lois, whatever the hell your name is.

(This last to the TV.)

JOEL   ...What was divorce number three?

LEE   Number three was she ate a bottle of sleeping pills on my birthday.

(LEE downs his beer and calls GRADY over.)

LEE   ...Hey. Brady. Hey. ...Who'sat?

(GRADY shrugs, gets LEE a beer.)

LEE   Regular?

GRADY   Occasional.

LEE   What's she drinkin'?

GRADY   Rye.

LEE   Damn.

(Pause. LEE looks at the WOMAN; so does JOEL.)

LEE   ...See what she's...see what she's doing?

JOEL   *(No)* ...Yeah.

LEE   See it? ...She's rubbin' her finger 'round the...'round the rim of her glass. What's it mean, a woman rubbin' her finger 'round the...rim of her glass like that.

JOEL   ...Uhh.

LEE   *(To the WOMAN)* Hey. Hey. ...Hey Miss. ...You wanna drink?

WOMAN   ...No thank you.

LEE   I'll buy you a drink. What's your name.

WOMAN   I have a drink.

LEE   My treat. —Give 'er another one a' whatever it is.

WOMAN   *No, I. ...No. But thank you.*

LEE   My pleasure. Lee Valeo.

(She just smiles.)

LEE   *(To JOEL, ironically)* …Chicks dig me.

(Pause. LEE returns to the TV:)

LEE   *Okay, Lois, go down swingin', go down swingin', here we go.*

WOMAN   It's Luis.

LEE   …What's that?

WOMAN   *Luis.*

LEE   …Oh. Well, nice to meet ya, Louise! You wanna join us?

WOMAN   I'm sorry, have I seen you before?

LEE   I don't know, have you?

WOMAN   You look…

LEE   Lee Valeo, come on over, have a drink.

WOMAN   I'm, uh, waiting. For someone.

LEE   So am I, what the hell. Come on over.

(But she just smiles, sips her drink and looks elsewhere.)

LEE   …This is what you call "mixed signals."

JOEL   She's got a ring.

LEE   So what? Whatta you think a woman like that comes in here for, a "rye"?

JOEL   So you go over.

LEE   I don't wanna go over.

(Pause. LEE catches the WOMAN looking at him; then they both look away. To JOEL:)

LEE   …You know what Einstein said about this?

JOEL   Einstein?

LEE   Evil. This is what he said. *Evil*…does not know its own mind. Evil is *inconsistent*. That's why it's evil.

(Pause. Then LEE and the WOMAN catch each other's eyes again. LEE waves and smiles. She turns away again. He sighs and shakes his head. End scene.)

Scene 5

(At the restaurant: BARBARA is still at her table. The WAITRESS now sits at the table listening, exhausted and uncomfortable. ARTHUR is still gone.)

BARBARA   It was the night before our wedding. I heard his voice beneath my window, so I *ran* downstairs but by the time I got there, there was only this package on the doorstep, all wrapped in white—a birdcage! And inside was a little—a parrot, a baby, with green and orange feathers and bright yellow eyes. Which you have to admit was very sweet, don't you think that's the sweetest thing you ever heard?

(The WAITRESS nods, shrugs.)

BARBARA   There was a card tied to the cage that said…"I…I wish I was your bird." Which was also very sweet but actually sort of…sort of *dopey*. For Arthur, I mean. I mean I would have expected something a little more…I don't know…*clever* than "I wish I was your bird." I made a joke about it, and he said it was an "illusion." …Which I thought was rather…unkind, for Arthur.

WAITRESS   "…Allusion"?

BARBARA   Hm?

WAITRESS   Maybe he said "*allusion.*" Like, to a book.

BARBARA   …Hmm!   …Well that would explain why the card was signed "Romeo," wouldn't it. I thought that was his *name.*

(She considers that a moment, then presses on:)

BARBARA   …Huh! …He would eat out of Arthur's hand, Romeo would, but he wouldn't let *me* come near him. Birds are like that, they *bond* with one person, for their entire *life,* and that's who they go to. He would whistle, Arthur would, and Romeo would come *flying* through the house. It got to be a game with Chelsea and me, whenever Arthur was out of town. We would whistle and Romeo would *fly* through the house looking for—are you sure I'm not keeping you from something?

WAITRESS   Um, no.

BARBARA   Do you need to go home? I don't mean to keep you.

WAITRESS   I'm waiting for my ride.

BARBARA   What a coincidence. What do you suppose happened to mine?

(The WAITRESS shrugs.)

BARBARA   …He'll come back. He allllways comes back. It's a wonderful thing, marriage is. I almost fucked one of his friends once. In a bathroom. I wanted to, too. I came *thiiiis* close. But I stopped myself, I *made* myself…say no. …And I can tell you there are nights I wish I'd just gone ahead and…done it, but I…I *remind* myself…that you cannot mistake *ecstasy*…for…*happiness.* And you can't have *both,* for Christ's sake, you just…you just *can't.* And people are *meant* to be together. If they weren't, then what would…what would there *be,* what would you *live* for?

WAITRESS   …I don't know.

BARBARA   I feel sorry for those people who get divorced after only a few years, for what they miss. It's not what you think it is, you can't know what you're saying "yes" to, but really, marriage is, it's, it's a—

WAITRESS   I *know.* …I'm married.

BARBARA   …You're not wearing your ring.

WAITRESS   No, I uh—

BARBARA   You get bigger tips.

(The WAITRESS shrugs.)

BARBARA   Ahahaha. They're all such idiots. With their little winks and calling
               you "darling" and staring down your shirt while you're pouring their
               drinks. I'll bet you make out like a little thief, don't you.

(Pause. BARBARA regards her with some contempt, then snaps herself out of it.)

BARBARA   …Well. *Anyway.* One day, when Chelsea is about eight or nine,
               we're in the kitchen, and she whistles, and Romeo flies in and runs
               smack into the window and lays there in a twisted heap on the floor,
               at which point she starts *howling* like, like I don't know what, which
               thank God Arthur wasn't home yet, he hates "displays." So: skip
               to the funeral. We're standing there, at sundown, the three of us,
               staring down at the *open grave.* Chelsea is, she's…she's crying
               but…there's a word for it. She's holding Romeo in her arms, not
               wailing but…it starts with a "K."

(The WAITRESS doesn't know.)

BARBARA   …Oh well. We have a prayer, and she wants to have another, so we
               have another, and this goes on for about forty-five minutes. *Finally,*
               Arthur's had enough, so he slooooowly peels her fingers away from
               Romeo, and he slides him into the sacred argyle burial sock, and
               he *places the sock in the grave.* As soon as he touches the shovel,
               she *throws* her arms around him and buries her face in his chest and
               starts that…*sound* again.

(Pause.)

BARBARA   …Well. We're standing there, Arthur and I. Looking at each other.
               Down at the sock. Back and forth.

(Pause.)

BARBARA   …The sock…starts to *move.* …I look at Arthur. He's holding Chelsea.
               She's delirious. I look at the sock. It's *moving.* …So. …You know
               what I did?

(Pause.)

BARBARA   …I…I stepped on it.

(Pause. BARBARA takes a long sip from her drink, trembling, and puts it down. The WAITRESS has straightened almost imperceptibly, and is looking at her. BARBARA remembers:)

BARBARA   "…Keening." …Keening.

(Pause. End scene.)

Scene 6

(Back at the bar, GRADY and the WOMAN, who will now be called LOUISE, are leaning in, having a private conversation; we can't hear much of it—only an occasional swell of intimate laughter or small talk. LEE will watch them out of one eye, but JOEL is oblivious to them.)

LEE   You're a lapdog.

JOEL   Nooooo—

LEE   You are, you're a lapdog. You don't see this as a problem?

JOEL   She gets upset, she can't handle it.

LEE   No fights, no arguments, you don't—

JOEL   Any sort of conflict—

LEE   You're a pussy.

JOEL   —she *leaves*, she goes out "walking."

LEE   You're a vagina.

JOEL   Hey fuck you.

LEE   "Walking."

JOEL   No, fuck you.

LEE   She's stonewallin' you, ace. Passion aggression.

JOEL   Forget it.

LEE   I'm tryin' to help here. Gotta stand up for your rights here. Where's she go, these "walks"?

JOEL   How would I know.

LEE   What, you don't tail her?

(JOEL scoffs. Lee scoffs back.)

LEE   Jesus Christ. How you know she ain't gettin' a little on the side? Huh? How you know she ain't walkin' down the street give the neighbor kid a blowjob?

JOEL   She *isn't*, she's—

LEE   What's she doin'.

JOEL   She's "thinking."

LEE   Oof.

JOEL   I *used* to. I used to go out and—but *fuck* it, you know? Let *her* work it out. I don't even ask. Let *her* come to *me*.

LEE   Well alright.

JOEL   It *is* a fight, it's a *fight*. She comes back, sometimes it goes on for days, *I'm* not saying anything.

LEE   Fuck it.

JOEL   Fuck it. Fuck it. …And then we make up, and that's, you know, *that's* okay… But then the whole thing starts all over again. Nothing gets *resolved*, nothing gets *discussed*. Sometimes I think...sometimes I think she really *does* hate me.

LEE   ...Well that's okay.

JOEL   No it isn't. I don't, I mean, I mean...I'm not a bad guy.

LEE   I know.

JOEL   I gave up a lot.

LEE   You were too young.

JOEL   I quit baseball, right? So I could get a *job*. And I was, I was—

LEE   You were good.

JOEL   I *was* good.

LEE   I know.

JOEL   So now I play *softball*. Which she *also* hates. She *used* to come watch me, she used to come out all the *time*, all the home games. Now she... I don't know. ...Maybe we *were*, maybe we were too—

LEE   More people get divorced in their twenties than they do in their fifties.

(Pause. JOEL is taken somewhat aback.)

LEE   ...More people cheat the first two years than any other time. And that's a fact.

JOEL   ...Well, I don't know if—

LEE   Human scientists, they got it all boiled down. Boy meets girl, boy thinks, "oooo," hands get all clammy, heart pounding, "I'm in *loooove*," remember that? Know what that is? ...Biology It's a hormone. It's Charles Darwin rubbin' your dick. Know how long that lasts, how long it's detectable in your blood?

(JOEL doesn't know.)

LEE   *Two* years. Two years. Statistically, hey: you haven't got a prayer.

JOEL   Well... But. It's like. ...My grandparents, okay? They were like *seventeen* when they—

LEE   You can't compare that.

JOEL   —when they, when he *dies*, right? Why not? When *he* dies, *she* dies like *four days* later. They put it in the *paper*. In their will, they wanted their ashes mixed in *champagne* and poured around their apple tree. They stuck it out like sixty *years*. They used to hold *hands*. That's *love*, man, that's—

LEE   My folks, they stuck it out forty-three.

JOEL   That's what I'm saying.

LEE   Their fortieth wedding day, anniversary, whatever, right? Ma looks over at him, she says, "You know, Ed? I'm real proud of you." Pop looks at her, he's hard of hearing, he says, "Yeah, well. I'm pretty tired of you too." Coupla years later he writes me a letter: "I'm stone deaf, and it's *such* a relief."

(JOEL smiles.)

LEE   *She* dies, right? Pop sits there in his recliner all night. Used to watch porno movies. Happy as a clam. Come over one morning, still sittin' there. Beer in his hand, baloney sandwich, eyes glued to the screen. "Pop?" ...He's *dead*. ...I called the cops but I left the TV on.

(LOUISE cackles wickedly, or GRADY laughs knowingly. Pause.)

LEE   ...You watchin' this?

JOEL   Uh-huh.

LEE   Two-faced bastard. "Waiting for someone."

JOEL   Huh.

LEE   ...See what he's, see his hands?

JOEL   Yeah.

| LEE | Always moving. Touch his hair. His lip, got something on his lip. Older guys, guys with money, it's the watch, class ring: ornaments. Brady's got...what's Brady got: his *lip*. |

(Pause. They watch:)

| LEE | ...Voices. Hands. Eyes—watch the eyes. She ain't interested, they *drift*, they wander. She's interested, they like, they *focus*, they *stare*. For a split second she thinks you're looking at her mouth. You *are*. |

| JOEL | ...He said he didn't. |

| LEE | Didn't what. |

| JOEL | Cheat. |

| LEE | Well he lied, didn't he. That's why they call it cheating. Some cultures, in France? They don't call it cheating. |

| JOEL | What do they call it? |

| LEE | "Sex." |

(Pause. They watch.)

| JOEL | *(Abruptly)* I gotta go. |

| LEE | You got time. |

| JOEL | I gotta pick her up. |

| LEE | You're already late. Let *her* wait for *you*, see. |

| JOEL | She's gonna kill me. |

| LEE | So what. Lapdog. I'm sittin' here alone, think I wanna watch *this* all night? |

(He indicates GRADY and LOUISE, who at this moment are stealing a short, soft kiss. LEE and JOEL watch. Pause.)

| LEE | ...Bitch. |

(LEE takes a big swig of beer and keeps watching. Then, abruptly:)

LEE   Ever cheat on her?

JOEL   …Me? …No.

LEE   Not even once. Not even a little bit.

JOEL   Huh. Nooooo.

LEE   Never even thought about it. Guy like you. Big baseball stud.

JOEL   …Well, yeah, I, you know. I *thought* about it.

LEE   Who with.

(Pause. JOEL is surprised at the question.)

LEE   …Who *with*? Little sideline cheerleader chicky?

(JOEL shakes his head sheepishly.)

LEE   …Pick one.

JOEL   *(Shrugging)* …This girl at…this girl I used to.

LEE   Nice lookin'. Hot little body.

JOEL   Yeah.

LEE   You fool around? …Just a little. Little foolin' around between friends, everybody does it, no harm done.

JOEL   Jees.

LEE   Second base. …Triple? Huh? Huh? You scurvy fuckin' dog. You *hound*.

JOEL   *(Embarrassed)* Shut up.

LEE   You hit a home run.

JOEL   Noooo.

LEE   Aaah: say you *did*.

JOEL   I didn't.

LEE   Say you did. Say you *parked* it. Say you smacked it over left
                 center.

(JOEL chuckles, despite himself.)

LEE   Knocked out the stadium lights. Let's say you broke windshields in
                 the fuckin' parkin' lot. ...Let's just...let's just say. Okay?

(Pause.)

JOEL   ...Okay.

LEE   It's okay. It's not your fault. ...It's not your fault. It's natural.

(Pause. JOEL listens:)

LEE   ...You say, this is what you say: "I take this woman, better or worse,
                 death till we part." ...And you're not *lying*. No one, no one *lies*
                 about this, right? You mean every *word*.

JOEL   ...Okay.

LEE   But. But *what*. ...Years go by. Things...things *change*. Things
                 happen. You were *mistaken*. You didn't *know*. It's not *her* fault,
                 it's not *yours*. ...Things fall apart, Joe. Because everything must fall
                 apart. Second law of thermodynamics.

JOEL   ...I...I don't—

LEE   "Love is forever."

(Pause. JOEL has no idea what to say.)

LEE   "Love is forever." This is what we say. This is what we mean, this is
                 what we *want*. We don't lie about this. In your whole life, listen to
                 this: your whole life, how many hearts you break. Probably a lot.

JOEL   I don't know.

LEE   Think about 'em. Those girls who *loved* you. What'd they do. After
                 all the—"Ooooo, I'll never be happy again!" What'd they *do*.

(Pause. Before JOEL can answer:)

LEE   They spend their life—did they grow *old*—mourning and pining the loss of their one true love? …No. Fuck no. Who does? Two years, they can't even see your *face*. Five years, ten years: you're not even a memory. You're a story maybe they heard once a long time ago they can't even barely *remember*. Why. …Why.

JOEL   …Life goes on.

LEE   Yes. Yes. And why does life go on. …It goes on because it's indifferent. It goes on because life doesn't give a shit. About you, about them, about what you said and what you meant. Love, okay, dies. This is what they don't tell you. Because it doesn't give a shit either. It's a chemical. It's a rumor. It's a word you said once. And that's all it is.

(Pause.)

LEE   …Love is *loss*. Family is pain. Marriage is loneliness. …We've all been lied to.

(Long, gloomy pause; JOEL breaks the spell.)

JOEL   …What are you, like a, like a biologist?

LEE   Me? Noooo.

JOEL   Psychologist? What.

LEE   Me?

JOEL   Yeah.

LEE   I'm a private investigator.

(Pause.)

JOEL   …No kidding.

LEE   No kidding.

JOEL   …Like a, like a detective.

LEE   Yeah. Well, "investigator." Detective sounds like a cop. "Dick" sounds like…well it sounds like a dick. Valeo's not my real name, either. I'm just tryin' it out, like a professional name. "Valeo."

JOEL	What's your real name.
LEE	My business, you gotta have a cool name. Cool name and a video camera.
JOEL	Really. …What kinda, what kinda work do you…
LEE	You mean like cases? What kinda cases?
JOEL	Yeah.
LEE	All kinds. Domestic shit mostly. You wouldn't believe all the domestic shit. Wives, ex-wives, husbands, fiances, babysitters: I got work every night of the week. I know more about what goes on in people's bedrooms and backseats and office supply rooms than Dear Abby. I'm a spy in the house of love. I could be a therapist if I weren't so pissed off all the time.
JOEL	Are you uh…you working now?
LEE	What, you mean here?
JOEL	Yeah.
LEE	Like on a case?
JOEL	*Yeah.*
LEE	Actually, if I was, I couldn't tell you.
JOEL	How come?
LEE	Ethics. Difference 'tween me and most guys? I try'n instill some ethics into it. Make it, you know, more sportsmanlike.
JOEL	How do you, how—
LEE	More "above board." Make myself, you know, more conspicuous, let 'em see my face. You spend that much time tailin' somebody, it's nice to say hello.
JOEL	You talk to 'em?

LEE   All the time. Shit, I usually try n' buy 'em a *drink*. I'm a, you know, I'm a good guy. People are shameless when you're sittin' right next to 'em. Somebody tells you something, that's admissable. Sometimes all you gotta do is *ask*.

JOEL   …Really.

LEE   People'll tell a total stranger anything they wanna know.

(Uncomfortable pause. GRADY and LOUISE have moved in very close to one another.)

JOEL   …Anybody ever…anybody ever catch you?

LEE   Catch me what?

JOEL   Spyin' on 'em. Fuckin' with 'em.

LEE   Hey man, I *tell* 'em. …If they *ask*, I just tell 'em.

(Pause.)

LEE   …I don't fuck with people.

(Pause. JOEL looks at him. LEE grins and drinks his beer. End scene.)

Scene 7

(Night: lights up half on an empty living room—no more than a stuffed chair and TV/VCR unit facing upstage.

Elsewhere: lights up half on BARBARA and ARTHUR, in their bedroom. BARBARA is sitting at her vanity, facing the audience, staring into what we assume is her mirror, brushing her hair languidly, absently. Behind her, in bed, ARTHUR is reading a folded newspaper or flipping channels with a remote. From time to time, she will look at him in her mirror.

Elsewhere: lights up full on JOEL and the WAITRESS, who is his wife MARIE, sitting beside one another. They are either in their car, JOEL driving, or on their couch. MARIE, exhausted and disgusted, is drinking a beer and rubbing her eyes and temples.)

JOEL   …I'm sorry.

MARIE   And these *stories* she was—this *bird*, when they were *young*, this *guy*
               she—talking, talking, *talking*: "Why are you *telling* me this!" Until
               finally it's just me and Rudy—Angie's gone, grill's *closed*, we're stuck
               there with—like *hostages*. And *smiling*! "Oh, he'll come back! He
               always comes back!"

JOEL   ...I'm sorry.

(MARIE scoffs. Pause.)

MARIE   ...A bar.

JOEL   ...Yuh.

MARIE   ...*Which* bar.

JOEL   Right down the street.

MARIE   The whole time.

JOEL   *Yeah.*

(Pause. She drinks her beer.)

MARIE   ...So finally he *does*, right? Real polite too, I felt sorry for him. Rudy
               has to like...*fetch* her, he has to like *pull* her out of her chair—he says
               she *hit* on him—she's like: "Goodnight, everyone! Thank you ev—"

JOEL   Spanish guy.

MARIE   Hm?

JOEL   Rudy. With the ponytail.

MARIE   Oh. Yeah. "Cath-tilian." "Rodolfo." "Angelica." They say they get
               bigger tips. ...Oh, and then she wants Friday off because "Anthony"
               is coming in. Can't get "Anthony" within a hundred miles without.
               They're like *rabbits*.

JOEL   Where's your ring?

MARIE   Oh.

(She digs it out of her pocket and puts it on.)

MARIE   So I got a study group that afternoon, *then* I get to cover *her* shift. I mean, and she's such a *bitch* about it. She'll come in *gloating* about "what a wonderful guy" he is.

(Pause. She shakes her head in disgust.)

MARIE   ...So how was "the game."

JOEL   *Fine.*

MARIE   You stink like beer. I hope you take a shower.

(The lights on JOEL and MARIE come to half.

Elsewhere, lights come up full on the living room. LEE enters or is standing beside the TV. He removes from his gift box a small video camera, which he connects quickly to the VCR. He picks up the remote, plops himself down in the chair and turns the TV on.

Elsewhere, lights come up immediately on a neutral space—or perhaps in front of a motel room door. GRADY and LOUISE enter the space and begin slow, silent, sensuous maneuvers. Perhaps she dangles the room key in front of him and drops it down her blouse; he responds by rubbing her breasts or going in after it, and then kissing her very passionately. Or perhaps he holds the key in his teeth, pulls her to him as if in a tango, she taking the key from his mouth with hers, then kissing him as he rubs her body. Eventually, they move out of the space—or into the room—into darkness.

LEE sits staring at the screen.

Lights come to full on ARTHUR and BARBARA. Sitting in bed, ARTHUR has become aware that BARBARA has been watching him in her mirror.)

ARTHUR   *(Pleasantly)* ...What are you looking at?

BARBARA   ...Hmm?

ARTHUR   ...What are you looking at.

BARBARA   ...Nothing.

(She brushes her hair. ARTHUR watches her. Eventually, she feels his eyes upon her and looks at him in her mirror.)

BARBARA   ...What are *you* looking at.

ARTHUR   *(Tenderly)* ...You.

(Pause: she smiles, weakly. He completes the thought, ominously:)

ARTHUR   ...Your lips. ...Your eyes. ...Eternity.

(BARBARA's smile fades. She and ARTHUR watch one another in the mirror. Then, all lights fade to black except for a few moments the half-light on LEE, slouched in his chair. Then that too fades. End Act I.)

ACT TWO
Scene 1

(In an airport terminal: perhaps we hear a departure announcement over a loudspeaker.

LEE and a MAN are standing or sitting next to each other. We cannot see the MAN behind the newspaper he's reading. LEE is reading a magazine and has found something in it amusing:)

LEE   *(Chuckling to himself)*   ...Huh. ...Huh. ...Huh!

(The MAN eventually lowers his paper: he is ARTHUR.)

LEE   ...Listen to this. Guy in Israel: "Yihya Av...Avaram." Spends thirty-two years in prison—thirty-two *years*—for, for "disobeying a rab, rabbin—"

ARTHUR   Rabbinical?

LEE   "—a rabbinical order to grant his wife a divorce." He *dies* there.

ARTHUR   Hm.

(Pause. LEE reads further:)

LEE   ...All he had to do—listen to this—all he had to do was say three words: "I am willing." Just *say* it, and they let him go.

(Pause. No response.)

LEE   ...Eighty-one years *old*. What a clown.

(Pause. No response.)

LEE   ...Boy, he musta hated her *guts*, huh?

ARTHUR   Or loved her very much.

LEE   ...I don't know. Thirty two *years*, man. That's like...that's like bein' a *Cubs* fan.

(ARTHUR nods politely and goes back to his reading.)

LEE   ...You married?

ARTHUR   ...Yes. Yes I am.

LEE   I was. ...Three fuckin' times.

(ARTHUR smiles politely. Pause.)

LEE   ...Same woman, too.

(Pause. No response.)

LEE   ...It's a bitch.

(Pause. No response. LEE extends a hand.)

LEE   ...Lee Coltrane.

ARTHUR   Pleasure.

(They shake. Pause.)

LEE   ...Not a Cubs fan, are ya?

(End scene.)

Scene 2

(Mid-day. LOUISE sits at a table at a burger joint. She wears sunglasses, which she may not take off, and her hand is bandaged. She's strung out. Nearby are one or two identical tables; MARIE sits at one of them having her lunch and reading a textbook.

Perhaps we hear the ambient noise of children in the play area. Presently, GRADY enters with a tray of burgers and stuff and sits across from LOUISE. He gives her a drink with a straw; otherwise, the rest of the food is his.)

GRADY   …You okay? This table okay?

(LOUISE shakes her head in disgust.)

GRADY   …Okay, I know, look.

LOUISE   What's this.

GRADY   Diet Pepsi.

(She pushes it away.)

GRADY   Look. Just. Okay? The thing we gotta do. I been giving this some thought.

LOUISE   *Have* you.

GRADY   Don't, see, this is exactly what—

LOUISE   *(Overlapping)* You've given it—you've given it some *thought*. You've given it some *thought*, and you meet me at, at—

GRADY   Don't, don't, don't—

LOUISE   I know why you wanted to come here. I know why you—what do you think I am?

GRADY   You called *me*, you said *you*—

LOUISE   Do I have "dumbass" stenciled on my forehead?

GRADY   You said *you* wanted—

LOUISE   Do I? Do you see the word "dumbass" on my—

GRADY   No! No! No! ...Okay? ...Jesus.

(Pause. LOUISE gets out a cigarette and lights it.)

LOUISE   ...I can't believe this.

GRADY   What'd you do to your hand.

LOUISE   Don't be helpful.

GRADY   I'm asking.

LOUISE   Don't embarrass yourself.

(Pause. LOUISE smokes.)

GRADY   ...This is no smoking.

LOUISE   Oh! I'm sorry. I thought this was the Dirty Laundry section.

GRADY   Keep your—

LOUISE   *(Loudly)* I thought this was the Lurid Details section.

GRADY   Sssssshh, ssssssshhhh, sssshush! ...Christ!

(Pause. LOUISE smokes. GRADY glances over at MARIE; she quickly turns away.)

LOUISE   ...You're on it. ...Did you hear me? You're on it. Squeezing my boob.

GRADY   Lemme see it.

LOUISE   I showed it to my friend Chuck. Chuck says—it's a Latin word, I think it means "shit creek."

GRADY   Who the hell's Chuck.

LOUISE   Chuck is a lawyer. Wanna see it?

GRADY   You got it?

LOUISE   Maybe we could go to Sears and plug it in. We could put it up on the big screen, pull up some lawn chairs, all the happy shoppers could watch you squeeze my boob.

Barbara Lowrance Hughes (Barbara), Fannie Hungerford (Waitress/Marie)
and Houston McMillion (Arthur) at the restaurant.
Photo: Joceyln Sanders.

GRADY   Hey.

LOUISE   You think I'm going to give it to you?   You fucking boneless fucking...*squid.*

(LOUISE flicks a fry at him. MARIE is chewing, staring straight ahead.)

GRADY   ...I thought you said he ignored you. He didn't "pay attention" to you.

LOUISE   What I *meant.*

GRADY   Obviously this is not "ignoring" you. Is it.

(LOUISE starts to speak, says nothing, shakes her head, maybe flicks another fry at him.)

GRADY   ...Who took it.

LOUISE   A guy.

GRADY   What guy.

LOUISE   I don't know, some guy he *paid*, how do I know what *guy?*

GRADY   Where is he, John.

LOUISE   His sister.

GRADY   What does he want.

LOUISE   ...A *divorce.*

GRADY   ...He *said* that.

LOUISE   What do you think he *wants?*

GRADY   You *talked* to him?

LOUISE   I can't.

GRADY   You *haven't* talked to him.

LOUISE   I *can't* talk to him.

GRADY   You *have* to talk to him. What do you think, you think he's gonna—

LOUISE   He got a *restraining* order, okay? He got a court order, I *can't* talk
            to him.

(Pause. GRADY sighs—more of a blow, really.)

LOUISE   ...She said if I call there again, he'll file charges.

GRADY   Jesus. What'd you *do* to him?

(LOUISE has caught MARIE looking at them.)

LOUISE   *(To MARIE)* Hello.

(MARIE smiles sheepishly and looks away.)

GRADY   What'd you—did you *hurt* him?

LOUISE   Let's just go.

GRADY   We're getting, no, let's—

LOUISE   I'm not staying here, let's go.

GRADY   We're not, when we, our *relationship*, when—

LOUISE   Let's go fuck.

GRADY   —when we, just listen, just listen for a—

LOUISE   You're my whore. Our "relationship?"

(Pause.)

LOUISE   ...Aren't you? Say yes. You're my whore.

(LOUISE flicks a fry at him.)

GRADY   ...Why are you talking to me this way?

LOUISE   Because you're my whore.

(She spits an ice cube at him.)

GRADY   Hey.

LOUISE   Whore. Squid.

GRADY   Quit. Calling me that.

LOUISE   Do you think I have no dignity? You fucking gelding?

(She flicks him in the forehead with her finger.)

GRADY   You wanna leave? You wanna—

LOUISE   *Yes.*

GRADY   So go. ...Go ahead.

(Pause. Not what she meant.)

GRADY   ...I mean it. Go. Get outta here.

(Pause.)

LOUISE   …You were never any good in bed, do you know that?

GRADY   So?

LOUISE   …Fuck you.

GRADY   Fuck *you*. So what?

(She starts to flick him again; he bats her hand away. She tries to slap him; he bats her hand away hard. MARIE is looking at them again.)

LOUISE   *(To MARIE)*   …Is this smoke bothering you?

(MARIE turns away quickly.)

GRADY   I don't understand why you're doing this.

LOUISE   He hurt *me*. Why don't you ask me if—

GRADY   *How?*

LOUISE   —he hurt *me*? Do you think I have no *feelings*, you think I—

GRADY   *(Interspersed)*   How. What did he do? How did he hurt you?

LOUISE   …Can we please…just…leave? Please?

GRADY   …I can't.

LOUISE   Just…somewhere we can, where we can—

GRADY   I can't, I'm not—I, I, I *can't*. …Okay?

LOUISE   …You can't what.

GRADY   …I can't. *Be.*

LOUISE   …Be what.

GRADY   When we got into this—

LOUISE   I don't know what that means, you can't—

GRADY   When we got into this—I'm trying to *tell* you.

(Pause.)

GRADY   …When we got into this. …Okay? We never. …Said. …We never *said*. That. …*We*.

(Pause.)

LOUISE   …What is this, the fine print?

GRADY   You knew this.

LOUISE   I didn't read the fine print?

GRADY   I have a *wife*. …You knew this. …You *knew* this.

LOUISE   …Well, *you* knew that. Didn't you know that?

GRADY   What are you asking me.

LOUISE   You *hate* your wife.

GRADY   Think about what you're asking me.

LOUISE   She hates *you*, this is a quote, isn't it? She "hates" you, she doesn't "want" you anymore. This is something you *said*. …Do you think you can just walk away? *Now*? You can just.

GRADY   I have a family.

LOUISE   …I gave up my marriage for you.

GRADY   No, technically, you did not.

LOUISE   Obviously yes, I did, technically.

GRADY   No, no, I was, I was…"incidental" to it. …I was an accessory. …Or yes: I was your whore. Yes.

LOUISE   …Mmm. …You *have* been giving this some thought. …And what was I?

GRADY   What were you?

LOUISE   Yes.

GRADY   *(As diplomatically as possible)* …You. Were the one. You were the
              one…who got caught. First.

(Pause. She looks at him—hard. End scene.)

Scene 3

*(Afternoon. LEE and BARBARA are in LEE's living room, looking at the TV. She is sitting
in the chair; he is standing beside her, drinking a beer.)*

BARBARA   …That's her?

LEE   That's her. …That's *him*, right?

BARBARA   …Mm-hmm.

LEE   Once I filmed the wrong guy. She was all over him. I was like: this
              is too easy. Turns out they were newlyweds.

BARBARA   She's certainly not…very pretty, is she.

LEE   Usually they aren't. Sometimes they're dogs. Sometimes they look
              just like the wife. I find that very disturbing.

BARBARA   She's…heavy.

LEE   Well, camera's gonna add a few pounds. Watch how I zoom out:
              nnnnnn.

BARBARA   …What are they drinking?

LEE   Champagne.

BARBARA   Champagne? …He *hates* champagne.

(LEE shrugs.)

BARBARA   …What are they saying.

LEE   Beats me. Camera's inside a box, won't pick up a thing.

BARBARA.   He's *laughing.*

LEE   Great color though. Nice composition, too. I oughta start doing weddings.

BARBARA   …They're certainly having a grand time, aren't they.

LEE   Married men are more romantic. Flowers, gifts. Better in the sack, too.

(Pause. She looks at him.)

LEE   …You know, so I hear. Sure you don't want a beer?

(She says nothing, so he picks up the remote, aims it at the TV and hits fast-forward.)

LEE   …Okay. So that's dinner. Then they take a stroll on back to the Hyatt, but I didn't get that. I take the stairs, stake out a position around the—

BARBARA   Did he touch her?

LEE   What, when—

BARBARA   On their "stroll," did he…hold her hand or.

LEE   What's the difference, he took her to his room.

(He hits "play" on the remote.)

LEE   That's it, on the right. Watch the elevator.

BARBARA   What is that…green fog?

LEE   Fake ficus tree. This is why I prefer motels.

(Pause. They watch.)

BARBARA   …Who is she.

LEE   Beats me. Ever seen her?

BARBARA   Have…? No, I haven't *seen* her. You mean *you* don't—

LEE   Sometimes they have. Like some guy's wife or somebody's daughter they know.

BARBARA   …Is she…is she a "hooker"?

LEE   Her?

BARBARA   Yes. *Her.*

LEE   No way. Hookers you can spot a mile off, strap up in them leather skirts, look like a pot roast. Plus, see how he's got his—see how he's got his hand there on her back? He ain't even in a hurry, look at him. My money, this is somebody he knows, some regular thing, somebody he feels safe with. …See? Says somethin' in her ear… aaaand a little smooch.

BARBARA   *(Slight groans)* …Mm. Mm.

(Pause. They watch.)

LEE   …There's this theory. According to which, *watching* an event, watching it take place…changes the *nature* of that event. It's called the Uncertainty Principle.

(Pause. She watches grimly. He stops the tape with the remote.)

LEE   Wanna see it again?

BARBARA   That's it?

LEE   Plus when she comes out. He's not in that, though. Probably conked out.

BARBARA   …This is all you have.

LEE   Well. Yeah. That's.

BARBARA   I could have got this myself.

LEE   True.

BARBARA   …How long was she there?

LEE	Three hours, twelve minutes.
BARBARA	Was she there both nights?
LEE	Doesn't matter.
BARBARA	Did...did they have *sex*?
LEE	Didn't ask.
BARBARA	...You don't, if they had *sex*, you don't even know if—
LEE	Well, I coulda kicked down the door and flung back the covers. *Or* I coulda hung by one arm and shot through the window. But that means I get arrested *and* lose my license. On top of which, it's not admissible.
BARBARA	And this is. Footage of, of, of a *hallway* with—
LEE	Hey, you wanna home movie of this broad ridin' your husband bareback across the lone prair-ree, I can get that. You wanna see him exercising her Schnauzer on her front porch, I'll be there—when he *does* that. Right now, *this* is what he does.
BARBARA	Then could you please tell me what the hell it is I'm paying you for?

(A long pause. LEE's demeanor changes, darkens.)

LEE	...Sure. Opportunity and Inclination.

(She starts to speak; he cuts her off:)

LEE	All you gotta prove.

(Again, she starts to speak, but:)

LEE	"Opportunity": was your husband in a hotel room with a woman who was not his beloved wife, long enough to have "intimate relations": yes. Is he "inclined" to have intimate relations with a woman: yes. Unless he suddenly decides he's queer, which is *also* grounds for divorce.

(Pause. He bears down on her now with a startling intensity and clarity:)

LEE ...You got the fucker. Right? Here's what else you got: you got maybe sixty percent of the proceeds from the sale of your house and mutual assets, less than forty percent of the debt, *none* of it that's in his name, and that's if you *settle.* You got your *car.* Woman your age, you got periodic alimony, which means for the rest of your *life,* according to the manner you're accustomed, which is a *lot,* unless you get married, which statistically you probably will. He pays the cost of the action: that's judges, that's his lawyer, that's *your* lawyer, bailiffs, assessors, mediators, *real* estate guys. You can sue his *company.* You want, you can sue *her* for alienation of affection, even if she *marries* him, which statistically he'll die alone.

(Pause.)

LEE ...It's an industry, okay? It's an industry, designed to chop him *up,* because *he's* the movie star now.

BARBARA ...I apologize.

LEE You ever cheat on him?

BARBARA Have—?

LEE *Have* you?

BARBARA ...No.

LEE From here to the trial, you stay outta *bars,* you stay outta *hotels,* men's houses, *locker* rooms, any place you have Opportunity. You're a *nun,* okay? You're not, and he proves it, that's no alimony, that's an even split, you blow the deal, you waste your money, you waste my time. You got all that?

BARBARA ...Yes.

LEE Here's another thing. This is the most important thing: you listen to this: you got like *two* days to move out. You don't *touch* him, you don't *sleep* with him—better you don't even go in the same *house.* You do, that's what they call "condonation."

BARBARA *(Confused, overwhelmed)* I...I—

LEE   Condonation means committing Forgiveness. Forgiveness means you got no legal cause, which means you blow the deal. You understand what I just told you?

BARBARA   I...I want—

LEE   What.

BARBARA   I want to know who she—

LEE   Why.

BARBARA   ...I want to know about the money.

LEE   What money?

BARBARA   Our money. I want to know if he's—

LEE   He is. It's gone.

BARBARA   Can you—

LEE   I can find out anything you want. I can get his bank statements, credit card receipts, phone calls, I can get his health records, find out if he's freebasing Viagra. That means you get out your checkbook.

BARBARA   ...How much?

LEE   Inadmissable.

BARBARA   How *much*?

LEE   This is free: your *husband* is *cheating* on you.

BARBARA   I know he's cheating on me! I told you that! I want to know who she is!

LEE   Whattaya think you're gonna do, you gonna blackmail him? ...Into what? *Not* cheating on you? You can rub that lamp all you want, sweetheart, he's gonna spend your money, he's gonna fuck strange women and he's gonna *lie* about it till the day he *dies*. You wanna know why?

(Pause. She looks at him.)

LEE   ...Because he *can*. ...Your marriage is garbage.

BARBARA   *(Softly)* …I know.

LEE   *(Backing off now, perhaps even sympathetic)* …Good. …Okay.
                …That's what you're paying me for.

(Pause. End scene.)

Scene 4

(Early evening: the bedroom, with exit to adjoining bathroom, of JOEL and MARIE's apartment. MARIE is sitting at what we assume is her vanity, facing the audience, hastily brushing or putting up her hair. JOEL is sitting on a bed or chair behind her, watching her. From a further room, we hear romantic if somewhat hokey music.)

MARIE   I *told* you.

JOEL   No you didn't.

MARIE   Yes I *did*. The other night. I said I had a study group and I'd be late.

JOEL   Well I don't remember.

MARIE   Well that's not my fault.

(Pause.)

MARIE   …Then of course there was lunch, *that* was lovely. There was this, this *woman*, this couple, they're having this, this, I mean it was *awful*, she *throws* her coke in—

JOEL   Where.

MARIE   At *lunch*. She throws her coke in his face, she starts *screaming* at him like—they get into this huge…*fight*, this—

JOEL   Who with?

MARIE   Each *other*. She starts *swinging* at him, I mean *belting* him, *pounding*, *screaming* like—

JOEL   No. The study group. Who with.

MARIE   …Who *with*? …Nobody. I was alone.

JOEL   You just said "study group."

MARIE   He stood me up, okay? I went over my notes. So then the manager comes over, everybody's *watching*, he like *pulls* her off this guy, she's *screaming* at him, she calls him a *squid—*

JOEL   He who?

MARIE   I'm trying to tell you something.

JOEL   You said "group."

MARIE   What do you *want* me to call it, it's a study group. We do it all the time.

JOEL   Just you and him.

MARIE   Is this like a big deal or something?

JOEL   …No.

MARIE   …Well, then…okay. Right?

(He shrugs. She stands, perhaps retrieves some clothes from the bed, and exits to the bathroom. JOEL sits.)

JOEL   …I made spaghetti.

MARIE   *(Off)* And you rented some porn, I saw.

JOEL   …It's not porn. …It's a…romance. Sort of.

(No answer. JOEL sits. Lights to half on the bedroom.

Elsewhere, lights come up full on a sidewalk, perhaps with ambient street noise. LEE enters from one side, smartly dressed. He carries the gift box. LOUISE enters from the other, still wearing sunglasses and the bandage on her hand. They cross and exit. Then, LOUISE reappears and looks off in LEE's direction. She processes something, then follows LEE off—all of this while the music plays in the apartment. Lights to black on the sidewalk.

The lights come back up on the bedroom as MARIE enters from the bathroom, wearing a bra and pulling on her pants or skirt for work.)

MARIE	You need the car?
JOEL	…What?
MARIE	If you're going to watch that, I'll just drive myself. If Rudy calls tell him whatever, make something up.
JOEL	…What are you doing?
MARIE	*(Obviously)* …I'm getting ready.
JOEL	…It's Friday.
MARIE	Angie wanted off, I took her shift. …I *told* you this.
JOEL	…W—. I thought.
MARIE	What do you think I've been doing?
JOEL	I *thought*. *We.*
MARIE	Joel, I know I told you.
JOEL	Who do you think I made dinner for?
MARIE	*You.*
JOEL	…Well.
MARIE	I'm sorry.
JOEL	…How late?
MARIE	Late.
JOEL	*How—*
MARIE	I gotta close. Look, I'll make it up. Tomorrow night, we'll…I don't know, watch your movie or whatever. I'm really, really sorry.

(She is putting on her blouse, pausing to fumble with the buttons on the cuffs. Meanwhile, he places his hand on her breast, awkwardly, and keeps it there. She's completely oblivious to it. Then she starts buttoning her blouse. He removes his hand and watches as she finishes getting dressed.)

JOEL   …Does he hit on you?

MARIE   Who?

JOEL   …I don't know. Whoever.

MARIE   Rudy?

JOEL   I didn't say Rudy.

MARIE   Noooooo.

JOEL   Nobody?

MARIE   No. …Well, I mean, guys ask me my name.

JOEL   Do you tell them?

MARIE   What do you want me to do, *lie*?

(Pause: no answer.)

MARIE   …What are you asking me?

(Pause: no answer.)

MARIE   …*No. Okay? No.*

(Pause. To JOEL, this was no help at all.)

JOEL   …I got something…I gotta tell you something. I got something I gotta tell you.

(Pause. She waits.)

JOEL   …I can't tomorrow night. I have…I have plans.

MARIE   …Fine. Okay. …Have fun.

JOEL   I will.

MARIE   Okay. …What, you got a game?

JOEL   What's the difference?

MARIE   I'm supposed to come watch, is that it?

JOEL   You hate to watch.

MARIE   No, I don't.

JOEL   Yes you do, you said you—

MARIE   I said it gets *boring*. It gets boring. Fast. But I *will*.

JOEL   …It didn't used to.

MARIE   Yes, it did. It was always boring. I just didn't tell you.

JOEL   Why not.

MARIE   What are we talking about?

JOEL   Are you bored?

MARIE   I'm confused.

JOEL   Why are you telling me now?

MARIE   …Look. I told you I'm sorry. I'm sorry I have to go. I'm sorry I was late, I'm sorry I didn't want to wear that, that *thing* the other night, I'm sorry I'm not the—

JOEL   I'm not talking about that.

MARIE   Yes you are. You've been weird all week—yes you have. You got all pissed off because—

JOEL   I got all pissed off bec—

MARIE   —I had a bad day.

JOEL   A bad day.

MARIE   Yes. Okay? I get to have a—

JOEL   Do you know how it, how it makes me feel, when you—

MARIE   Oh let's *please* not—

JOEL   "Your hands are cold." "I'm tired." "Don't."

MARIE   I said I was—

JOEL   "Don't."

MARIE   I'm *sorry*, alright? I'm *sorry*!

JOEL   Why do you keep apologizing?

MARIE   *(A savage groan)* Aaaaaaarrrgh!

JOEL   You always have a bad day, every day is bad.

MARIE   I *work*, Joel.

JOEL   *I* work.

MARIE   I work, I go to school—

JOEL   Do you know how degrading it—to have your wife—

MARIE   Don't make *me*, don't make *me* the—

JOEL   —do you know how humiliating it—*shut* up! *Shut up! Shut the fuck up!*

(Pause. MARIE stands stunned. The music plays in the background.)

JOEL   …You wanna know something? Can I tell you something? …I didn't sign up for this. …Okay? I didn't sign up for this.

MARIE   …What does that mean? …Yes you did. What does that mean?

JOEL   …Nothing. You want the car? You can have the car. Here.

(He tosses her the keys or slams them down somewhere.)

MARIE   No. What does that, what does—

JOEL   Forget it.

MARIE   No, no, no, you think you can just *say* that, you can just—I'm sorry, is your life not *perfect*? Is your life not, not *perfect* enough for you? Am I not—is this *inconvenient* or, or—

JOEL   Just, no, forget it—

MARIE   What do you think I signed—*shut up!* *You* shut up!

(Pause.)

MARIE   …Do you think I *belong* to you? I'm supposed to—I'll, I'll, I'll *beg*, I'm *afraid*? No, no, *fuck* you, you put the paper down I'll sign it. You want out—you go ahead. You go ahead. I'll sign it.

(Pause.)

MARIE   …Do you think I *like* this, I *enjoy* this anymore than—

JOEL   No.

MARIE   Do you think I *need* you? I—I—I—I *need* you?

JOEL   …I know.

MARIE   I don't!

JOEL   I *know*!

(Pause. He approaches her. Softly:)

JOEL   …I know. I'm—

MARIE   *Don't.* …Okay? …Just…just.

(He stops. Pause. They look at each other. Music plays. Then she exits: a door closes offstage. He stands. End scene.)

Scene 5

(Evening. Lights up on the bar. BARBARA is perched on a barstool, all dressed up, working on a shot and reading a small card. GRADY is behind the bar; he has a black eye and/or a big scratch on his face. While she talks, he will steal an occasional glance at the ballgame on the TV.)

BARBARA   *(Reading the card)* "I would…I would I were thy *bird.*" "I would *I* were thy bird." …It's what Romeo says to Juliet on the balcony. It's an "allusion."

GRADY   Ah.

BARBARA   *(Consulting the back of the card)* And she says, I looked it up, she says: "Sweet, so would I. Yet I should…kill thee with…much cherishing. Parting is such sweet sorrow… That I shall say goodnight…till it be morrow."

GRADY   Very nice.

BARBARA   The night before our *wedding.* Isn't that amazing? How many men do you know who'd—would *you* think of this? It took me thirty years to figure out what it *meant.* Most men I know—what I could never *understand,* what I could *never* understand: they treat the, the, the *garbage man* with more—my cousin, *her* husband? Now there's an asshole. Do you mind if I swear Grady?

(His gesture says "okay, whatever.")

BARBARA   A miserable asshole. Goddam, grabass, shit prick bastard goddam I used to swear so well. He'd tell her how "disgusting" she was, how fat, stupid goddam *baboon* she was. I mean she is a little heavy and she doesn't exactly "light up the room" but you just don't…*talk* that way to—you don't talk that way to *anyone.* In thirty years, I'll give him this, Arthur cannot *bring* himself to say an unkind word to me. And he's one of the best fathers you've ever seen.

(She downs her shot.)

BARBARA   He used to read to Chelsea every night, same goddam story too, because children, he says there's a…there's a great *comfort* in being told a familiar story. What did you say this was?

GRADY   Jagermeister.

BARBARA   I would like another Jagermaster please. So: one morning, listen to this: my cousin, she gets up, she cooks him this big, spectacular breakfast: blueberry pancakes, eggs benedictine, the whole— grapefruit juice—whole thing. They're sitting there, she takes a deep breath, she says, "...Hubert. If you're not nice to me. If you're not *nice* to me. I will leave you."

(Pause. GRADY draws her a cola in a tall glass.)

BARBARA   ...Isn't that...isn't that incredible? "If you're not nice to me, I will *leave* you." She *meant* it, too. In business, this is what Arthur says: you cannot negotiate, if you're not prepared, at any moment, to walk away from the table. You see what I'm saying?

GRADY   Uh-huh.

BARBARA   If I stuck a gun, if I stuck a gun at your head and said, uhh... "repent!" "Put the toilet seat down!" Would you rather watch the baseball?

GRADY   Uh, no, I'm.

BARBARA   Fooooor...two years now, *three* years, Hubert has been this—cards, backrubs, considerate, affectionate, born again, Norman Vincent Rockwell, perfect...perfect husband. The perfect marriage. His girlfriend must be the silent type. He thinks I talk too much. I *do* talk too much. Even in bed, he hates noise. It embarrasses him. If I was boring in bed, I bet he'd still—actually he won't hardly even *touch* me now. I *spoiled* him, is what it is. Grady. But, I mean, it's not like I *defrauded* him. It's not as if I didn't...hold my end up. What's this?

GRADY   Diet Pepsi.

BARBARA   I'd like another one of these please, Grady. Don't you, don't you turn tail on me now, you bastard son-of-a-bitch.

(GRADY gets her another shot. As he does, JOEL enters the bar, tired and angry. He trudges to a barstool away from BARBARA and sits. GRADY will get him a beer.)

GRADY   Hey. ...Where you been?

JOEL   *(Shrugs)* Walkin'. …What happened to you?

(He means GRADY's shiner.)

BARBARA   He's not saying. …He had an "accident."

(JOEL looks at her. She smiles at him. Pause. Then JOEL smiles awkwardly and focuses on the game overhead. BARBARA returns to GRADY.)

BARBARA   …What were we talking about?

GRADY   *(No idea)* Birds.

BARBARA   I never cry anymore. Isn't that strange? Except once, when I was chopping onions. I was chopping onions and tears were streaming down my face and I thought how…how *wonderful* it would be to feel that…strongly about something anymore. That…*passionate* or—

(Pause.)

BARBARA   …There was a man, though, once. A friend of Arthur's, actually. We were at this party. I met him coming out of the bathroom and the next thing you know he's got his tongue in my mouth and his hands on my tits and then there was a great deal of fffffurious buttoning and unbuttoning and it. Felt… That…anticipation. That's passion, is what that is. It leaves a…leaves a taste in your mouth. And you miss that, you miss it, that's the thing you…miss when you've been…

(Pause. The men exchange a glance.)

BARBARA   …I never told Arthur. I was going to. I was going to confess everything and maybe I should but. But…*guilt*. The words, "I'm sorry. I am *sorry*, my love." It's only a selfish thing to say sometimes, don't you think? If you're sorry, don't…don't *do* it. And if you did it, you must have *wanted* to.

GRADY   …I don't know.

BARBARA   People forgive too easily. If we didn't forgive…there would be only…only devotion.

(Pause. She considers that, glances briefly at JOEL, then changes tacks:)

BARBARA   …So. Ssssylvia, you say.

GRADY   Yuh.

BARBARA   That's a pretty name. "Ssssylvia." …Is she pretty?

GRADY   …Yeah. She's.

BARBARA   Mmm. …Have you been married long?

GRADY   Yeah, we've—actually, I kinda don't like to talk about…my uh.

BARBARA   Well, I don't mean to *pry*. …How pretty is she?

GRADY   Well, like I say, I don't…

BARBARA   You don't have much of a barside manner, do you Grady. I thought this was how you were supposed to make the big tips, you barkeeps.

(Pause. GRADY shrugs or ignores the comment.)

BARBARA   …Does she make you happy?

GRADY   *Yes*. She makes me *happy*. She's a *great* wife, Sylvia, she's real pretty, we've been married a *long* time, we're real happy all the time, me and Sylvia, alright?

BARBARA   …You don't know how refreshing it is to hear a man volunteer these things about his wife. You don't know how rare it is. She's a lucky, lucky woman, this…Sylvia.

(Pause. The exchange has caught JOEL's attention. He's looking at them when BARBARA glances at him; then he turns quickly back to the TV.)

BARBARA   …I know a man who *makes* his wife have sex with his friends. He *makes* her! He bought her some new boobs and takes her to the gym and picks out her clothes himself.

(Pause.)

BARBARA   …Drunks. Wife-beaters. …Women who, I know women who will only date married men. *Couples* who go on these—"swingers"—they go on these cruises so they can…*meet* people. I know a man who became *transfixed*, *fixated* on this, this *girl*, I mean he *pursued* her, *openly*! He *talked* about her! To his *wife*! And she would…what can you say to her? People like that, all of them, how do they—they must *hate* each other, they're, they're, they're *hollow*, they're sick— they *should* hate each other. ...But you know what bothers me? You know what...what the worst, the absolute worst thing is?

(Pause.)

BARBARA   ...This is the worst thing of all. This is what I cannot understand. ...Arthur and I, we're...we're *good* people. We're not...we're... we're...*moral* people, we're *good* to each other, we *are*, we just *are*. ...If we weren't, then I could...that's what...

(Long pause. She ponders it. Then she snaps back:)

BARBARA   ...I would like another one of these, please.

GRADY   I think...that's probably.

BARBARA   Ha! ...What, are you "cutting me off," Grady?

GRADY   No, ma'am, I don't th—

BARBARA   "Ma'am"? Are you new at this, Grady?

GRADY   I'm just, hey, I don't want to see you—

BARBARA   I would like a glass of bord—bordeaux. Please. I think I know what I'm doing.

GRADY   I can't do that—

BARBARA   —"ma'am." I am a woman, sitting in a bar, *alone*, asking for a drink.

GRADY   Look, lady.

BARBARA   "Lady"?

GRADY   Look.

BARBARA   You look. Look at this, look-look-look. I went to the bank, I went to the bank—

(She reaches into her purse and produces a wad of cash.)

BARBARA   —and I got *this*. This is what, I'm *sitting* here, this is what I'm going to drink. I have spelled out to you—

GRADY   Hey.

BARBARA   —that I, how *good* I am, how *good* I am. Grady. Do I need to draw you a fucking compass?

GRADY   No, I'm just—

BARBARA   This is indelicate.

GRADY   Yes.

BARBARA   I would like a drink.

GRADY   No.

BARBARA   One glass. I'm asking. For me, for—

GRADY   *No.*

BARBARA   Do you think I'm repulsive? Do you think—

GRADY   Here, here's a Pepsi, here's—

(GRADY puts the glass back in front of her.)

BARBARA   —think I'm, no, you tell me, you think—

GRADY   —no, no, there you go—

BARBARA   I'm asking you, one glass, I'm offering, I'm offering, to just have—

GRADY   *(Completely unnerved)* No! No! No, I'm *not*, no, I'm, no. Nnnn-nno. ...I'm sorry. No. ...I'm sorry.

(Pause. BARBARA composes herself, musters some dignity.)

BARBARA   ...I ffff—. Huh. I...forgive you. You are...absolved...and forgiven.

(She takes her cash and, as she speaks, stuffs it into his tip jar.)

BARBARA   …And for the rest of the evening. Grady. I would like for you…to
               call me Barbara. And I would like…I would like for you…to be nice
               to me.

(Pause. She looks over at JOEL, and smiles a sad, cringing smile at him. He turns away. She watches him for a few more moments, sips her cola, and then looks up at the game on TV.)

BARBARA   …I don't know how you can stand to watch this every night. I really
               don't.

(Pause. End scene.)

Scene 6

(Evening. LEE sits at a table in the restaurant. In the background, strings are playing. On the table is a lighted candle and, near his elbow, the gift box. MARIE is pouring a beer into his glass—aware that he is eyeing her.)

LEE   …Time you got, darlin'?

MARIE   Ummm…ten after.

LEE   …Huh.

MARIE   Would you like to order, or are you waiting for someone?

LEE   Oh, I'm waitin' for someone. …*Everybody's* waitin' for someone.
               Right?

MARIE   I'll be back in a few minutes for—

LEE   What's your name.

MARIE   …My name? …Mmmmary.

LEE   Do me a favor, Mary. See the hairdo over there holdin' hands with
               the wingtips?

(She looks: he means across the restaurant, in the direction he's facing.)

LEE   Send 'em a bottle of the house champagne, on me. They ask who it's from, you say, "a fellow romantic." Think you can do that, Mary?

MARIE   …Okay.

LEE   Thanks, Mary.

(He winks at her. MARIE smiles uncomfortably and exits. Pause. LEE sips his beer, maybe takes out his notepad and makes a notation, adjusts the position of the gift box on the table, and then looks over the menu. Presently, LOUISE enters, locates LEE, then saunters over nonchalantly to his table.)

LOUISE   …Well. Hello. …It's…Lee, isn't it?

LEE   *(Obviously uncomfortable)* …Uhh. Yeah.

LOUISE   Remember me?

LEE   …Lllllouise.

LOUISE   Very good. May I…join you?

LEE   …Uhh.

LOUISE   For a drink. You did offer.

LEE   …Well. Well. Actually.

(Too late: she sits herself down across from him, right in the direction the gift box is "aimed" and then immediately notices it, touches it.)

LOUISE   Oh, I'm sorry, is this for someone? I thought you were alone.

LEE   Actually—don't, don't—

LOUISE   You're not married, are you? Married men don't usually offer to buy me a drink. Well, that's a lie. Happily married men don't usually—

LEE   I'm not.

LOUISE   Married? Or happy.

LEE   Buying you a drink.

LOUISE	…Oh. …Well, then I'll buy *you* one. How about that? Is that too forward?
LEE	…You're married, Louise.
LOUISE	That didn't seem to bother you the other night.
LEE	Didn't seem to bother you either.
LOUISE	…Well, yes, technically, I am. My husband and I aaaare…separated.
LEE	Really.
LOUISE	Very recently, actually. And rather badly, too. As you might imagine.
LEE	's a shame.
LOUISE	And I know you…saw, I know you—
LEE	I see it a lot.
LOUISE	And I know what you must be thinking. And you're right, you're—
LEE	Tell you the truth, Louise: I don't give a shit.

(Pause.)

LOUISE	…Huh. This is awkward, isn't it… Well, I'll tell *you* the truth. The truth is: I followed you. I saw you, and I thought we'd—
LEE	You followed *me*.
LOUISE	…Yes. I thought we could…*discuss* what…*happened* the other night. I felt that I could…you know, that I *owed* you. I wanted to…make it up to you…somehow.
LEE	…Make it up to me.
LOUISE	Yes. …So what do you say?
LEE	…What do I say.
LOUISE	Yes. …Say yes.

LEE   *(Grinning, as if accepting a challenge)* …Alright. Sure.

LOUISE   …Good!

(She resituates herself, gets comfortable. Pause. They look at each other. She smiles.)

LOUISE   …You look good tonight.

LEE   I'm a good guy.

LOUISE   I sat there, the other night, did you know I was looking at you?

LEE   Likewise.

LOUISE   I kept thinking, I…I've seen this man before.

LEE   I got a familiar face.

LOUISE   You do. You do, and I felt that I…I *knew* you somehow.

LEE   I get that a lot. You hurt yourself?

(He means her bandaged hand.)

LOUISE   Oh. I…yes. I was…fixing something.

(MARIE enters and comes to the table. Before she can say anything, she and LOUISE recognize one another.)

LOUISE   …Hello.

MARIE   *(Grimly)* …Can I get you something?

LOUISE   I would like a rye. Neat. And the gentleman will have another one of tho—

LEE   The gentleman wants a double Glenlivet on the rocks. No, two, actually.

LOUISE   …Two. "Please." "Thank you."

(LOUISE smiles sweetly at MARIE; MARIE exits.)

LOUISE   …I think we should get a little drunk. What do you think?

LEE   Knock yourself out.

*Gene Aimone (Grady) and Barbara Lowrance-Hughes (Barbara)
commiserate at the bar. Photo: Jocelyn Sanders.*

LOUISE   I've been feeling so...you know, cooped up, caged up. And now suddenly it feels like I've just been...*released*.

LEE   Technically you have.

(LOUISE produces a cigarette and leans forward at some point during the following so he can light it—which he does, with the candle.)

LOUISE   Well that's true, isn't it. ...And maybe it's a "weakness," it's a, a "failing," I'm sorry, I know all that, but there are...things. In my life. That I *desire*, that's all. My father used to say you "measure" yourself against your desires, you "measure" yourself, and that's...that's exactly what I'm saying. And I don't think most people measure up. I think that's why they're unhappy. And they are, most people. I just...*refuse*...to be unhappy.

LEE   ...Why are you telling me this.

LOUISE   I just wanted you to understand. I'm *not* sorry, really. It's not *weakness*, this is my theory: it takes...it takes...great *courage* to, to *see* something, to see something you *want*...and risk your whole *life* on it. It's an act of great, of great...*strength* to *yield* to what you desire. To say *yes* to what you want.

(Pause. She smiles)

LOUISE   But you don't give a shit, do you.

(Pause. He smiles.)

LOUISE   ...My name isn't really Louise, by the way.

LEE   Really.

LOUISE   I'm not going to tell you what it is. Later, maybe.

LEE   Later.

LOUISE   Maybe.

(She smiles. Pause.)

LEE   …What are you doing, Louise.

LOUISE   What am I doing? …I don't know, what do you think I'm doing?

LEE   I think you're jerkin' me around.

LOUISE   Why would I—were *you*? …Were you jerking me around?

(Pause. No answer.)

LOUISE   …Well, I'm being too forward again, aren't I. Let's talk about you.
               Tell me about you.

LEE   …About me.

LOUISE   Yes. What you do.

LEE   What I do.

LOUISE   Yes.

(Pause.)

LEE   …I'm a social worker.

LOUISE   Really. Like…family counseling, that sort of thing.

LEE   Sort of.

LOUISE   You must find that very fulfilling.

LEE   I like to help people.

LOUISE   Huh. It's a shame I didn't know about you before.

LEE   I'd say so.

(MARIE enters, places their drinks on the table, and tosses a menu in front of LOUISE.)

MARIE   I'll be back for your order.

(MARIE exits. An awkward pause.)

LOUISE   …Well. So. If I came to you, as a client, let's say.

LEE   I'd say you were a little late.

LOUISE   Let's say I wasn't. Let's say I…needed your help. Your…*assistance*…
              with something.

LEE   …What?

*(LOUISE begins rubbing her finger around the rim of her glass. Through the following,
LEE will begin unconsciously tugging his ear or drumming his fingers, touching his
nose, and so on.)*

LOUISE   Well, you tell me. I mean, is it…advice, is it therapy, would you…ask
              me questions, would I…would I lie *down*, would I stand *up*, what sort
              of, you know…*things*…would we do.

LEE   …Well. That's. We'd. Do any fuckin' thing you wanted.

LOUISE   Any fuckin' thing.

LEE   …Yuh.

LOUISE   Uh-*huh*. Uh-huh. …And are you…you know…good?

LEE   …Huh. …You wanna find out?

LOUISE   I don't know. Are you available?

LEE   I could find an opening.

LOUISE   I'll bet you could.

LEE   Huh.

LOUISE   It would have to be soon, though.

LEE   You in a hurry?

LOUISE   Yes, I am. I'd have to…squeeze you in.

LEE   I'll bet you would.

LOUISE   Would that make it hard?

LEE   …Huh. …Uh. Huh.

LOUISE   Would it? ...Lee? Would it be...hard?

LEE   ...You're pissin' me off here, Louise.

(LOUISE laughs.)

LEE   You got something you wanna say, you say it. But let me tell you
something: let me tell you something: there's not one goddam thing
you can do to me.

(Pause.)

LOUISE   ...Is something wrong, Lee?

LEE   Knock it off.

LOUISE   I'm sorry, I don't understand.

LEE   Just...say what you got to say.

(Pause. LOUISE just looks at him. LEE is thoroughly perplexed. He sits for a moment, looking at her. Then he abruptly stands and mutters to himself:)

LEE   ...Jesus. This is, *fuck* this, *fuck* this, this is...

(He starts away, then returns:)

LEE   Look. Look.

(Long pause. He fumbles for something to say:)

LEE   ...I'm...I'm *sorry*. Okay? I'm sorry. ...I'm—

(Pause. They look at each other.)

LOUISE   ...For what, Lee?

(He looks at her, speechless. Then he starts to exit.)

LOUISE   You forgot your package.

(He quickly returns, grabs his gift box, and exits. Pause. LOUISE sits, smoking. She smiles. MARIE enters and comes to the table, looking around for a moment for LEE. LOUISE downs her drink and holds the glass up to MARIE.)

LOUISE   …Well! I believe I'm…ready for another!

(End scene.)

Scene 7

(Late evening. A soft or gobo window-light comes up on BARBARA, disheveled and half-drunk, sitting on a marble bench in her back yard. A shovel is propped up nearby.

From inside her home, we hear soft, romantic music playing, and then, once that picture is established, ARTHUR's voice, calling from within:)

ARTHUR   *(Off)* …Barbara? …Hello? …Barbara?

BARBARA   *[To herself]* …I divorce thee.

ARTHUR   *(Off)* Barbara…?

BARBARA   …I divorce thee, I div…

(She trails off. ARTHUR's voice sounds more alarmed:)

ARTHUR   *(Off)* What the…Barbara?

BARBARA   I'm out here, dear.

(Pause. Then ARTHUR enters from the house. He stands.)

BARBARA   …Hello. Darling.

ARTHUR   …Hello.

BARBARA   How are you?

ARTHUR   …Fine.

BARBARA   How was your trip? Did you have a wonderful time?

ARTHUR   …Yes. I did.

BARBARA   Would you like a drink?

ARTHUR   Did you know there was glass on the floor?

BARBARA   Oh. Yes. That was me. I threw one of the cordials at the TV.

(He sighs and joins her on the bench.)

ARTHUR   ...May I ask why?

BARBARA   ...Not yet.

ARTHUR   I'm sorry I was late. If that's what this is about. But I told—

BARBARA   No-no. You said you'd be late. Yes you did. Apology entirely
              unnecessary.

ARTHUR   ...Did you know your hand is bleeding?

BARBARA   Oh. Yes. I cut myself.

ARTHUR   Is it deep?

BARBARA   Sort of. I used this.

(She holds up a glass shard.)

BARBARA   ...It's the crystal. And look: I've been exc...excavating. I dug...two,
              three, four holes. I thought I knew where he was. It got to be very
              discouraging.

ARTHUR   Where *who* was?

BARBARA   And then I thought, maybe I'm not digging deep enough.

ARTHUR   ...Would you like to come in?

(She looks at him sadly.)

BARBARA   ...I can't.

(She leans gently into him.

*Elsewhere, lights come up on the bar, where GRADY and JOEL sit in silence,
watching the TV.*

Elsewhere, lights come up on LEE's living room. LEE enters, opens his giftbox, plugs the camera into the VCR, slouches in his chair, picks up his remote, hits play—and stares. Perhaps we hear a little of his conversation with LOUISE— "Well. Hello. ...It's...Lee, isn't it?"—before he mutes it.

Now, in the back yard:)

BARBARA   ...Arthur. Do you think...

ARTHUR   ...What.

BARBARA   ...Do you think it's...possible. For us to speak to one another. And tell the truth. No matter what the truth may be.

ARTHUR   ...Is that what you'd like?

BARBARA   ...I think so.

ARTHUR   ...Alright.

(Pause. She considers where to begin.)

BARBARA   ...Do I...do I hurt you?

ARTHUR   ...Yes. Sometimes. You do.

BARBARA   I don't mean to. Usually.

ARTHUR   ...I know.

BARBARA   Do you mean to hurt me?

ARTHUR   ...Never.

BARBARA   ...Do you think...this is what...being married is?

ARTHUR   ...I don't know. It may be.

BARBARA   It's supposed to be...it's supposed to be *different*, isn't it? I see it, sometimes. ...Not very often, though. Some people.

(Pause.)

BARBARA   ...Do you love me?

ARTHUR   …Yes.

BARBARA   …Say it?

ARTHUR   *(Gently, sincerely, looking at her)* …I love you, Barbara. …I have always loved you. I always will, I think.

(Pause. BARBARA takes ARTHUR's hand in hers turns the palm over, looks at it, and gently strokes it.)

BARBARA   …Suppose I told you…

ARTHUR   …What.

BARBARA   Suppose I told you. That I had…that I had been…unfaithful to you. Suppose I told you I had cheated on you. …Would that…would it hurt you?

ARTHUR   …Yes. It would.

BARBARA   But you'd still love me.

ARTHUR   …Yes.

BARBARA   Would you leave me?

ARTHUR   …I don't know. …Have you?

BARBARA   What if I asked you.

ARTHUR   …Are you?

BARBARA   What if I am?

(Pause.)

ARTHUR   …If I told you I had, would it—

BARBARA   *Yes.*

ARTHUR   …Would you leave me?

BARBARA   *(A moment's hesitation, then resolutely:)* …Yes.

(Long pause. She looks deeply into his eyes.)

ARTHUR   ...No. Barbara. ...I haven't.

(BARBARA has been running her finger over ARTHUR's palm. Now, she places the glass shard in his hand and squeezes his hand closed around it. He resists only slightly, looking at her in wonder while, trembling and tearful, she keeps squeezing it. Then she opens his hand, sees that it's bleeding, and softly kisses it.

Lights up full on the bar. JOEL and GRADY watch the TV. Presently, MARIE enters, tentatively. GRADY notices her first. Perhaps JOEL doesn't notice her at all. She approaches JOEL, gently places the car keys down beside him, sits next to him and takes his hand. They regard each other for a moment. Then she looks up at the baseball game on the TV. JOEL looks at her for a moment, then silently joins in watching the game with her.

Lights go to half on the bar, and then on LEE, in his living room. Pause.)

ARTHUR   ...Why don't we go in now. ...Barbara. Why don't we go in.

(Pause.)

BARBARA   ...Alright. Yes. ...I'm almost...almost ready. ...Arthur?

ARTHUR   Hm?

BARBARA   Are you happy?

ARTHUR   ...Sometimes. ...Are you?

(Long pause.)

BARBARA   ...I don't know. ...The ground here has...gotten very hard.

(Pause. Then all lights to black. End of play.)

Holy Ghost

Time passes, and little by little everything
that we have spoken in falsehood becomes true.

> — Marcel Proust

Little by little we were taught these things.
We grew into them.

> — Adolph Eichmann

GENESIS/SETTING: During World War II, German and other prisoners-of-war were warehoused in 500 camps across the United States and "re-educated" according to American values. *Holy Ghost* imagines one such camp in the lowcountry of South Carolina—and environs—in October 1944.

A NOTE ON LANGUAGE: Though these languages are spoken at various points in the play, it is assumed that an audience will understand not a word of German, Serbian or Yiddish. What's important is that the intention (or *intension*) behind what's said is made clear. Sometimes characters will speak variations on English—for instance Gullah, a black dialect particular to the lowcountry. Each should be understood as the code language it is but should be at least somewhat comprehensible to an audience.

Where not provided by the context, translations are indicated as follows:

Šta radiš! Nísam, ništa uradio! [What are you doing! I've done nothing!]

Translations of the several songs requiring it are appended.

ACKNOWLEDGEMENTS: This play's debts are many. It was funded in part by a grant from the Florence Regional Arts Alliance and the South Carolina Arts Commission, which receives support from the National Endowment for the Arts. I am also grateful to the wonderful cast and crew of the premiere production at Trustus Theatre, especially Dewey Scott-Wiley and Noël Parkinson, who were tireless; to George E. Harding, Virginia Mixson Geraty, Malcolm Cohen, Larry Falck and Senad Ademovi , who served as translators and advisors; to Fred Carter, Rich Chapman, Chris Johnson and indeed everyone else at Francis Marion University, for their constant and generous support; to Tom Mack and the James & Mary Oswald Distinguished Writers Series at the University of South Carolina Aiken, which honored me with a residency; to the Sprenger-Lang Foundation, for sponsoring the Nathan Miller History Play competition; to Nick Olcott, Alyse Rothman and the casts of the staged readings by Tribute and Reverie Productions; to those scholars whose research on the subject made this play possible, particularly John Hammond Moore, Arnold Krammer, Ron Robin, Lewis Carlson, and Judith Gansberg; and most particularly to Cheryl, Staci, Jill and Josh, for their many indulgences and for thinking that what I do is really interesting.

Portions of Robert Sherwood's *Abe Lincoln in Illinois* are reprinted herein with permission of The Robert Freedman Agency, Inc.

CHARACTERS
Suggestions for casting are appended.

PRIVATE HENRY	black male, early 20s.
CETNIK	(pronounced "Chetnik"; his real name is Juraj Eras, pronounced "Yur-ai Eddas"): white male, 20s. Speaks Serbian.
LIEUTENANT BERGEN	white male, late 20s. Small.
PATTY	white, teenager.
CORPORAL MULLER	white.
SERGEANT WATERS	black.
COMMANDING OFFICER	a colonel, white, middle-aged.
LIEUTENANT REIKER	white.
PRIVATE ABD-AL QAISER	black.
CORPORAL WEISZ	white.
PROFESSOR	white.
AGENT MARKS	white.
SHERIFF LOKER	white.
PAPA	white.
GULLAH WOMAN	black.
KING	white.
DUKE	black.

BILLY	white.
DEL	white.
REVEREND	white, middle-aged.

VARIOUS GERMAN PRISONERS:

anonymous white males, various ages. No more than three to five need appear at a time. Typically, they wear blue pants and shirts with "PW" stitched prominently front and back.

HOLY GHOST was the winner of the 2004 Sprenger/Lang History Play national contest and premiered at Trustus Theatre in Columbia, South Carolina, on August 12, 2005, as the Trustus Playwrights' Festival production. It was directed by Dewey Scott-Wiley. The cast was as follows:

PRIVATE HENRY	DeRante Parker
CETNIK	Dylan Barton
LIEUTENANT BERGEN	Alex Smith
COMMANDING OFFICER, REVEREND, PAPA	Bob Hungerford
SERGEANT WATERS, DUKE	Maxwell Highsmith
LIEUTENANT REIKER, AGENT MARKS	Andre Rogers
PRIVATE ABD-AL QAISER, GULLAH WOMAN	Seena Hodges
PATTY, PRISONER	Elisabeth Gray Heard
CORPORAL MÜLLER, DEL, KING, PRISONER	Charlie Harrell
CORPORAL WEISZ, BILLY, PROFESSOR	Ben Compton
SHERIFF LOKER, PRISONER	Tim Csuti
PRISONER	Jade Jennings
PRISONER	Amy Catalino

Production Staff:

Artistic Director	Jim Thigpen
Managing Director	Kay Thigpen
Stage Manager	Noël Parkinson
Technical Director	Larry McMullen
Set Design/Assistant Technical Director	Brandon McIver
Lighting Designer	Todd Clark
Costume Designer	Corinne Robinson
Properties Manager	Andre Rogers
Assistant Stage Manager	Jade Jennings
Technical Assistant	Amy Catalino
Sound Designer	Dewey Scott-Wiley
Sound Board Operator	Korinne Collins
Master Electrician	Teddy Palmer

HOLY GHOST

ACT ONE
Scene 1
Holy Ghost

(Night: an empty room. A noose hangs about seven feet from the floor. In the distance we hear a train approaching. As it nears, we hear a voice or voices singing:)

VOICE/S   *(Off)*   By the waters, the waters
                            Of Babylon
                            We lay down and wept
                            And wept
                            For thee, Zion.

                            We remember
                            We remember—

(The song is drowned out by the train grinding to a halt. Special up on PATTY, a white-trash southern teenager.)

PATTY   When I seen the crowd all gathered there at the station, I wonnered what President Roosevelt'd think. I mean, I hope he don't think we ain't patriotic or nothin'. I mean, they was Boy Scouts and po-lice—like it was the carnival come to town. And when the whistle blew and the train come to a stop, we all crowded 'round to see and ever'thin', and ever'thin' got real quiet. Finally some American soldiers started openin' up the cars, and that's when they aaaall started comin' out: *Germans.* Whole long line of 'em, maybe two hunnerd in all.

(As she speaks, a line of GERMAN PRISONERS files into the room, each wearing blue pants and shirt with 'PW' stitched prominently front and back. They stand somberly in a line against the back wall. The last to enter is REIKER, wearing a tattered Wehrmacht lieutenant's uniform.)

PATTY   I looked at 'em real hard, tryin' to read their faces for...for meanness or evil, but mostly they just looked like regular boys. I even felt kinda sorry for 'em—all packed inta a train like that, and so far from home. And I wonnered if maybe they warn't just like us. Just nice, y' know? So I waved, and a couple of 'em even waved back!

(*Special down on PATTY, waving. One of the prisoners, MÜLLER, stands at attention in the center of the room until REIKER signals to him with a nod. Then MÜLLER looks around for something and, not finding it, turns to the line of prisoners. He grabs one—CETNIK—and pulls him toward the noose. CETNIK is frightened:*)

CETNIK   Šta radiš? ...Šta radiš! Nísam, ništa uradio! [What are you doing? ...What are you doing! I've done nothing!]

MÜLLER   Es ist schon entschlossen worden. [It's already been decided.]

CETNIK   Ja ne razumijem. [I don't understand.]

MÜLLER   Keine Rede, Juraj! Nieder! [Stop babbling, Juraj! Get down!]

CETNIK   Ja ne razumijem! Ne! Nein! [I don't understand! No! No!]

(*MÜLLER punches CETNIK and throws him onto his hands and knees beneath the noose.*)

MÜLLER   ...Es tut mir leid, Juraj. Aber ich muss. [I am sorry, Juraj. This is something I must do.]

(*MÜLLER stands on CETNIK's back and fixes the noose around his own neck. While he prepares to hang himself, REIKER leads the prisoners in the "Horst Wessel Lied." He sings heartily, they glumly, as much of the song as necessary until:*)

MÜLLER   (*Over the singing*) ...Na, gut...ich bin fertig. [...It's alright. ...I am ready.]

CETNIK   ...Ja ne razumijem! [...I don't understand!]

MÜLLER   'Sist schon gut, Juraj. Jetzt! Los! [It's alright, Juraj. Now. ...Do it!]

CETNIK   Ne! Nein! Nein! Necu! [No! No! No! I can't!]

(*MÜLLER kicks CETNIK hard in the ribs, then again, then again.*)

CETNIK   Ne! Stanite! Molim vas! Nein! [No! Don't do this! Stop! Please! No!]

(*The scene can end here—a blackout at the instant that CETNIK appears finally to collapse, the singing coming to an abrupt stop.*

BERGEN   It's Norwegian, actu—

REIKER   You speak German.

BERGEN   High school. Mrs. Spevak. What, uh—

(REIKER tosses several books onto the desk.)

REIKER   Thomas Mann. Karl Zuckmayer. If you were German you would know these authors are disgraced.

BERGEN   But I'm—

REIKER   Saroyan, Crane, Remarque: Americans.

BERGEN   Remarque is Germ—

REIKER   Zwieg, Werfel, Frank: Jews. I am told you can explain this to me.

BERGEN   Explain wh—

REIKER   Why certain books have been removed from our library, why these have taken their place. I am told you are responsible.

BERGEN   Who told you that.

REIKER   The commandant. He says you are here to force American culture on the prisoners.

BERGEN   Well that's.

REIKER   You are here to brainwash them with American propaganda.

(He refers to the newspaper:)

REIKER   Praise for the plot to assassinate Der Führer. A drawing of Hermann Goering wearing cosmetics.

BERGEN   *(Interspersed)* I'm not—. I didn't draw th—.

REIKER   A comparison of Lebensraum to *Zionism*. This is Jewish libel. This is in direct violation of the Geneva Convention. I am camp spokesman, I speak for all the pr—

BERGEN   That's—. Just hold up a—. Would you just! …Wait a minute?

(BERGEN sighs, capitulates, indicates the newspaper:)

BERGEN   …Uhh…alright. Look. …*Der Ruf*. I don't have anything to do with this. It comes out of Fort Kearney. It's written by prisoners, for pris—

REIKER   It's written by traitors to coerce other traitors. It will be removed, the books will all be removed, and the others—

BERGEN   I can't.

REIKER   —Miklen, Dinter, Zillich, *Mein Kampf*—they will all be ret—

BERGEN   They've been destroyed. …They were identified as sub…versive.

REIKER   …And in your next breath you will condemn the Reich for censorship.

BERGEN   It wasn't just—I mean, Jack London, Shaw, Ayn Rand—it was, you know, morale, they were bad for—

REIKER   Whose.

BERGEN   Yours! The uh, we, we, we thought that—

REIKER   We-we-we?

BERGEN   …We! Umm, the uh—

REIKER   I intend to register a complaint with the Swiss legation.

BERGEN   Look, no, we've got, we've got classes, field trips, we've got…movies, *good* movies, we've got—

REIKER   *Casablanca. Watch on the Rhine. Bambi.* More Jewish filth.

BERGEN   Did he tell you I'm—?

REIKER   …You're what? …Norwegian?

(Pause. REIKER smiles, then continues, indicating the flyer:)

REIKER   …One last thing. This…play of yours. I would suggest a different one, perhaps *Schlageter* or *Sharnhorst*.

BERGEN   Never heard of 'em.

REIKER   I'm sure you would receive better cooperation.

BERGEN   What's that supposed to mean?

REIKER   ...My honor, Herr Bergen, is my loyalty. Oh, and: Remarque is a German no more. Guten Tag.

(REIKER issues the Nazi salute and exits. BERGEN is deflated. End scene.)

Scene 5
Basic Training

(Evening: black guards' mess hall. HENRY and QAISER sit at a table, eating. WATERS enters with a tray and joins them.)

WATERS   Well alright. Private Ohn-ree. The fightin' French Legionnaire! And Kaiser Abdul, the righteous black Mormon!

QAISER   I am Muslim.

WATERS   Muslim. I forget. And I'm aaaa—what's that you—

QAISER   Accommodationist.

WATERS   No, no, the—.

QAISER   Assimilationist. Infidel.

WATERS   Infidel! I'm a infidel! Got ourselves an international brigade here! How's it goin' out in the field there, mon frer? You kill anybody yet?

HENRY   Noooo. Like to have a heat stroke out there. And I axed you to quit callin' me that.

WATERS   You "axed" me?

HENRY   Didn't sign up for this shit, stand in a plantation all day. Got Mexicans do this shit.

WATERS   *(To QAISER)* Ohn-ree here's thinks he's better'n us.

HENRY   Paintin' *flowers* on a wall. They *told* me I was gonna get to fight. I mean, how am I supposed to get *my* chance? Or *you*? You know? Why they even give us a uniform?

WATERS   Why'nt you wear your Daddy's?

HENRY   No serious.

WATERS   I *am* serious. Bet he had a real pretty uniform. Big French war hero, his daddy. Killed him—how many Nazis he kill? Ten, twelve-thousand?

HENRY   Didn't say he was Fr—.

WATERS   There *weren't* any *Nazis* in that war, boy! Nigger tell you this shit? Daddy killin' him all them Nazis. Oughta look this shit up before you go—

QAISER   Maybe you should leave him alone.

WATERS   Well I didn't "axe" you, did I?

QAISER   And quit calling him that.

WATERS   ...Don't you get uppity with me. Nigger. You both niggers and I'm a sergeant. Kaiser here thinks he's better'n us. You gonna eat that pork?

HENRY   Nah, man, I'm sick a' pork! How is it we gotta eat *pork* every night? Ham hocks, pork loins—what the hell's a *loin*, anyway?

WATERS   Poor ol' Kaiser here can't even eat pork. Hell, you oughta sign on with him, join the big Righteous Revolution, let you kill you anybody you want.

HENRY   Who?

WATERS   Mormons. They gonna wipe out everybody—all the white folk, they're all of 'em Nazis.

HENRY   No shit?

WATERS	Yeah man. Mormons hate white folk. —Ain't that right, Kaiser?
QAISER	I am *Muslim*. My name is Abd-al *Qaiser*, I am a citizen of the Nation of Islam, and the loin is the crotch of a pig. You are eating the crotch of a pig.
HENRY	Maaaan. I don't know how much more a' this I can take. Gonna bust outta here, I swear to God.

(WATERS scoffs.)

HENRY	…I'll do it! I don't care. Gonna go find where the war is. You watch.
WATERS	Well when you get there they'll just throw your black ass in jail.
HENRY	So *what*. I ain't afraid a no jail, I *been* in jail. Jail ain't no worse'n this.
WATERS	*Hhhhaaa!*
HENRY	What.
WATERS	You been to ja—when you been to jail?
HENRY	Before.
WATERS	*When* before? For what? What you go to jail—
HENRY	I did. For murder.
WATER	*Murder.*
HENRY	Twenty-five to life. But I broke out.
WATER	I ain't even listenin' to you.
HENRY	I killed me somebody before.
WATERS	Sh—! Who?
HENRY	Some cat. …I did! I swear to God I did!
WATERS	Which cat? Where?
HENRY	Little white cat. Siamese I think. Big blue eyes. Ran him right over.

(QAISER smiles—and WATERS knows he's been had.)

HENRY   ...Lady calls the police, police haul me away. Judge say, "You can pay this lady thirty dollar, or you can do thirty days." So I say, "Your honor, ain't no white pussy worth no thirty dollar."

(QAISER busts out laughing.)

HENRY   That went over real well. Boom. Twenty-five to life. Them boys in prison though, I was like a legend. Call me Thirty Dollar, that was my name. "Here come Thirty Dollar." They wrote a song about me, give me all their—

WATERS   *(Angrily) Shut up Private!* Just *shut up!* ...Nigger, can you even hear yourself? ...You wouldn't last two weeks in jail, ignorant little fuck like you.

HENRY   ...Just jokin' around, Sarge.

WATERS   Well it isn't funny. You wouldn't last two *nights.* You'd hang yourself with your own *belt.*

(QAISER and HENRY exchanged a surprised look. Pause: WATERS cools down.)

WATERS   ...Alright. Look here. Mr. Thirty Dollar. You're so unhappy, tell you what I'm gonna do. Next week, you knock off a little early, take the kriegs into Drayton, get everybody an ice cream cone.

HENRY   ...Right.

WATERS   Place downtown, they practically give it away to boys in uniform. They even have raspberry. I love raspberry.

HENRY   This a white joint. They gonna let me walk in a white ice cream joint and eat ice cream.

WATERS   Well you're the man now, Ohn-ree. You're a private in the United States Army, they can't kick you out.

HENRY   ...Serious.

WATERS   Hell yeah serious. Thought you knew that. I'll set it up for you, get the CO to make a call. Get you a big double scoop.

HENRY   …Well, alright. Thanks, Sarge.

(Pause. They eat. QAISER shoots WATERS a disgusted look.)

HENRY   …What's it mean, "schwarzer."

WATERS   Schwarzer? …Why, they calling you that?

HENRY   Yeah. What's it mean?

WATERS   …Well…it means, "big master." Like "head honcho." They really calling you that?

HENRY   Yeah.

WATERS   …Well that's good, then. They're showing you their respect.

HENRY   No shit.

WATERS   They're probably afraid of you.

HENRY   …Well alright. …What's it mean, inf…inf—

QAISER   Infidel. …Disloyal. A traitor.

(Pause. End scene.)

Scene 6
Another Jew

(Mid-day: the dayroom. BERGEN is posting notices on a bulletin board—onto which a swastika has been painted. A prisoner, WEISZ, enters with CETNIK and approaches him tentatively.)

WEISZ   …Herr Bergen? Ich möchte mit Ihnen sprech— [I would like to speak with you.]

BERGEN   English, please.

WEISZ   I would speak with you.

BERGEN   "I would *like* to speak with you."

WEISZ   I would like to speak with you also. I would like to…to give you something.

BERGEN   …What is your uh—

WEISZ   I would like to give you first.

(WEISZ hesitates, then hands BERGEN a sheet of paper.)

BERGEN   …Numbers?

WEISZ   They…did not like to write their names. They would like to be in your play. My number is there—there.

BERGEN   …Oh! Well, this is…this is great. Why didn't you just—?

WEISZ   They would like for you to…to pick them. Like this. Numbers. But not Abe Lincoln, no one wants Abe Lincoln.

BERGEN   Why not?

WEISZ   They are afraid. But…this man. This man, he is different. He will be Abe Lincoln.

(WEISZ pulls CETNIK over.)

BERGEN   Hello.

CETNIK   I am Cetnik.

WEISZ   He is Cetnik. He is…ehh…he is different.

BERGEN   Well…thank you, uh…?

WEISZ   Weisz. Werner Weisz. I am corporal.

BERGEN   Thank you, Corporal. What's everyone so afraid of?

WEISZ   …I have something else.

(With a nod or gesture from WEISZ, CETNIK exits.)

BERGEN   …Ooookay.

WEISZ First I must ask. …You will forgive me… …Sholem aleichem.

BERGEN …What did you say?

WEISZ Nothing. I—I'm sorry.

BERGEN You speak Yiddish.

WEISZ No, no, I'm sorry I bother you.

(WEISZ starts away.)

BERGEN …Aleichem sholem.

WEISZ …I knew it! Du bist a Yid!

BERGEN Yes! Well, no, but—you're—?

WEISZ Yes. …I'm not the only one. There are two others here. More, maybe, I don't know.

BERGEN You're in the German *army*.

WEISZ There are thousands of Jews in the German army. Some, they are…out in the open. Most of us—

BERGEN How?

WEISZ *(Shrugs)* Hitler knows. They say he decides who is a Jew and who is not. My own father, he is a Nazi.

BERGEN …Why?

WEISZ …Why do you think? …I am ashamed, Herr Bergen. I give myself up because I am ashamed. I am worse than meshumad. …I give you this because I am ashamed.

(WEISZ presents a half-potato.)

BERGEN …A potato.

WEISZ That is not a potato. It *is* a potato, but it's… What I am about to tell you, you must not tell anyone. He will kill me. He will kill me for being a Jew, probably. But he will kill me for this definitely.

BERGEN   Who?

WEISZ   …I have your promise.

BERGEN   …Yes.

(Lights to black. End scene.)

Scene 7
The New Camp

(Afternoon: BERGEN's office. BERGEN sits nervously at his desk, shuffling files or something—obviously waiting. Finally, a knock on the door.)

BERGEN   …Come.

(HENRY enters and salutes.)

HENRY   Krieg you wanted, sir.

BERGEN   Thank you, Private. You can uh…I'd like you to stay, actually.

HENRY   Yes sir.

(HENRY shows REIKER in and stands to the side. REIKER stands at attention and issues the Nazi salute.)

BERGEN   Get that out of my face, Lieutenant. This is a courtesy call. Since you're camp spokesman, I thought I'd fill you in on a few changes around here. Number one: have a walnut.

(BERGEN places one on the desk.)

REIKER   I prefer not—

BERGEN   *Have a walnut… Open it. …Read it.*

(Inside the walnut is a small slip of paper.)

REIKER   *(Reading:)* "Das Vaterland wird siegen. Mut halt— "

BERGEN   "The Fatherland will prevail. Keep your chin up and your mouth shut." I've asked the Colonel to suspend all shipments from the German Red Cross.

REIKER   I'm afraid that would violate the Gen—.

BERGEN   The Red Cross has already violated the Geneva Convention. Number two: there will be extension courses offered through the university in literature, economics, horticulture, and history. The Reich Ministry of Education has agreed to honor grades at face value.

REIKER   Whose.

BERGEN   …Whose what?

REIKER   Whose history.

BERGEN   American. Of course. Taught by a Professor Compton. I understand he likes to dress up as some of our forefathers.

REIKER   Whose literature, whose economics and for that matter whose horticulture.

BERGEN   Three: we've arranged a course in square dancing, the culmination of which will be a trip to Charleston, where the prisoners will get to dance with actual American women.

REIKER   That would be very bad for morale, Herr Bergen.

BERGEN   They're just as good as your hefty Bavarian fräuleins.

REIKER   No, Herr Bergen. The men are…very lonely. They are engaging in…behaviors.

BERGEN   …Aaaoooh.

REIKER   It is bad for discipline.

BERGEN   Well, they're prisoners.

REIKER   They are soldiers of the Reich.

BERGEN   And you can't explain that to them?

REIKER   I think you overestimate my influence.

BERGEN   Yyyess, and then there's *that*. How is it you're camp spokesman and you're outranked by, what, twelve officers?

REIKER   I was elected.

BERGEN   By a huge majority, I'm told.

REIKER   It's the American way.

BERGEN   (*Consulting his notes*) The day I got here, a prisoner—81G-42—was found hanged in the warehouse.

REIKER   Corporal Müller. A homosexual.

BERGEN   Three months ago another one dove off a roof and broke his neck. Various reports of prisoners trying to starve or cut themselves.

REIKER   Traitors and cowards.

BERGEN   Holy Ghosts, they're called. A person comes to them in the night with talk of salvaging their honor. Or with threats against their families in das Vaterland. Or you just beat them to death.

REIKER   Who told you th—?

BERGEN   There will be no more Holy Ghosts and no more Nazi brainwashing.

REIKER   Instead there will be only American brainwashing.

BERGEN   Public relations. Take your shirt off. …You heard me.

REIKER   …I prefer not—

BERGEN   You want the private to do it for you?

(*Pause. REIKER looks at HENRY. Then REIKER removes his blue shirt; beneath it he wears a sleeveless undershirt.*)

BERGEN   …You said something interesting the other day. "My honor is my loyalty." Sounded familiar. Raise your arm. …That was Himmler, wasn't it?

(*BERGEN will inspect both his armpits, using a pen.*)

REIKER   It is...how do you say. Axiomatic.

BERGEN   Other arm. How is it you speak English so well?

REIKER   Gymnasium. Fräulein Jones.

BERGEN   (*Having found what he was looking for:*) ...Uh-*huh.*

REIKER   The tattoo indicates my blood type.

BERGEN   SS? Your blood type is SS?

REIKER   I am Wehrmacht.

(BERGEN consults a file on his desk.)

BERGEN   You are from Duisburg, and until you were captured, a lieutenant in an anti-aircraft unit under General Rommel.

REIKER   Yes.

BERGEN   I don't think so. I think you're Waffen-SS, probably a Captain. When you saw Eisenhower closing in, you swapped uniforms with the guy standing next to you. I'm going to request your immediate transfer to Camp Alva, where you'll be investigated for war crimes.

REIKER   I think you overestimate *your* influence, Lieut—

BERGEN   You are *dismissed.*

(Pause. Reiker thinks for a moment, then issues the Nazi salute. BERGEN doesn't return it, but gets in his face:)

BERGEN   ...Listen to this: "Your child belongs to us already. You will pass on. Your descendants now stand in the new camp. And soon they will know nothing but this new community."

REIKER   Herr Bergen has read his Hitler.

(BERGEN salutes; REIKER exits. HENRY smiles at BERGEN, impressed, and exits. Lights to black on BERGEN's office.

A musical interlude: the camp band, playing badly.

Elsewhere, in a barrack, THREE PRISONERS crawl into their bunks for the night, covering themselves with blankets.

Elsewhere, special comes up in the dayroom on the PROFESSOR, in an elaborate colonial costume—and overacting.)

PROFESSOR   I am Thomas Paine, and these are the times that try men's souls! The summer soldier and the sunshine patriot will, in this crisis, *shrink* from the service of his country, but he that *stands up now* deserves the thanks of man and woman!

(The FIRST PRISONER begins to masturbate, his blanket bouncing furiously.)

PROFESSOR   Tyranny is not easily conquered, yet we know that the *harder* the conflict, the more *glorious* the triumph!

(SECOND PRISONER begins to masturbate—then the THIRD.)

PROFESSOR   The British army was beaten back by a woman, Joan of Arc! Would that heaven might now inspire some maiden to *spirit up* her countrymen, and save her fellow sufferers from *ravage* and *ravishment!*

(Special down on the PROFESSOR. The band music stops, but the THREE PRISONERS keep masturbating.

Lights up on CO's office: the CO and BERGEN.)

CO   ...Alva? Where's that, Arkansas?

BERGEN   Oklahoma, sir. It's where we quarantine the unsalvageables.

CO   ...Well, I'll look into it.

BERGEN   ...Sir, the PMG's orders stipulate—

CO   Quit beatin' me over the head with the PMG. You need to remember your place, Bergen.

BERGEN   My—?

CO   You're 1-A-O. I read up on you, college boy. How the hell'd you make lieutenant?

BERGEN   It came with the posting, sir.

CO   Well you're no officer, Bergen. You let me worry about Reiker.

BERGEN   Sir, he intimidates the prisoners, he bullies them and he—

CO   Before he got here I was stampin' out brush fires all over the place. Had the Catholics and Lutherans at each other's throats, Austrians and Bavarians—shit, they kept goin' on *strike*, said they weren't gonna be *slaves*. Reiker shows up—that's about fifteen fewer headaches I gotta deal with.

BERGEN   Sir, he's SS.

CO   All them flowers out there? Those were *his* idea.

BERGEN   He's *S! S!* ...You gotta be kidding.

CO   I know what—

BERGEN   Sir, in the beginning, magnificent, super-human Aryans emerged from something called 'eternal ice' to turn the world into their own biocratic utopia. ...That's what they tell their children. It's not a military unit, it's a religious order, with its own liturgy, its own icons, it's own bizarre rituals, and Himmler is archbishop, and Hitler is God. ...Colonel. He's a fully indoctrinated instrument of artificial selection.

CO   Well, apparently so are you. I said I'd look into it. You're dismissed. Go worry about your...little play.

(Lights down on CO's office.

Band music begins again. The THREE PRISONERS keep masturbating.

Elsewhere: Special up on the PROFESSOR, now as John Adams:)

PROFESSOR   I am John Adams! And I say let the pulpit sound, let the bar proclaim, let the colleges join in the same delightful concert!

(FIRST PRISONER climaxes loudly.)

PROFESSOR   Let the public dispute the means of preserving good and demolishing evil! Let all these exercises spread far and wide the ideas of right and the *sensations* of *freedom*!

(SECOND PRISONER climaxes loudly.)

PROFESSOR   In a word, let every sluice of knowledge be opened and set a-flowing!

(Lights down on the PROFESSOR as the THIRD PRISONER climaxes very loudly—in the same moment that the music reaches its crescendo and stops. Pause. In the silence:)

FIRST PRISONER   Mein Gott, Helmut! [My God, Helmut!]

(THIRD PRISONER giggles, and lights come down on their barrack.

Elsewhere: lights up on BERGEN and CETNIK in the dayroom, rehearsing.)

BERGEN   "The mud wagon's in!"

CETNIK   "The mood wahgonen!"

BERGEN   "The *mud* wagon's *in.*"

CETNIK   "The *mood* wahgon *sin*"

BERGEN   "Hello Jack! Hello boys! Ain't you fellers drunk yet?"

CETNIK   "Ant yoofallurs dronget?"

BERGEN   "Seid ihr noch nicht besoffen?" ["Ain't you fellers drunk yet?"] Yes? No? Don't you speak German?

CETNIK   I am Cetnik.

BERGEN   Cetnik, you are Cetnik, I know that. Okay. Again: "The mud wagon's in!"

CETNIK   "The mood wahgonsin! Hallo, Jack! Hallo, boyss!"

(Lights down on BERGEN and CETNIK.

Elsewhere: lights up on the cotton field. HENRY and QAISER stand guard.)

QAISER   In the beginning, all men were created black. And all there was was black people, 'til a scientist named Yakub made the white people. And these white people turned out to be the devil. First they was all Jews, then Jesus came and made some of 'em Christians, but they was all still the devil. And then they took over the world.

HENRY   …So you gonna kill all the white people.

QAISER   They took us from our homes, from the Tribe of Shabazz, and they made us into slaves, and they made us into Christians. And as long as we're Christians, we'll be their slaves.

HENRY   …So you gonna kill aaaaall the white people.

QAISER   Yes. Well, most. Allah will allow the followers of Elijah Mohammed to rise up and reclaim their kingdom. But only if you believe. If you don't, you'll be lost.

HENRY   Sergeant says you're a strange motherfucker.

QAISER   The sergeant is lost.

HENRY   …Well, so, what does that mean, if you're lost? I mean, if you're lost, what's that mean?

QAISER   …It means you don't know it.

(QAISER exits. HENRY ponders. A special stays on him through the rest of the scene.

Lights up on rehearsal, where BERGEN directs CETNIK and WEISZ, sitting beside one another and reading from scripts. WEISZ, playing Ann, wears a woman's wig and perhaps a shawl. Otherwise each is still in his blue POW uniform.)

WEISZ   "…Are you saying you're in luff with me, Abe?"

CETNIK   "Yes, siam."

BERGEN   Takes her hands.

(CETNIK takes WEISZ's hands, faces him, reads:)

CETNIK   "I'fe been luffing yoo…a lonk time, vith all my heart. Yoo see, Ann, yoor a partic-ally fine girl. An yoor goot to look at too."

WEISZ   "I thought I knew you pretty well, Abe, but I didn't."

CETNIK   "I'm not expectink yoo to feel anytink for me. I'd nefer dream of such a think… But ef I cood vin yoo, Ann, I'd be—"

BERGEN   (*Providing a line reading*) "If I could win *you*—," you love her—er liebt, er liebt!

CETNIK   (*Still badly*) "Ef I cood vin you."

BERGEN   (*Rhapsodically*) "If *I* could win *yooou*."

CETNIK   "Ef *aaah* cooood...win *yoooo*...I'd be willink to disbelief eferytink I'fe efer seen vith my own eyes, and haf faith in everythink wonnerful I efer read in poetry books."

BERGEN   Good, turns away.

(*CETNIK turns away, demurely.*)

WEISZ   "Abe! What are you doink?"

CETNIK   "I'm goink to tell Bowlink Green I'm a can, I'm a canid—"

BERGEN   (*Exasperated*)   "I'm a *candidate* for the *assembly* of the State of *Illinois*!" Ooookay! Let's—let's stop there.

CETNIK   Ja trebam imati bradu, jelde? Bradu? [I should have a beard, yes? ...A beard`?]

BERGEN   I don't—what—

WEISZ   I think he wants to have a beard. Like Lincoln.

BERGEN   Oh. He didn't—Lincoln didn't have a beard yet. He grows one in the last scene, when he goes off to—you know what? Okay. Sie werden einen Bart haben, ja. [We'll get you a beard. Yes.]

(*WEISZ gives CETNIK a happy thumbs up. CETNIK smiles and starts off.*)

CETNIK   Goot! Goot! Ookay!

(*CETNIK exits—crossing over to that part of the stage which is the field. There, as we can see from his gestures, he sits silently rehearsing his lines in his head.*)

BERGEN   ...What's wrong with him?

WEISZ   Wrong? There is nothing wrong with him.

BERGEN   Why doesn't he understand German?

WEISZ   Because he is not German.

BERGEN   …He's not?

WEISZ   He's been trying to tell you.

BERGEN   …What is he?

(Lights to black on rehearsal. HENRY, standing guard over the field, has been watching CETNIK and now approaches:)

HENRY   Alright. That's enough. Let's go.

CETNIK   *(Friendly)* Um, ehhh… "Hallo Jack! Hallo boys! Ant you fallers dronkyit?"

HENRY   …Huh? Let's go—back to work. …What are you doing?

(CETNIK recognizes the cue, thinks for a moment, and then in a tone that echoes Bergen's earlier exasperation:)

CETNIK   …Vhat are you—oh! Ehh: "I'm goink Bowlink!" Ehhh, ehhh, "I'm goink, I'm goink *tell* Bowlink, I'm canniday, I'm a can—"

HENRY   You get smart with me I bust your fuckin' head, fuckin' Nazi.

CETNIK   No, no. I am Cetnik. Cetnik.

HENRY   Ain't gonna tell you again.

(CETNIK searches for a line, smiling nervously, panicking.)

HENRY   …You hear what I said? What you lookin' at? …Huh? …*Huh?*

(HENRY hits him in the head with his rifle. CETNIK falls.)

HENRY   See what you made me do? Huh? You see what you made me do?

(HENRY stands over CETNIK. End scene.)

Scene 8
Indoctrination

(Late afternoon: the cab of a truck. HENRY is driving; REIKER sits beside him. They ride in silence. Several POW's are in back. CETNIK is one of them; he has a black eye. Finally:)

REIKER   …You are upset. …You are upset about the private. You shouldn't be. They say there's something wrong with that one. You can see by looking at him.

(Pause. No response. He tries another angle:)

REIKER   …So. Where you from?

(HENRY just looks at him. Pause.)

REIKER   …If I were you, I wouldn't let it—

HENRY   I ain't upset about the private. Feel damned good about the private. I'm the schwarzer here. Do any damn thing I want.

REIKER   …You're—?

HENRY   You heard me. Shoulda shot the fuckin' private.

REIKER   *(Smiling)* Mmm. …So why didn't you?

HENRY   What.

REIKER   Shoot the fucking private. Teach him a lesson. You're the schwarzer.

HENRY   …You mean you want me to shoot one'a your own men.

REIKER   They aren't my men. I have no idea who he is. Most of them are Strafbataillon. You know Strafbataillon? Criminals, drunkards—the niggers of Germany. You must put them on their knees, it's the only language they understand. If I were you, I'd have done the same thing. If I were you, I'd—

HENRY   Well you ain't me. I ain't a Nazi. …And quit sayin' that word.

REIKER   Which word.

HENRY   You know. You ain't even supposed to be talkin' to me.

REIKER   I'm only trying to—

HENRY   Sparta. That's where I'm from. You ain't heard of it. Town called Sparta.

REIKER   …You're from *Sparta*?

HENRY   You know it?

REIKER   Pffff—everyone knows Sparta. Very famous. A great garrison once, the whole town, a great fortress. From seven years old every boy trained as a soldier. You must be a great warrior.

HENRY   …I am.

REIKER   You don't look Greek.

HENRY   Huh?

REIKER   The Fuhrer, you know, he is a great admirer of your culture. It's his model for the Reich, in fact.

HENRY   The hell you talkin' about.

REIKER   Sparta, Athens, the body and mind—a total culture, where everyone is better, everyone is stronger, everyone belongs. It's where we get our idea of the Volk.

HENRY   The folk.

REIKER   *Volk*, das Volk. It means—you have no word for it. It means a people, the *force* of one people who are…who are the same and united.

HENRY   That's folk. I *got* folk. I got folk in Sparta *and* Athens. The *fuck* you keep smiling at?

REIKER   …I think maybe you are a Nazi.

HENRY   What?

REIKER   You heard me. Turn here.

(HENRY turns the truck. Pause.)

REIKER   …"To be a Nazi…is to have clarity." Hitler wrote this. And if you think clearly for just a few moments, you will admit you are a Nazi. Everyone would.

HENRY   Yeah well. You can count me out. I hear about you all. All that shit you got goin' on.

REIKER   I don't know what you mean.

HENRY   All that sick shit. "Everyone belongs." Ain't what I hear.

REIKER   Well no, not yet, of course. First we must …cleanse our country of those who don't. Men like that one—the one you hit—the defectives—they are…what is it…castrated. By law. We chop off their balls, I'm saying.

HENRY   Well that's some sick shit.

REIKER   It is, yes. …Of course, you have the same laws.

HENRY   Who?

REIKER   Here, America. Where everyone is equal. You take your defectives and you chop off their balls. South Carolina, many states have these laws—long before Germany. A professor from Chicago—he invented this. *Our* people learned this from *your* people.

HENRY   Ain't my people.

REIKER   We have other laws. They restrict—they *forbid* people from our country.

HENRY   Yeah, the, the Jews.

REIKER   The Jews, the Slavs, many people, but so do you—the *same* people—long before Germany. The Johnson Act. The Webb Act. Still in effect.

HENRY   That ain't what—

REIKER   We forbid marriage between Germans and Jews, Germans and whoever. Terrible, you say. So now tell me what happens—here, right here, where everyone is equal—when a nigger tries to marry a white woman, when a nigger even *looks* at a white woman, or gets on a bus, or—

HENRY   I told you quit sayin' that word! …You don't get to say that word.
               Now on, you say "Negro."

(REIKER shrugs: "as you wish.")

HENRY   …I heard you put 'em in camps.

REIKER   Negroes?

HENRY   Jews. You put Jews in camps.

REIKER   You put us in camps.

HENRY   Maaaan.

REIKER   You put us in camps.

HENRY   But you the enemy.

REIKER   The Jews are our enemy.

HENRY   They ain't even a country.

REIKER   They are political prisoners. You think you have no political prisoners?
               Your Japanese, thousands of them, where are they?

HENRY   But they the enemy too.

REIKER   They are Americans—all in camps. Or your Indians. Where are
               they? They aren't they enemy.

HENRY   But that's different.

REIKER   Every country has its own Jews. It's no different. How many Negroes
               are in jail who are *not* political prisoners? …You see? You are the
               Jews of America.

HENRY   Don't call me a Jew. I ain't a Jew.

REIKER   Well then you must be a Nazi.

(Pause. They drive. HENRY listens.)

REIKER   …You should be proud of that, Private. You should take pride in what you are. I am a Nazi, I'm not ashamed. Because "if I am not for myself, then who will be for me?" Yes? …Who wrote this, do you think, if I am not for myself—

HENRY   Hitler.

REIKER   The Jews. The *Talmud*. And you would say yes: they are entitled to, to assert their right to exist.

HENRY   That's right.

REIKER   Why then am not I? Or you? If everyone is equal, why should we allow them to destroy us? The Jews are conspiring—yes—to destroy Christianity, to rule *many* countries. They have infiltrated the banks, the schools—Hollywood, even baseball! They are a cancer, they are *evil*. Who wrote this? Hitler?

(HENRY stammers—he doesn't know.)

REIKER   Henry Ford. Henry Ford. Famous American. His picture hangs over Hitler's *desk*. Because he had the courage to admit he was *better* than those who would *destroy* him if he did *not*. …And this is the essence of Nazism: that people *are not equal*. And you know this.

HENRY   Okay.

REIKER   You can look around and say: "That man is beneath me. I am the better man." You Negroes, you hate other Negroes because they are not as black. Or they are more black, who is the better Negro, I don't know. But no race, no country—

HENRY   *Okay.*

REIKER   —no Volk will achieve its perfection unless it cleanses itself of its useless and unwanted. In Sparta, when a child was born weak or deformed, its father would smash it on the rocks. He would take his child—

HENRY   Just—just shut up, man! Just shut the fuck up or I'll bust your head too, you understand me?

REIKER   *(Smiles broadly)* …Oh, I understand you perfectly. …Just ahead. With the window.

(REIKER points ahead. HENRY pulls over, gets out, goes to the rear of the truck.)

HENRY   Alright. One ice-cream cone, back in the truck. Let's go.

(The PRISONERS leap out of the truck and head offstage—into the 'ice cream shop'— save for CETNIK, who sits there, uncertain.)

HENRY   Let's go, boy! What'sa matter with you?

CETNIK   I am Cetnik.

HENRY   Get the fuck out the truck.

(HENRY pulls CETNIK from the truck, throws him in the direction the others have gone. REIKER stands smiling at him—then turns and joins the others. Pause.

HENRY hesitates, then steels himself and strides bravely into the ice cream shop. He is quickly pushed back onstage and reels onto his back. He sits stunned.)

HENRY   …I'm in the Army! …I'm a soldier in the United States Army!

(Laughter from inside the shop. Then REIKER returns with two ice cream cones—and holds one out to HENRY. End scene.)

Scene 9
Enunciation

(Evening: the prisoner's mess. CO and REIKER sit eating dinner, laughing. REIKER wears his tattered lieutenant's uniform.)

REIKER   …So now he has fifty eggs beneath his bunk. He was going to trade them with the guards, you know, but he waits too long—one morning he gets up—he has fifty little chickens running around the—

CO   Bergen.

(BERGEN has entered with a tray and joins them.)

BERGEN   Colonel. May I?

CO   This is a surprise. You know Lieutenant Reiker.

BERGEN   Guten Abend, Herr Reiker. Have you been in an accident?

REIKER   GI's, souvenir hunters. Two hours after I'd been captured they'd taken my Soldbuch and all my insignia. Somewhere I think there's a little American boy wearing my medals to school.

CO   Here to see how the other half lives, Lieutenant?

BERGEN   I'm not entirely sure what this is.

REIKER   Sauerbraten and Spätzle. I bought some Mosel at the canteen, let me pour you some.

BERGEN   No—thank you.

REIKER   I was telling the colonel, I've gained four kilograms since I came here. Last night we had pork knuckles, this morning there were oranges! Do you know how hard it is to find oranges in Germany?

BERGEN   I hear that American prisoners in Germany are eating rats. ...I hear they're freezing to death.

(REIKER fills BERGEN's cup with wine.)

REIKER   I hear that *Berliners* are eating rats and freezing to death. Have some wine, Lieutenant.

BERGEN   ...My condolences on the death of your friend.

CO   Who's that?

REIKER   General Rommel.

CO   Rommel! No kidding.

REIKER   He was shot. In his car.

BERGEN   Actually, no.

(BERGEN tosses an open news magazine onto the table.)

BERGEN   Actually, two Gestapo showed up at his door and told him they'd be back in an hour to arrest him—if he was still alive.

CO   Rommel?

BERGEN   For plotting to kill Hitler. He was one of them. So he drank some poison and announced to his family he had fifteen minutes to live. A Holy Ghost.

REIKER   Das sind Lügen natürlich. [These are lies, of course.]

BERGEN   Mir ist egal, wenn Sie es nicht glauben. [I don't care if you believe it.] ...You can have that. Look at the cover: our infantry's inside your borders. We just bombed your hometown.

(Pause. REIKER stands.)

REIKER   ...Gentlemen.

(REIKER exits. Pause.)

CO   ...Kinda *like* bein' an asshole, don't you, Bergen?

(Lights down on the prisoners' mess.

Elsewhere, lights up on guards' mess. HENRY and QAISER sit eating. WATERS enters with his tray and joins them.)

WATERS   ...Well alright. Here we are again. Private Ohn-ree! You enjoy your ice cream? Huh? ...Musta tasted pretty good on a hot day. ...I *axed* you a question, Private.

HENRY   ...I thought you were my friend.

WATERS   I'm your *sergeant*. Trying to shape you up. Been here a month, all bitchin' and whinin'—you're in the best place you can be, Private, three squares and a roof. ...And quit all this shit about your French daddy. Shit's wearin' a little thin around here.

HENRY   He wasn't Fr—

WATERS   When did that war end? Huh? When it end? ...You don't even know. You're how old—nineteen, twenty? That means he got killed like ten years before you're even born. Now how'd he do that? How'd he get killed ten years before—

HENRY   Didn't say he got killed, said he—

WATERS   Said he never came back!

(HENRY starts to speak—but there's nothing he can say. He stands to leave.)

WATERS   …Just tryin' to help you out, mon frer. Tryin' to help you get along.

HENRY   Don't call me that.

WATERS   Mon frer? That means "my brother."

HENRY   I know what it means.

WATERS   Well, alright. That's alright, ain't it? …Huh? …We alright, brother?

HENRY   …Yeah. Alright.

(WATERS tousles HENRY's hair. HENRY grins sheepishly and exits. When he's gone:)

WATERS   …That is one baffled motherfucker.

QAISER   Why do you do him like that?

WATERS   …White man looks at you, white man looks at me, what do you think
             he sees? …Henry. That's what. Henry's the reason for the back door.
             Henry's the reason for "colored only." That's why. He's an ignorant
             nigger. He's so ignorant, he don't know he's a nigger.

(Pause. WATERS eats.)

WATERS   …An' you quit lookin' at me.

(Pause. Lights down on black guards' mess.

Elsewhere, lights up on the rehearsal space. CETNIK has a black eye and is in
costume: black pants and shirt, black hat, and an obviously fake beard. BERGEN
is providing a grand, declamatory reading of a speech, affecting different accents
and gestures, which CETNIK tries to mimic. While his pronunciation has improved,
CETNIK still understands little of what he says).

BERGEN   "As a nation, we began by declaring, 'All men are created equal!'
             But now we practically read it, 'all men are created equal—except
             Negroes!'"

CETNIK   *(Interspersed, parroting Bergen's delivery)* "All men creeted eekal! …essept Negroes!"

BERGEN   "That is the conclusion toward which the advocates of slavery are driving us. But I advise you to *watch out*! When you enslave any of your fellow beings, and place him among the beasts—"

CETNIK   "…slafery are drifin' us! …*washout*! …fellow beans! …the beets!"

BERGEN   "—are you quite sure the demon you have created will not turn and rend *you*?"

(Here BERGEN might turn threateningly toward CETNIK—who panics and backpedals.)

BERGEN   "I am not preaching civil war! All I am trying to do is state the fundamental *virtues* of *dem-o-cracy*!"

CETNIK   "…voodoo of *dem-o-cassy*!"

BERGEN   "Because I believe those virtues are endangered not only by slavery, but by those who shout 'leave it alone!'"

CETNIK   "…slafery! …leef it alone!"

BERGEN   "This is a policy of indifference to *eeevil*, which enables our enemies to *taunt* us as *hypocrites*!"

CETNIK   "…*eeefil*! …*hippocriss*!"

(BERGEN chuckles warmly, pats CETNIK on the back, opens a cooler and produces two beers.)

BERGEN   …You're missing a really great play here, pal. This is great stuff.

CETNIK   *(Meaning the beer)* Thiss iss great stuff.

(They sit on the cooler and settle in for a drink. BERGEN sighs heavily—more of a long blow, really; CETNIK does the same.)

BERGEN   Hooooo. …Well, maybe you're lucky. At the end of the play, you get on a train, and you're gonna go to war, and you're gonna die, and everybody knows it but you. …And the ironic thing is, you don't want any of it.

CETNIK   Don wann any offit.

BERGEN   That's right. And I know how you feel, you know? I'm a pacifist. I
                mean, I don't mind serving my country, I know there's evil in the world,
                but I don't want to add to it. I think humanity would get along just fine
                if clearer heads prevailed and we just...we just *listened* to each other.

(CETNIK nods, oblivious but increasingly fascinated.)

BERGEN   That's why I gave up being a Jew even. My grandmother, maaaan,
                she was: "how can you do this!   Think of the Jews who were
                slaughtered!"   Goes on and on about how we're supposed to
                be a *people*, one common, equal *people*. But that's bullshit. The
                Sadducees, the Maccabbees and Pharisees, the, the, the Essenes—
                we were never one people. Orthodox, Reform, Conservatives—they
                can't stand each other. And I don't *want* to get slaughtered. ...So
                now she calls me a meshumad.

CETNIK   Meshumad.

BERGEN   Which means I don't even *exist*. ...Pfff.

(BERGEN drinks his beer in disgust. CETNIK does the same.)

BERGEN   ...It's not like I didn't try, you know? I took my bar mitzvah. And my
                rabbi, we talked about "davar," which means "word" and "event,"
                that words *are* events, how when God speaks, you know, "let there be
                light," it *activates* something. And I *wanted* that. I kept *waiting* for Him
                to *speak* to me. But He never did. ...So one day I go to a football game.
                Philadelphia: Independence Hall, Liberty Bell, beh. Then we go to
                Municipal Stadium. Eagles and Bears. Sweltering. The whole place, this
                big...bowl of...*people* just... shaking, all this...*power*, you could *feel* it.
                That's when something spoke to me. *That's* what I wanted to be a *part*
                of. I wanted to...just be an *American*, just an *American*, you know?

CETNIK   ...American. Yah.

BERGEN   Yeah. Just...just...*belong*.

CETNIK   *(Enchanted)* ...American. ...Belong. ...Yah.

(Pause. CETNIK beams. End scene.)

Scene 10
Emancipation

(Late afternoon: the cotton field. HENRY stands alone, obviously bored or lost in thought. A PRISONER is pushed suddenly on and stumbles to his knees. QAISER follows.)

QAISER   Count 'em.

HENRY   Wha—?

QAISER   Count 'em. Go ahead. Tell him.

(This last to the PRISONER while HENRY quickly counts heads in the field.)

PRISONER   He walk away.

HENRY   Wai-wai-wai-wait.

QAISER   Tell him where.

PRISONER   There—in there. Mit…Kleider, Kostüm. [With a costume.]

QAISER   We missing one. Right here, right in front of your nose, just walked off into the woods.

(QAISER throws a blue POW uniform at HENRY's feet.)

HENRY   Just—what—

QAISER   Got clothes on under his uniform. You count all you want. We're one short, you just standin' here daydreamin'.

HENRY   …Oh man.

QAISER   That's right.

(HENRY grabs the prisoner.)

HENRY   Where's he headed? …Huh? Where's he goin?

QAISER   I already did that. He don't know.

HENRY   Well…what do we do now?

QAISER   Go back and tell the sergeant.

HENRY   Oh *man*.

QAISER   That's right.

HENRY   Okay. …Okay. You take 'em back.

QAISER   Where you goin'?

HENRY   Where you think? …Gonna get me a runaway.

(HENRY exits and lights come down on field. Special up on BERGEN, in the dayroom, beginning rehearsal. He looks out into the audience and checks off the characters he names.)

BERGEN   Werner? We got Ann? …Okay. …Josh Speed? …Bowling Green?
                …Abe?

(Pause.)

BERGEN   …Where is he? …Abe Lincoln? You here? …We can't start without
                him. Anybody seen Abe?

(Elsewhere: special up on PATTY. She addresses the audience:)

PATTY   When I first seen him, he come walkin' outta the woods, down there
                by the railroad, but kinda slow and scared, like a deer.

(Special up on CETNIK, standing in his black clothes and fake beard, peering around carefully.)

BERGEN   …Wo bleibt Abe? …Wo bliebt Abe Lincoln?   […Where is Abe?
                …Where is Abe Lincoln?]

(Special fades on BERGEN, searching the audience, as PATTY continues:)

PATTY   He was a tall, skinny feller with a black eye and a fake beard, all soakin'
                wet from the rain, but when he saw me his eyes lit up and he says, "Hello
                Ann!" And I says, "My name ain't Ann," and he give me the biggest smile
                and says "The mud wagon's in." …And I don't care what anybody says,
                I could tell right then he warn't no bad man. And I wasn't afraid.

(She smiles at CETNIK, who smiles back. Then she saddens:)

PATTY   …But I didn't mean for it all to work out like it did.

(She saunters off, wistfully looking over her shoulder. He watches her go—then follows her offstage. Pause. The sound of thunder in the distance.

Then HENRY emerges, his rifle at the ready, searching the woods.

Lights to black. End Act One.)

Alex Smith (Bergen) and DeRante Parker (Henry) in Scene I.3: Cotton Field.
Photo: Kim Kim Foster/The State.

ACT TWO
Scene 1
My German Solder

(A voice, PAPA, calls from the darkness.)

PAPA   …Patty. …Patty. …Patty!

(Lights up on a porch, where PAPA stands with HENRY, who's looking a little ragged.)

PAPA   …Patty, come out here a minute.

(PATTY joins them on the porch.)

PAPA   …This boy wants to know if we seen somebody unfamiliar.

PATTY   You in the Army?

PAPA   Just answer the question and go on in.

PATTY   …I ain't seen nobody.

HENRY   Folks down the road said they—

PAPA   Don't look at her.

HENRY   …Folks down the road said they seen—

PAPA   We answered your question. I respect the uniform. We ain't seen nobody.

HENRY   *(To PATTY)* You sure?

PAPA   I said don't look at her.

PATTY   …I ain't seen nobody.

HENRY   You mind if I look around your property?

PAPA   Yes I do. Now that's twice we answered your question. I respect the uniform.

HENRY   That's twice you said that, too.

PATTY   Who is he?

PAPA   Don't talk to him. Go on in.

PATTY   I'm just *askin'*.

HENRY   German prisoner. Ran away coupla days ago.

PATTY   (*Deliciously*) Is he dangerous?

PAPA   We done our duty. We ain't seen nobody.

PATTY   I think I seen him... I just remembered. I seen a man like that, headin' inta the woods, 'bout a half-mile up. Like he was hidin'. ...This mornin'. I seen him.

PAPA   I said—hey!—don't you fuckin' look at her. We done our duty. We're all patriots here. Now you git offa my porch.

HENRY   Yeah. Folks down the road said that too.

(*Pause. Then HENRY turns and exits. PAPA strikes PATTY.*)

PAPA   ...Don't you look at him!

PATTY   O-*kay*!

(*PAPA exits. Patty tries to collect herself, sniffling a little.*

Elsewhere, lights come up on a hayloft, where CETNIK sits in his underwear and socks, and wrapped in a blanket, eating apple pie. His black Abe Lincoln outfit and beard hang on a wire overhead. Patty joins CETNIK in the barn and addresses the audience:)

PATTY   ...I strung up a wire to dry out his clothes and made him some pot roast and potatoes and fresh apple pie. He didn't say much right at first. Just smiled at me while he ate and I told him 'bout how I didn't like school and how all the boys 'round here all went overseas to fight the likes a' him, and here he was, right here in my barn! ...But I know he's a good man. I can tell by the way he looks at me.

(*She smiles at him dreamily and sniffles a little. He gets nervous.*)

CETNIK   ...Hello, Ann.

PATTY   He always calls me Ann.

CETNIK   Mud wagon's in.

PATTY   I don't know *what* that means.

(She sniffles a little. CETNIK watches her, thinks, recites:)

CETNIK   Ehhh, "it appear to me you haf bin cryin'. It make me sad sometink cood hurt you."

PATTY   *(At first astounded)* ...Well! I ain't...I ain't been cryin'. But that's sweet enough to say.

CETNIK   Emm, "The ting is, I tink quite lot of you. Efer sinz I come here. I wooden mention it, but...ehh...ehh...is comfort to find ears pour trouble into. And Lord knows my ears big enough!"

PATTY   Oh, now.

CETNIK   "I'm plain, common sucker with shirt-tail I can't sit on it."

PATTY   Well, you ain't so plain.

CETNIK   "Why, it be a pleasure."

PATTY   What would.

CETNIK   "...Well I don' even say anyting. A person juss look at me."

PATTY   ...Are you flirtin' with me?

CETNIK   "I wooden say that, Ann."

PATTY   Patty.

CETNIK   "Probably I don't."

PATTY   It's okay. I don't mind.

CETNIK   "I'fe got...kind of fanity myself."

PATTY   Well, I seen boys without their clothes on before. I mean, I ain't easy or nothin', but—

CETNIK   "I don' lack be snickered at either."

PATTY   I ain't snickerin'.

CETNIK   "I know what I yam. I know I'fe got nothink to offer girl that—"

(She touches his face or puts her hands on his knee.)

PATTY   I know what you are too. ...I don't mind. In spite of everything, I still believe that...people are really good at heart.

(CETNIK thinks, nervously, until he finds a spot to continue:)

CETNIK   Ehhh. "...Yes. Siam."

(Per his blocking, he takes her hands and faces her.)

CETNIK   "...I'fe been luffing yoo...a lonk time, vith all my heart."

PATTY   You *are* flirtin' with me.

CETNIK   "Yoo see, Ann, yoor a partic-ally fine girl."

PATTY   Patty.

CETNIK   "An' yoor good to look at too. I'm not expectink yoo to feel anytink for me. I'd nefer dream of such a think... But if I...if aaah cood—if I cood vin yooou—"

(She swoons, he pours it on:)

CETNIK   "—If aaaah cooood vin yooooo... I'd be villink to disbelief eferyting I'fe efer seen vith my own eyes, and haf fai— "

(She can't take it anymore. She puts a big, long kiss on him. His eyes stay wide open—and he smiles. He places his hand on her breast; she pushes it away. Again. Finally, with a few groans or "oh my" or "I can't," she stands and pulls away. He too turns away, per his blocking, his blanket falling away. He has an obvious erection. They both look at it. Pause.)

CETNIK   Ehhh... "De mud wagon's in."

PATTY   I can see that.

CETNIK   *(To his crotch)* "Hello, Jack. Hello boys."

(PATTY laughs a little. He wraps up and smiles sheepishly. Awkward pause. She touches his face.)

PATTY   Tell me again? ...Say...say you love me?

CETNIK   ...You luff me?

PATTY   Yes. ...I think I do. In spite of ever'thing. I do.

(She takes his hand and places it back on her breast. She kisses him and lies down on her back, pulling him with her. End scene.)

Scene 2
Gestapo

(Mid-day: the CO's office. CO and BERGEN are joined by FBI AGENT MARKS and SHERIFF LOKER.)

BERGEN   His name is Eras. Juraj Eras. He's not a Nazi. He's not even German. He's Cetnik.

LOKER   Hell's a Cetnik?

CO   A Serbian.

LOKER   Hell's a Serbian?

MARKS   A Yugoslavian. So he's a communist.

BERGEN   No. The Croats are communist.

CO   Serbians are fascist.

BERGEN   *Some* Serbians are fascist.

MARKS   And some fascists are Nazis.

CO   And some Nazis are Yugoslavian.

BERGEN   But not if they're Cetnik.

LOKER   Wait.

BERGEN   Look—his whole country, it's just a bunch of factions who hate each
                other. The Germans just let 'em all shoot it out, conscript the survivors
                and stick 'em in a trench next to—I don't know, Poles, Hungarians—
                they don't know who they're fighting with or against or why. When
                the British process these guys they just lump 'em together and send
                'em over. His file is pretty much empty.

LOKER   We got any idea where this man might be headed?

BERGEN   No.

CO   Well.

BERGEN   No. We have no idea.

MARKS   …Are you protecting this man, Lieutenant?

BERGEN   No.

MARKS   Because it sounds like you are. You sound like you sympathize with
                this Nazi. You sound like a Nazi sympathizer.

BERGEN   (*Interspersed*) I'm not, I'm—*no*—he's *not* a—

CO   Alright. Look here.

(CO opens a drawer, withdraws a half-potato and a magazine.)

BERGEN   Sir, we agr—

CO   Turns out there's a committee in camp—an escape committee. Draws
                up plans, pools the money, procures supplies like civilian clothing.
                And this.

LOKER   …A potato.

CO   A stamp. Put India ink on it and you can validate a fake passport or ID. That's an article from *American* magazine.

MARKS   "Enemies at Large."

CO   By your boss, J. Edgar Hoover. Talks about prisoner escapes around the country, typical MOs, that sorta thing. Hoover wrote it as a warning, but the kriegs've been using it as sort of a…how-to manual. How to get out, how to fit in. …Ironic, ain't it?

BERGEN   But we don't think Eras had access to that. He couldn't read it, and nobody could read it to him. We think he just walked—

MARKS   How'd you get this?

BERGEN   We can't say.

MARKS   …I'm sorry, what?

BERGEN   We can't say… You can have that, you have his description, you know everyth—

MARKS   "We" who? Who's this, who's this "we"?

BERGEN   *We,* uh—the uh—

CO   Lieutenant's got him a mole. One of the kriegs.

BERGEN   I promised him. I told him I'd protect him.

MARKS   That's not our problem.

BERGEN   He's not even on the committee.

LOKER   But he knows who is. And they may know where this man's headed.

BERGEN   He's afraid.

LOKER   We won't hurt him.

BERGEN   They will.

MARKS   That's not our problem either.

BERGEN   …I promised.

(Pause. AGENT MARKS and SHERIFF LOKER look at the CO.)

CO   …Won't tell me.

(An impasse. AGENT MARKS turns back to BERGEN:)

MARKS   …Bergen. …Bergen. …That's a…German name, isn't it?

CO   Noooo, it's a Jew name.

(BERGEN throws his head back and sighs—or some other gesture of disbelief.)

LOKER   I thought he looked like a Jew.

BERGEN   Kush meer in toches. [Kiss my ass.]

CO   But he speaks German.

LOKER   Sounded Jewish.

MARKS   It's both. It's Yiddish. He's fucking with us. Here's another language you might understand, you little kike: fraternization. Aiding and abetting.

BERGEN   Gey tren zich. [Go fuck yourself.]

MARKS   You're in violation of the Articles of War.

BERGEN   Not unless I defy a direct order.

(AGENT MARKS and SHERIFF LOKER turn to the CO and wait. The CO groans.)

CO   …Arrrr, Jesus. Alright. Tell you what. Let me handle this.

BERGEN   I think I'm handling it, sir.

CO   You're dismissed. Dammit. Tell…whoever's at the desk to come on in here.

(Pause. Then BERGEN stands, salutes and exits.)

MARKS   …What kinda American is he?

CO   Look, fellas: I'm gonna check into this, see what I can root out. Alright?

LOKER   Hell of an operation, Colonel. Half-Jewified, half-negrified, and Nazis roamin' around free.

CO   I'm lookin' *into* it, and I'll get *back* to you.

(WATERS has appeared in the door and saluted. AGENT MARKS points menacingly at the CO, starts to say something, then decides against it. He and SHERIFF LOKER exit.)

WATERS   Wanted to see me, sir?

CO   …Yeah. Is Bergen gone?

WATERS   Yes, sir.

CO   …Go get Reiker. Tell him I…tell him I need his help with something.

(WATERS salutes and exits. End scene.)

Scene 3
Formless Fears

(Night in a pine forest. HENRY staggers on. He is missing a shoe, his pants are soaked, and he's exhausted. He sees a stump or a rock, sits and removes his remaining shoe and shakes it out.)

HENRY   …Fuckin' jungle, man. Snakes. Spiders. Raccoons. White folks.

(He peels a leech off his calf.)

HENRY   Leeches. …Fuckin' swamp. Probably got malaria.

(From offstage, very faintly, PAPA's voice:)

PAPA   *(Off)* …Patty.

HENRY   …Can't see the moon. Can't see shit. …This is not America! … Where am I! …Anybody hear me?

PAPA   *(Off) …Patty? …Patty, where are you?*

HENRY   *Hello! …Anybody!*

(Lights to half on HENRY.

Elsewhere: lights up on the hayloft. Morning: CETNIK and PATTY are asleep in the hay, half-dressed. At the sound of PAPA's voice, now closer, they awake. CETNIK realizes—begins scrambling for his clothes.)

PAPA   *(Off) …Patty? …Where the…Patty?*

PATTY   Not that way—this—! This! Go!

(CETNIK grabs his clothes and beard and runs off. PATTY, wearing perhaps only her underclothes, also scrambles to cover herself—but too late: PAPA has entered the barn with AGENT MARKS and SHERIFF LOKER.)

PAPA   Patt—? …What are you doing?

PATTY   Um… Nothing. I'm—

PAPA   These men here say they're lookin' for the—what the hell's goin' on?

PATTY   I—I—I—fell asleep, I was—

PAPA   What are you doing out *here*?

PATTY   It's not what it—it's not—I'm not doing anything.

(She starts to panic and cry.)

PAPA   …For Christ's sake!

PATTY   Leave me alone!

PAPA   Stand up.

PATTY   No!

PAPA   Don't you look at her!

(She stands. AGENT MARKS and SHERIFF LOKER avert their eyes—sort of—as PATTY tries to cover herself.)

PAPA   ...Who. ...Patty. ...Who.

PATTY   It's not what—

(PAPA strikes her.)

PAPA   ...*Who.*

(He strikes her again.)

PAPA   ...*Who!*

(Lights to black on barn.

Lights full on HENRY, in the forest, wringing out his socks. A rustling in the bushes behind him:)

HENRY   ...What the—who's there? Come on out. ...Come outta there!

(He peers into the bushes, grabs his gun and takes aim—then lowers it.)

HENRY   ...Squirrel. Great. You run, little brother.

(Settles back in—but then a rustling elsewhere.)

HENRY   ...Where the hell that—? ...*Who's in there! Hey!*

(In the distance, the baying of hounds. HENRY listens:)

HENRY   ...Wolves! ...That's just. ...*Get away from me! Just stay away from me!*

(The dogs continue howling, closing in. HENRY panics, abandons his shoes, runs off. End scene.)

Scene 4
Dutchmen

(Mid-day: a train boxcar. Crates, bales and a disheveled white man, KING, partially covered in a pile of burlap and sharpening a makeshift blade. When CETNIK climbs into the car, KING turns suddenly, wielding the blade, and a startled CETNIK starts off:)

KING   …No-no-no! Wai-wai-wai-wait! It's okay! It's…okay. This is, this is—I won't hurt you. I'm uh—you're fine, see? See? …Come in! Look, you want, you want an apple? …Huh? …Go ahead. Take it. It's okay.

(KING has put the blade aside, and CETNIK carefully takes the apple KING offers.)

KING   …We've got…uh, we've got cantaloupes, tangerines, I don't know what's over there. You help yourself. We're just uh. I mean, your timing is, I mean this is, this is great. You want another? Go ahead. As many as you want. You don't know how glad I am to see you.

(Pause. CETNIK sits and eats. He and KING watch each other.)

KING   …So I'm thinking you're…what. Amish, right? …No? Mennonite? It's okay, friend. I'm from Dutch country! I'm Quaker, my whole family. Name's King. Welcome, friend.

(KING extends a hand. CETNIK looks at it, then shakes it.)

KING   That's right. We're all friends here. I don't know what you're doing here, but it's certainly none of my business.

(A black man, DUKE, appears from beneath the burlap. He is feverish, weak and in pain.)

DUKE   Where are we?

KING   We haven't left yet. Train hasn't moved. This is Mr. Duke. He's sick. We got in some uh…

DUKE   Trouble.

(KING throws the burlap off from around his feet. He and DUKE are shackled together at the ankles.)

KING   Some trouble, yes, down in New Orleans. His leg is, well, he's in, he's in bad shape—

CETNIK   New Urleans?

KING   You know it?

CETNIK   …Emm. "Sure, I bin to New Urleans. And efery minnit vas dere, I vas scare."

DUKE   So were we.

KING   Shhh.

CETNIK   "I am scare dey vill kill me."

DUKE   No shit.

KING   Take it easy. …He's got gangrene. In his leg, he's burning up. He's not gonna make it if we don't. I don't know. I made this, from a hinge. I tried wire, I tried rocks, I can't, I, I, I can't. …I need to cut the chain and…I can't.

DUKE   Leg.

KING   No.

DUKE   My *leg*!

KING   I'm not cutting your—!   –He wants me to—you know. I can't do that, I can't…just *leave* him. …Can you help us? …Please. …Please?

(KING holds out the blade. CETNIK suddenly understands:)

CETNIK   Oooooh!

KING   Yes! Yes, thank you.

(CETNIK takes the blade and begins to saw on the chain.)

DUKE   No, no, my—

KING   Let him *try*. –Thank you. We really…you have no idea.

(CETNIK saws on the chain. Lights to black on box car.

Special up on BERGEN, at rehearsal in the dayroom.)

BERGEN May I have your attention please, gentlemen? ...I have an announcement to make. ...As you all probably know, Abe Lincoln has...emancipated himself. Which, of course, creates a problem. But the show, as they say, must go on. And in just a few days. Soooo, since I've rehearsed every damned line about...five hundred times...I will assume the role of Abe Lincoln... Any problems with that?

(Elsewhere, lights come up on the supply room—where a noose hangs from the ceiling. A line of PRISONERS files in solemnly.)

BERGEN ...Alright. From the top. I need Ann, Jack and the rest of the boys. We got everybody?

(The last to enter the supply room is WEISZ—who is shoved in and stumbles— followed by REIKER, in his uniform.)

BERGEN ...Where's Ann? ...Werner, are you here? ...Anybody seen Corporal Weisz?

(WEISZ gets to his feet and looks up at the noose. Lights to black on BERGEN, then on the supply room.

Lights back up on the boxcar, where CETNIK sits sawing on the chain. DUKE's eyes are closed and he looks worse. KING chatters nervously:)

KING ...Actually, I have a confession to make. I am not...technically...a Quaker. I *used* to be. They uh...they disagreed with...or they...didn't *approve*...well, they kicked me out. Is what they did. I "received disownment." Is what they call it. Which means I've been "forgotten." "The beast with many heads has butt me away!" ...Huh.

(Pause. He mops the sweat off DUKE's forehead; DUKE is unresponsive. CETNIK keeps sawing.)

KING ...The Society of Friends! ...You'd think it'd be pretty hard to get kicked outta something called the Society of Friends, you know? ...You'd be surprised. They got *four* different factions. Gurneyites, Wilburites, the...I don't know. You'd think something called the Society of Friends wouldn't have *factions*.

(Pause.)

KING   ...Buuut...fuck 'em. You know? "I banish you," quoth Coriolanus. "Thus I turn my back, there is a world elsewhere." We're actors. Anabaptists hate actors. ...Buncha *zombies.* Quakers, we're the ones just...*sit* there like that, you know? For hours, we just...we just *sit.* ...It's called "waiting," we're *waiting,* see. For what, you ask. For the "Holy Spirit." To "speak *through* us". ...But it never does. Not a goddam word. ...Or if it does, it's in some strange language you can't even understand.

(Pause.)

KING   ...Not a bad group though. I mean, nice folks. That whole Underground Railroad thing, that was us. –You know that? Huh? That was us. My people *saved* your people.

(He nudges DUKE. DUKE is barely responsive.)

KING   ...Hey. ...Hey. ...*Hey.* Stay with me, man. You alright? ...He's almost done. Look, look, he's—

(He means the chain, but CETNIK has made no progress.)

KING   ...Ah, God. Duke? You stay with me, man. I'm here. I'm stayin' with you. Can you hear me? ...Duke?

(He pulls DUKE close, holds him. DUKE manages at best a small whimper. Long pause. Then KING resigns himself. To CETNIK:)

KING   ...It's okay. You can go now. We're grateful. You tried. ...You can go. This part's...this part's just us.

CETNIK   ...Ja ne razumijem. [I don't understand.]

(KING produces a small wad of bills and holds it up for CETNIK, then stuffs it in one of CETNIK's pockets.)

KING   Here. You can take this, for your trouble. Don't tell anybody where you found us. Just leave us alone... Just leave us... Go on.

(CETNIK is confused.)

KING   ...Go on! ...Out! Get *out!* Get *out!*

(KING resorts to brandishing the blade; CETNIK is frightened and runs out. Pause. KING holds DUKE.)

KING   …It's okay. I'm here. I'll wait.

(DUKE weakly tugs on his own pant leg.)

KING   Shhh. …I know. …I'll try. …Just…wait. …My friend. Just…just wait.

(Long pause. Waiting. DUKE breathes heavily, his head on KING's shoulder. End scene.)

DeRante Parker (Henry), Maxwell Highsmith (Waters) and
Seena Hodges (Qaiser) in scene I.5: Basic Training.
Photo: Kim Kim Foster/The State.

Scene 5
Sanctuary

(Early evening: a small frame shack in a clearing in the forest. A placard above the door reads "Praise House." Outside it is an old GULLAH WOMAN stirring a pot and humming to herself. Her language is beautiful but only vaguely comprehensible. The door to the Praise House opens, and HENRY comes out, wearing plain work clothes—dark overalls over a white shirt—and putting on different shoes.)

GULLAH WOMAN   ….Dem tings fit, eh? [Those clothes fit, yes?]

HENRY   Yeah. I guess.

GULLAH WOMAN   Dey b'lonx tuh de elduh. He ent gwi' min'. Ef Uh tell'um Uh gib oonuh he gumbo, he ent gwi' like dat. …Attuh oonuh dun et, mebbe he gwi' gib oonuh uh ride tuh town. [They belong to the elder. He won't mind. If I tell him I gave you his gumbo, he won't like that. After you've eaten, maybe he'll give you a ride to town.]

HENRY   …I'm sorry, I didn't understand one word a'—

GULLAH WOMAN   Seddown. Hab sum cawnbread. [Sit down. Have some cornbread.]

(She hands him some cornbread. He's obviously famished.)

HENRY   Thanks. …Do you speak English?

GULLAH WOMAN   Wuh oonuh t'ink Uh duh "speak." [What do you think I speak?]

HENRY   I don't know what you're speakin'.

GULLAH WOMAN   Sho oonuh do. …Ef us lussen…ef us *lussen*, eh? Us onduhstan' one'nuddah. [Sure you do. If we listen…If we listen, yes? We can understand one another.]

(He nods, smiles She serves him a bowl of gumbo.)

GULLAH WOMAN   …Wuh dat oonuh duh do. …Trouble, oonuh een trouble. [What did you do? …Trouble, you're in trouble.]

HENRY   Trouble? Oh, no ma'am, I ain't in no trouble. I'm in the United States Army.

GULLAH WOMAN   (Dubious) Mm-hmm.

HENRY   I'm lookin' for a man—a white man. Maybe you seen him.

GULLAH WOMAN   Uh ent shum no buckruh. [I ain't seen no white man.]

HENRY   Kinda funny lookin, got a—

GULLAH WOMAN   ...Ent no buckruh come *dis* way. [Don't many white men come *this* way.]

HENRY   ...Well, I got to find him. And I can't go back without him. But I don't know where he is.

GULLAH WOMAN   Wuh oonuh gwi' do wid'um? [What are you going to do with him?]

HENRY   I don't know. I haven't figured that part out yet. Kill him maybe, if I have to.

GULLAH WOMAN   Mmm. Nyam you gumbo, chile. [Eat your gumbo, child.]

HENRY   ...What is it?

GULLAH WOMAN   Swimp, okry, cawn, rice. ...'E good, enty? [Shrimp, okra, corn, rice. ...It's good, isn't it?]

HENRY   ...Not bad. I ain't eat this good since... Hell, I don't 'member when I ate this good.

(Pause. She hums a song and watches him eat. Then:)

GULLAH WOMAN   ...Oonuh bes le'm gone, eh? ...De buckruh. Mebbe oonuh bes le'm gone. [You should let him go, yes? ... The white man. Maybe you should let him go.]

HENRY   ...Well, no, I...I can't just—

GULLAH WOMAN   Mebbe oonuh bes go on home, chile, go see you mammy. [...Maybe you can go home, child, and go see your mother.]

HENRY   ...My mama? She died a long time ago. I grew up at my cousins' mostly.

GULLAH WOMAN   Mm-mm-mm.

HENRY   Wouldn't mind seein' *them* though. Go back in my uniform, too, know what I'm sayin'? Gonna look straight. Say, "Looka me, assholes. I don't need you no more. I got *real* brothers now. I got people who *respect* me."

GULLAH WOMAN   ...Oonuh loss, enty. [You're lost, aren't you.]

HENRY   ...I'm sorry, I can't...

(The GULLAH WOMAN smiles sadly at him, begins softly singing, and serves him more gumbo.)

GULLAH WOMAN   Wade in duh watuh, chillun
Wade in duh watuh, chillun
Wade in duh watuh
Gawd gwi' trouble de watuh.

...Yeddy dat song? De ole folk sing'um w'en sumbody git free. Song tell oonuh to wade in de watuh, so de dawg cyan gitya. Dat bin dem sign, de ole folk. W'en duh mastuh yedde duh song, 'e t'ink somebody git baptize. 'E ent onduhstan um. Dat bin how dey talk t'one nudduh. Dat bin de way us talk stillyet. ...Onnuh ain' onduhstan um, needuh. [...You hear that song? The old folks sang it whenever somebody got free. The song told you to wade in the water, so the dogs can't get you. That was how they told each other, the slaves. When the master heard the song, he though it was somebody getting baptized. He didn't understand it. That was how they talked to each other. That's how we talk to each other still. ...But you can't understand it either.]

HENRY   *(Smiling)* ...Well, you lost me again.

GULLAH WOMAN   Mm-hmm. Nyam you dinuh, chile. [I know. Eat your dinner, child.]

(Pause. He eats. She hums the song. End scene.)

Scene 6
Uncle Tom's Tavern

(Afternoon in the Rebel Bar—a dive decorated with Confederate memorabilia. A radio plays country music. CETNIK, in his beard and black clothes, stands center, surveying it all in wonder. DEL, a young redneck, comes out of the back carrying a jar of pickled pigs' feet. His drawl is so thick and his syllables so squashed together that occasional translations will be necessary:)

DEL   …Ainope yit. …Ainope yit. …Looow. Say wainope yit. […Ain't open yet. Ain't _open_ yet. …Hello. Said we ain't open yet.]

(CETNIK squints at him—trying to discern some familiar word. DEL treats himself to a pig's foot.)

DEL   …J'hear whatahsed? Hellsamatta witchoo. [You hear what I said? The hell's the matter with you.]

CETNIK   …Eh. "Hello, Jack."

DEL   Whozjack? …Fkyuwah? Huh? [Who's Jack? …What the fuck do you want? Huh?]

(CETNIK looks intently at the pig's foot DEL is eating.)

CETNIK   …Pork nookle.

DEL   Huh?

CETNIK   *(Enunciating helpfully)* Poooorrk nookle.

DEL   Iss? Sspigsft. [This? This is a pig's foot.]

CETNIK   Spizzffft?

DEL   Piiigzzz ffffoo-t. Wahn one? …Huh? Zat it? Y'wahn one? [Pigs foot. Want one? …Huh? Is that it? You want one?]

(DEL dangles a pig's foot invitingly. BILLY, the proprietor, enters with a bottle or two of booze, which he sets down somewhere, and grunts hello. His conversation with DEL is almost completely unintelligible.)

BILLY   …Hnn. [Hey.]

DEL   Hnn. Too' y'slon? [Hey. What took you so long?]

BILLY   Roeclose. ...'sat? [Road was closed. Who's that?]

DEL   I'nno. Fuckn weerowannerin. Whutha roeclose? [I don't know. Fucking
             weirdo wandered in. Why was the road closed?]

BILLY   Roeblock. Fucknsherf loofer summun. S'wahn?   [Roadblock. Fucking
             sheriff's looking for someone. What's he want?]

DEL   I'nno. Hootha looknfur. [I don't know. Who are they looking for?]

BILLY   I'nno. Munkle binere? [I don't know. Has my uncle been here?]

DEL   Huh?

BILLY   Munkle! Munkle! [My uncle! My uncle!]

DEL   Nahyit. Jees! [Not yet. Jees!]

BILLY   (To CETNIK) ...Shoowahn, bo? ...Huh? Shoowahn? [What do you
             want, boy? ...Huh? What do you want?]

(CETNIK is mystified. Now he recites experimentally:)

CETNIK   "...Ass for you sir, I haffn't pleashure of your acquainance. But my
             name iss Abe Lincoln, I'd lack to shake hants vith brafe man."

(CETNIK shakes BILLY's hand.)

BILLY   ...Th' hell?

DEL   I'nno. Jus' wannerin ere. [I don't know. He just wandered in here.]

BILLY   ...Looks lak a reetarr. –Y'retarr bo? ...Huh? Reee-tarr?... [He looks
             like a retard. You a retard, boy? ...Huh? Retard?]

CETNIK   Reee-tarr?

(BILLY laughs—a snort. CETNIK laughs and snorts back. They get chummy, BILLY
tugging on CETNIK's beard.)

BILLY   ...You're a funny li'l fucker, aincha bo. Huh? Huh? –Looka this here. He's
             a funny li'l fucker. –Look here, bo: d'yew? Know? Wharrr? Yarrr?

DEL   Why don'cha gimma shot.

BILLY   Pfff.

DEL   C'mon, it'll be funny, gimma shot, let's fuck 'im up.

(DEL quickly gets a glass and a shot of booze is poured. BILLY will dangle and slosh it invitingly.)

BILLY   Looka here, reetarr, you wahn some hooch? Huh? Li'l John Barleycorn? Li'l hair a' the dog? Y'wahn that, don'tcha. Looka that.

(CETNIK takes it, drinks and reacts.)

CETNIK …This iss great stuff.

BILLY   Y'like that, doncha. Wahn some more? Let's give 'im some more.

(The REVEREND, a middle-aged white male, appears in the door, carrying an empty keg. He has a genteel southern accent.)

REVEREND Hello, boys!

CETNIK *(Hearing a cue and seizing on it)* "Hello, Jack! Hello, boyz!"

REVEREND How's everybody today!

CETNIK "An't you fallers dronk yet?"

BILLY   Tom.

REVEREND Need a refill here, if you please, Del.

(He hands the keg to DEL, who will convey it to the back.)

CETNIK "Where'd you get that keg, Fergus?"

DEL   Got us a retarr, Tom.

REVEREND A what?

DEL   *(As he exits to the back)* A ree-tarr-d.

REVEREND …So I see. …Looks rather like a pilgrim.

BILLY   Ask'm who he is. G'head, g'head.

REVEREND   Uh…pardon me, sir, I don't believe I've had the pleasure of your
               acquaintance.

CETNIK   (Delighted—picking up his line) "But my name iss Abe Lincoln. I'd
               lack to shake hants vith brafe man!"

(They shake hands. The REVEREND is astounded, of course.)

REVEREND   …Well! A genuine honor, sir! A genuine honor! I am the Reverend
               Thomas M. Bessinger, minister at the Grendel Baptist Church. It's not
               every day the commander in chief of the Union Army ambles into our
               tavern. I'm glad these boys saw fit to offer you a cocktail.

CETNIK   Cocktail!

REVEREND   Have you checked his…?

(BILLY leaps into action, as slyly as he can, searching CETNIK's pockets, as the
REVEREND distracts CETNIK:)

REVEREND   …It's a good thing I stopped by before my fishing expedition, Mr.
               President. There are a great many issues I have always wanted to discuss
               with you, sir, a great many issues. Because I believe history—drink your
               cocktail—I believe history has misremembered you, sir, and you are not
               at all the man you pretend to be. To your Yankee brethren, you are the
               Great Emancipator who saved the union and put an end to slavery!

CETNIK   "Slafery?"

REVEREND   That's what I said.

CETNIK   (Remembers, strikes a pose and declaims gallantly) "No! I am
               oppose to slafery! I belief in our democrack system, which open
               way to all!"

REVEREND   That's what you said, sir. –By God, he's quoting himself. –But in
               another speech you yourself delivered, you said, "I am not now nor
               have I ever been in favor of the equality of the white and black races."
               Indeed, before the War of Northern Aggression, our General Lee
               freed his slaves, but when it was over, your General Grant still had his.
               —Straight down to my boat please, Del.

(He refers to the full keg DEL now brings from the back. DEL continues out the front door with it.)

REVEREND   To sum up, Mr. Lincoln, you preside over a nation of *hypocrites!*

CETNIK   *(Recognizing the word, scowling)* "Hypocriss!"

(As the REVEREND pontificates. CETNIK will shadow him—as with Bergen in Act I— replicating gestures and repeating familiar or emphatic words, at the actor's discretion.)

REVEREND   That's what I said, sir! Ours is a Godly confederation—our own flag the cross of St. Andrew! And yet *you*, an avowed *atheist*, presumed to stand on Christian principles of liberty and brotherhood to justify the *burning* of our homes and *plunder* of our property!

CETNIK   *(Interspersed)*   ...Godly!   ...atheist!   ...liberty!   ...brotherhood! ...*burning*! ...plunder!

(BILLY finds the wad of bills in one of CETNIK's pockets and holds it up. REVEREND will take it and count it.)

REVEREND   You *plunged* this country into civil war, sending your boys and ours to slaughter, all in the name of putting an end to the very things you *believe*! The true ensign of hatred, the true banner of oppression, is the one flying over your White House in the Kingdom of Subjugation!

CETNIK   *(Interspersed)* Plunge!   ...slaughter!   ...belief!   ...hatred!   ... appression! ...Subbagation!

REVEREND   For as our Governor Tillman once said, "We Southerners are not a free people, for if we were, we would still have our slaves!"

(But CETNIK has stopped and is now staring at HENRY, who has just entered, dressed in his new clothes and cradling his rifle. The REVEREND follows his gaze across the room.)

REVEREND   ...Well, well. Speak of the devil.

BILLY   Fuck you think yer doin' bo?

HENRY   ...That man you got there. I been lookin' for him.

BILLY   Boy, I war you, I'd turn an' walk out, an' I mean rat now.

HENRY   I'm a soldier in the United States Army. I've come to take him back. He's a German prisoner of war.

CETNIK   Not German! Not German!

REVEREND   Sir, do you not recognize your Commander-in-Chief?

HENRY   His name's Cetnik. He knows who I am.

REVEREND   Mr. President, do you know this man?

CETNIK   …Schwarzer.

REVEREND   Schwarzer? Are you Jewish?

HENRY   …No I ain't Jewish. Now I don't want no trouble. So you just hand him over, we'll be on our way.

BILLY   Don' look lak no soldier, Tom.

REVEREND   No, he doesn't. –But I'll tell you what we'll do, Mr. Schwarzer. During the War of Southern Independence, there was such a thing as paroling a prisoner—setting him free, in exchange for his promise to lay down his arms. If you will help me for, say, two minutes to extract such a promise from Mr. Lincoln here, I will remand him to your custody.

BILLY   Ain't no nigga's 'lowed in my—

REVEREND   For *that* I will need a *sack* of *flour*, Billy. –And you will leave that gun by the door, Mr. Schwarzer. And for two minutes we will all promise not to lay so much as a finger on one another—and we'll keep that promise, sir, if you will.

(DEL has appeared in the door behind HENRY, surveyed the situation, and now places his hand on HENRY's rifle. HENRY pulls it back—then places it beside the door. Meanwhile, the REVEREND has placed two chairs in the center of the room.)

HENRY   …Two minutes.

(HENRY sits next to CETNIK; both are nervous.)

REVEREND   Alright then! If you were a Jew, Mr. Schwarzer, you would no doubt be well-versed in the stories of the Old Testament, particularly the one in Genesis about the Great Division of the Races.

HENRY   I ain't a—

REVEREND   How in the *beginning*, there were white people. How aaall there *was* was white people, until Ham was cast out to the land of Canaan and fathered all the dusky races, who were then conquered and made slaves by the Shemites. If you were a Jew, Mr. Schwarzer, you could remind Mr. Lincoln that the Bible is full of allusions to slavery—the Hebrews, of course, the Carthaginians, Macedonians—and nowhere is it said to be evil. We Christians know that Jesus himself had ample opportunity to condemn it, but never said a word. You are a Christian, aren't you sir?

HENRY   …One minute.

REVEREND   Alright then, as an African, you will recall that slaves were captured and sold by their fellow Africans—and so deeply did they love their plantation homes, they didn't want to leave. Indeed, as a gesture of humanity, many freed slaves bought slaves of their own. Now isn't that true, sir.

HENRY   I'm not an African.

REVEREND   Well, but you are.

HENRY   I'm an American.

REVEREND   Not according to your President. Your President believes there is, and I quote, "a physical difference between the white and black races which will forever forbid them from living together. If there must be a position of superiority, I am in favor of assigning it to the white man." Do you recall saying that, Mr. President? If so, say "Yes, I do."

CETNIK   "Yes sydo."

REVEREND   Given all the foregoing, are you ready pronounce your empathy with the Confederacy, renounce your previous hypocrisy, and join the Southern Baptist Convention? If so, say "Yes, I am."

CETNIK   "Yes siam."

(The REVEREND has taken a Confederate hat and coat from their displays and, pulling him to his feet, now puts them on CETNIK.)

REVEREND   Then by the power vested in me by...Anheuser-Busch Incorporated, I hereby commission you an honorary general in the Confederate army. Congratulations, General Lincoln!

(The REVEREND salutes; CETNIK returns it happily. BILLY and DEL have of course been delighted by all this.)

REVEREND   Mr. Schwarzer, we do truly appreciate your helping to end a hundred years of hostility between your people and ours. How are we doing on time?

HENRY   You're out.

REVEREND   In that case, without further ado, we would like to celebrate our new bonds of kinship by anointing you an honorary white man.

(From behind him, BILLY pours flour over HENRY. HENRY stands—enraged, howling. BILLY grabs a chair and wields it like a lion-tamer; the REVEREND hides behind him.)

BILLY & DEL   *(Some improvising here)* Oooo-ey! Watch out now! Now you done it! Think we made 'im mad! *[Etc.]*

REVEREND   *(Interspersed)* Settle down now, boy, we kept our promise, just like we said. ...We never laid a finger—you're only making it worse for yourself! ...We will defend ourselves! *[Etc.]*

(The baiting continues, HENRY lunging at them, BILLY and DEL whooping, until the REVEREND signals DEL, who tackles HENRY and brings him to the ground. BILLY immediately joins the fight. They begin to kick and punch HENRY, who curls up on the floor, covers his head and screams.)

BILLY & DEL   Whatcha gonna do now, boy! Mad Afercan Jewish white nigger! Told you stay out my bar! Whatcha gonna do now! *[Etc.]*

CETNIK   ...No! ...Ne! ...Ne radite to! Pusti tega! Pusti tega! [No! No! Don't do this! Let him go! Let him go!]

(The beating continues, BILLY and DEL dispensing kicks and punches while the REVEREND presides, smiling and laughing and improvising lines like "don't let him up" or "get his arm there, Del," etc. Meanwhile, CETNIK has edged toward the door. He thinks first to escape, but he sees HENRY's rifle beside the door, thinks, picks it up and aims it tentatively at BILLY and DEL.)

CETNIK   Stanite! Rekao sam da stanite, jer cu pucati! Stanite! [Stop! ...I said
                  stop or I'll shoot! ...Stop!]

(He fires once into the ceiling, then levels the rifle at the boys. The fighting immediately
stops. BILLY and DEL back away:)

BILLY   Hoo-hoo! Easy now there, General! Careful where y'point that now.

CETNIK   Spustite se! [Get down!]

(HENRY, bleeding from his nose or cheek, struggles to his feet.)

REVEREND   Let's just everyone simmer down now. It's his own fault. He went back
                  on his promise.

CETNIK   Spustite se—na zemjlu! [Get down—on the ground!]

DEL   The hell's he sayin'?

BILLY   I don't know!

(CETNIK prepares a careful aim, obviously intent on firing. There is nothing tentative
about him now.)

CETNIK   Spustite se, jer cu pucati! [Get down or I'll shoot!]

(BILLY and DEL drop to the ground instinctively, their hands up.)

BILLY & DEL   Okay! Okay! Take it easy there! [Etc.]

(HENRY has by now pulled himself somewhat together. He approaches CETNIK; the
two look at one another carefully, gathering an understanding. HENRY places his hand
on the rifle—and CETNIK surrenders it. HENRY turns to the others, straightens, and
stares them down. He wipes his face, walks up to the REVEREND, and glares at him.)

HENRY   ...On your knees...boy.

REVEREND   ...Now listen, son. We don't—

HENRY   Get! ...on your knees.

(The REVEREND drops to his knees. HENRY puts the rifle barrel to the back of the
REVEREND's head.)

HENRY   …That's right. …Now say, "I am beneath you, sir."

REVEREND   …I am beneath you…sir.

HENRY   "You are better'n me."

REVEREND   …You are better'n me.

HENRY   (*Now to BILLY*) "We are useless and unwanted."

(*Pause. BILLY hesitates.*)

HENRY   "…We are useless…and unwanted!"

DEL   Say it, Billy!

HENRY   "…We are *useless* and *unwanted!*"

(*BILLY clearly refuses to answer. HENRY steels himself to pull the trigger.*)

CETNIK   …No, Schwarzer.

HENRY   Say it! …Say it!

(*The REVEREND squeezes his eyes shut. HENRY tries, tries again—*)

CETNIK   No! …Nemoj te to raditi! [Don't do this!] …No!

(*—but he can't do it. He lowers the barrel in defeat. Pause. CETNIK, with a gesture or nod, pleads "Let's just go." HENRY understands and assents. He goes to the door, turns back, starts to say something. CETNIK stops him:*)

CETNIK   (*Warning, chastising*) No.

(*HENRY exits. CETNIK looks sadly at the men. He retrieves his money from the REVEREND or wherever it ended up, and puts it in his pocket.*)

CETNIK   …Ja ne razumijem. [I don't understand.]

(*CETNIK grabs the jar of pigsfeet and exits. Long pause. The REVEREND, BILLY and DEL collect themselves. None can speak. BILLY begins to put the place back together while DEL goes to the window.*)

DEL   …Tom.

REVEREND   Shut up, Del.

DEL   ...Tom. They're stealin' yer boat.

(End scene.)

Scene 7
On the River

(Evening on a river. HENRY and CETNIK in a johnboat. HENRY, his face cut and bruised, reclines, drinking a beer, while CETNIK languidly rows.)

HENRY   ...Guess this ain't so bad, is it. Ain't done this since I was a kid. Sun go down little more, we have us a moonlight cruise.

CETNIK   Cocktail?

HENRY   Sure thing, mon frer.

(He draws a beer for CETNIK and hands it to him—or perhaps they share the same cup.)

HENRY   ...My daddy, he took me out fishin' now and again on a night like this. Just lay back in the boat, actually, smoked him some reefer, say he could read the stars, say he could hear what they said. ...I got about...ten things I 'member 'bout my daddy. That's about number five. That's one of the good ones.

CETNIK   Sspssfft?

(He offers the jar of pigsfeet. HENRY waves it off.)

HENRY   ...I was a kid—I 'member this: used to sit inna chair, right by the door, waitin' for him to come home. Just me and him after mama died. Sat in that chair every night, waitin'. Finally he come in and rub my head and call me "sawloh."

CETNIK   Sawloh.

HENRY   That's right. 's French. Means "my son." Fought for the French—don't nobody believe me. Ninety-second infantry—got paid cash money to shoot all the white boys he wanted. He even got a medal for it, usedta let me wear it to school. That's a good one too, that's about number three.

(Pause. His smile fades.)

HENRY   …One night he's sittin' at the table…and he's runnin' his hand through a candle—right in the flame, y' know? Didn't flinch or nothin'. Sees me there, could see he been cryin', says, "C'mere, sawloh."

CETNIK   *(Softly)* Sawloh.

HENRY   He puts that medal on the table, and he says, "You want that?" I say, "Yes, I do."

CETNIK   Yes sydo.

HENRY   So he takes out his knife, and he opens it up, and he sticks it right in the wood—you know, like it means somethin'. And he say, he say, "Alright then, sawloh. Let's see what you made of." And he takes my hand—and he holds it right in that fire. …Took me a long time to understand this. I mean I was…screamin,' cryin'. But he held on, "You can't be afraid, sawloh! You do it! You show me what you made of!" …I *knew* what I was supposed to do. I pulled that knife out, laid it right up against his arm— "Can't be afraid, sawloh! Better do it!" …But I couldn't, I… So finally he just…lets go. And he picks up that medal and puts it in his pocket. And he says, "Well. Now you know."

CETNIK   Now you know.

HENRY   …That's right. –That's right, Pere! Now I know!

(This last he's shouted out to the stars; he's answered by the faraway barking of dogs.)

HENRY   …'Cause maybe a week later, one night after school, I'm sittin' in that chair, see. Waitin', waitin'. Next night too, maybe three nights in all, still see it: just sittin' there in the dark. …And *that's* when I understood. I picked up that chair…put it up against the wall. …And that's the thing I remember most. That chair against that wall.

(Pause. A dog barks in the distance.)

HENRY   ...Damn I'm tired... Wish I knew where this river went. Figure it's gotta come out somewhere. ...And what I'm gonna do is–you listenin'? ...I'm gonna turn my back. And you just gonna go. You understan' that? You just...be free.

CETNIK   Be free.

HENRY   That's right. And then I'm gonna...I don't know what I'm gonna do. I can't go back to camp. I don't...I don't wanna be in the Army no more.

CETNIK   ...Army no more.

HENRY   ...Huh. That's right, mon frer.

CETNIK   Mon frer.

HENRY   ...Mon frer. That's right. That's right.

(Pause. The dogs barks again—now much closer. HENRY turns his head slightly to listen. CETNIK is oblivious. End scene.)

Scene 8
Funeral

(Late afternoon: the camp cemetery. BERGEN stands to the side. In the distance, we hear the camp band playing. REIKER enters with a small funeral procession: a coffin, draped in a makeshift Nazi flag—a bedsheet with a painted swastika—is carried in by prisoners and placed near a simple grave marker reading "Werner Weisz/Soldat." Beside that are other markers. The CO and WATERS bring up the rear and join BERGEN. When the music stops, an informal—and inaudible—funeral begins (see Appendix).)

CO   Lieutenant. ...Friend of yours?

(BERGEN nods.)

CO   ...Well. I'm sorry.

(Pause.)

BERGEN   ...This is an obscenity.

CO   ...Flag he fought under, son.

BERGEN   If he died in combat they wouldn't—

CO   War Department says we bury him under the flag they choose.

BERGEN   Permission to speak freely, sir.

CO   Denied.

(Pause.)

CO   ...Sergeant here says this man was in your play.

(BERGEN nods.)

CO   ...So I guess that means it's—

BERGEN   No sir. One of the others stepped in to take his place. ...They admired him.

CO   ...This the one you were protecting?

(BERGEN nods.)

CO   ...Well. I'm...sorry. I'm sorry about this. ...Wasn't your fault.

BERGEN   No, sir. If you'd sent Reiker to Alva none of this—

CO   I said denied.

(Pause. BERGEN glowers.)

CO   ...Just tryin' to run a camp here, Lieutenant, just want everybody to—

WATERS   Ahem.

(REIKER has wandered away from the funeral and joined the group.)

REIKER   Colonel. Lieutenant. ...A shame, yes? ...Very sad. ...He must have been very desperate.

(Pause. The funeral proceeds.)

REIKER   ...I worry for these men, you know. They don't know what to do, they feel guilty and useless. Living in a camp, sometimes a soldier feels he is a coward, he loses a sense that his...his life has any purpose. And to die in a camp, well. ...It's as if you never even...existed at all. ...Do you see what I mean, Herr Bergen?

(BERGEN doesn't look at him. REIKER nods and rejoins the funeral.)

BERGEN   ...Colonel, you can still—

CO   He ain't the only hard-liner around here. If I send him to Alva, one of the others'd just step up in his place.

BERGEN   ...Friend of yours, sir?

CO   Damn good officer.

BERGEN   Sir, he's the enemy.

CO   ...Well so was this man, son.

(Long pause. BERGEN contemplates that. Then:)

BERGEN   ...Sir. ...Request permission for transfer.

CO   You're taking all this personally.

BERGEN   Sir! Request permission—

CO   Where.

BERGEN   The war, sir.

CO   ...You're kidding.

(Pause. BERGEN says nothing.)

CO   ...You wouldn't last a month.

BERGEN   Sir, request—

CO   Give me one good reason.

BERGEN   ...Because he's right sir.

(Pause. The funeral ends with the prisoners issuing a Nazi salute before the coffin. Two prisoners remain with shovels. The others exit back across the stage—REIKER among them, who exchanges a look with BERGEN. When he is gone:)

CO   …Granted.

(CO puts his hat on. BERGEN salutes; CO returns it—and exits. Pause. BERGEN approaches the coffin, addresses the two prisoners:)

BERGEN   …Lasst das. Geht weg. [...Go. Go away.]

A PRISONER   Wir sollten ihn begraben— [We're supposed to bury—]

WATERS   Raus! Jetzt! [Go! Now!]

(The prisoners lay their shovels down and exit. Pause. When they're gone, BERGEN removes the flag and throws it on the ground. Then he finds and places a stone on the coffin. He kneels and begins quietly praying the Kaddish—struggling to remember the words, and reciting as much as is necessary for the moment. As he prays, WATERS silently picks up the shovel, stands aside and waits.)

BERGEN   Yis'ga'dal v'yis'kadash sh'may ra'bbo,
              B'olmo dee'vro chir'usay
              V'yamlich malchu'say, B'chayaychon uv'yomay'chon
              Uv'chayay d'chol bais Yisroel,
              Ba'agolo u' viz'man koriv; vimru Omein.
              Y'hay shmay rabbo m'vorach l'olam ul'olmay olmayo.
              Y'hay shmay rabbo m'vorach l'olam ul'olmay olmayo…

(Lights fade to black with his prayer. End scene.)

Scene 9
Incarceration

(Evening: county jail. HENRY is in one cell, CETNIK the other. A hallway leading to an outer office divides their cells.)

HENRY   …Hey. …Out there? …I get a phone call. …Hey! Hello out there!

(SHERIFF LOKER calls from offstage:)

LOKER   *(Off)* You wanna hold it down!

HENRY   You call! Call the camp! Ask for Sergeant Wa—

LOKER   *(Off)* I'm on the phone shut up!

(Pause. HENRY and CETNIK look at each other.)

CETNIK   …Šta radiš? …Eh? Šta radiš? [...What are you doing? Eh? What are you doing?] …Eh? Schwarzer?

HENRY   Don't call me that.

CETNIK   Vant to be American… Schwarzer? Vant to be—

HENRY   I said don't call me that! My name's Henry! …I'm *Henry*, okay?

(SHERIFF LOKER enters with AGENT MARKS, nods toward CETNIK's cell.)

MARKS   You Err-ass? …Huh? Your name Err-ass?

CETNIK   *(Delighted—and correcting the pronunciation)* Eras! Yes! Yes! Juraj Eras! Juraj Eras!

MARKS   This the other one?

HENRY   My name's Henry. I'm a private in the United—

MARKS   We know who you are, Private. You say you apprehended this prisoner?

HENRY   …Well…yes, sir, I…I did. He—

MARKS   Ran away from the camp up by Drayton.

HENRY   That's right. He ran away, and I—I went after him, and—

MARKS   Looks like he put up quite a fight.

HENRY   Huh? …Oh, uh…well…he didn't want to go back, and I, well, when I found him—

MARKS   Looks like he smacked you around pretty good.

HENRY   …He put up a good fight. Yes sir.

LOKER   Private, can you explain you boys were trolling down the Savannah River in a johnboat?

(AGENT MARKS whips out a notepad and jots down notes.)

HENRY   Well, I—I—I was lost, I didn't know where—

MARKS   Can you explain why this man had a roll of cash on him?

HENRY   Uh…huh! I—

MARKS   You were deserting the United States Army and helping this man to escape.

HENRY   Oh, no, no sir! No, I—

LOKER   Where's your uniform? Why're you boys wearing those clothes?

HENRY   Well, there was—we—

MARKS   You know what we do to traitors in this county?

HENRY   No, no, it ain't like that! I got lost! I got—

MARKS   You got lost. You were lost, but now you are found.

HENRY   …That's the truth, yes, sir. …Yes, sir.

(Long pause. Then AGENT MARKS exchanges a knowing look with SHERIFF LOKER, then smiles and flips his notebook closed.)

MARKS   …Good job, Private.

(SHERIFF LOKER hands AGENT MARKS a form.)

LOKER   Sign there…and there.

(SHERIFF LOKER opens CETNIK's cell, pulls him out and starts to drag him down the hall, but CETNIK pulls away:)

CETNIK   Sacekaj. …Sacekaj te, molim vas. [Wait. Wait, please.]

(CETNIK returns to HENRY's cell. He smiles in at HENRY.)

CETNIK   …Henry?

MARKS   Looks like he wants to tell you something.

CETNIK   …You Henry, yes? Henry?

(CETNIK extends a hand through the bars for HENRY to shake.)

CETNIK   …I am Juraj. …Welcome, friend.

(HENRY feels the eyes of the others upon him. He doesn't move. CETNIK smiles and keeps his hand insistently through the bars. A long moment. CETNIK's smile gradually fades.)

CETNIK   Welcome, friend, yes? Yes? …Henry?

(HENRY doesn't move, but stares at CETNIK. Finally:)

LOKER   …Okay. That's enough.

(SHERIFF LOKER pulls CETNIK away and up the hall. CETNIK calls as he goes:

CETNIK   Henry? Šta se dešava…? Šta se dešava? …Reci mi štase dešava.
                [What's happening…? What's happening? …Tell me what's happening.]

HENRY   Wait! Wait, I—what's gonna happen?

MARKS   Sheriff's got someone out there waiting for you.

HENRY   To him, I mean, what's gonna—

MARKS   Oh. I'm takin' him back to camp. …Want me to give him a few licks
                for ya? Little payback for your trouble?

HENRY   …Uhh.

MARKS   Happy to do it. All on the same side here.

(HENRY hesitates, nods.)

MARKS   Alright. Yeah.

(AGENT MARKS winks and leaves. Pause. From the office we hear CETNIK calling:)

CETNIK   (off)…Ja ne razumijem. …Henry! Henry! …Ja ne razumijem!

(HENRY winces, closes his eyes and holds the bars of the cell. Pause. Then SHERIFF
LOKER enters with PATTY and her PAPA and leads them to HENRY.)

LOKER   That him?

PAPA   (To HENRY) …You motherfuckin'. I'mo tear you limb from—

LOKER   Eh-ehh! That him or ain't it.

PAPA   That's him. …Patty? That's him, ain't it?

(PATTY searches the floor, struggles to look at HENRY.)

PAPA   …Answer the man! He's the one, ain't he?

PATTY   …Papa?

PAPA   Answer the man! Say it! …Say it!

(One last time, PATTY looks up at HENRY—and nods weakly.)

LOKER   That a yes?

(PATTY nods.)

LOKER   Good enough.

(PAPA grabs through the bars at HENRY, who backs away.)

LOKER   Ah! C'mon now.

PAPA   'Git you, you filthy coon! Wish you never been born.

(SHERIFF LOKER directs PAPA back down the hall. PATTY turns and looks apologetically
at HENRY, who has no idea what just happened. Long moment.

Then she faces or even approaches the audience—and searches for some way to
explain all this. Finally, though, when SHERIFF LOKER returns to shepherd her off, she
starts to cry and runs off. SHERIFF LOKER turns to HENRY.)

LOKER   Private Henry, you're under arrest. You got a lawyer?

HENRY   ...No, I, no—

LOKER   Well, you better get one. Say you're in up to your neck.

HENRY   No! No, call the camp, call my camp, talk to my sergeant, or, or—

SHERIFF   Army ain't gonna help you. Sergeant says you went AWOL. ...Said
             he'd loan you thirty bucks, though, whatever that means.

*(SHERIFF LOKER exits. HENRY stands thinking—and realizing. Lights narrow to a
special on him.*

*Elsewhere: special up on BERGEN, wearing black clothes and a fake beard. He is
Abe Lincoln, delivering the closing address to "Abe Lincoln in Illinois." Perhaps the
camp band plays "Glory, Glory Hallelujah" softly and badly in the background:)*

BERGEN   "...I now leave, not knowing when or whether I may return. It is a
             grave duty I now face. In preparing for it, I have tried to enquire:
             what great principle is it that has kept this Union so long together?
             ...I believe it was the fulfillment of an ancient dream, which men have
             held through all time, that they might one day shake off their chains
             and find freedom in the brotherhood of life. We gained democracy,
             and now there is the question whether it is fit to survive. Perhaps
             we have come to the dreadful day of awakening, and the dream is
             ended. If so, I am afraid it must be ended forever. I cannot believe
             that ever again will men have the opportunity we have had. Perhaps
             we should admit that, and concede that our ideals of liberty and
             equality are doomed."

(He removes his hat—and now looks Hasidic.)

BERGEN   "...And yet, let us believe it is not true! Let us live to prove that we
             can cultivate the natural world about us...and the moral world within
             us...so we may secure an individual and social prosperity which,
             while the earth endures, shall not pass away."

*(From offstage, we hear the voice of the GULLAH WOMAN, singing, comes up over
the orchestra:)*

GULLAH WOMAN *(Off)* Wade in duh watuh, chillun
             Wade in duh watuh, chillun
             Wade in duh watuh
             Gawd's gwi' trouble duh watuh.

(BERGEN waves his hat in farewell. HENRY feels the cage closing in around him—and perhaps drops to his knees.)

BERGEN   *(Continuing, over the singing)* "...I commend you to the care of the Almighty, as I hope that in your prayers you will remember me... Goodbye, my friends and neighbors."

(As the song continues, the special on each man fades to black, and we hear the sound of a train pulling away from the station.)

GULLAH WOMAN *(Off)* If a you don' believe Ah been redeem
                    Gawd's gwi' trouble duh watuh
                    Folla me down to Jurdun stream
                    Gawd's gwi' trouble duh watuh.

(The train rolls into the distance. End play.)

Andre Rogers (Reiker) and DeRante Parker (Henry) in scene I.8: Indoctrination.
Photo: Kim Kim Foster/The State.

APPENDIX
SONGS

THE HORST WESSEL SONG
[Act One, Scene 1]

Die Fahne hoch die Reihen fest geschlossen
S.A. marschiert mit ruhig festem Schritt—
Kam'raden die Rotfront und Reaktion erschossen
Marshier'n im Geist in unsern Reihen mit.
Kam'raden die Rotfront und Reaktion erschossen
Marshier'n im Geist in unsern Reihen mit.

Die Strasse frei dem braunen Batallionen
Die Strasse frei dem Sturmabteilungsmann
Es schau'n auf's Hakenkreuz voll Hoffnung schon Millionen
Der Tag für Freiheit und für Brot bricht an.
Es schau'n auf's Hakenkreuz voll Hoffnung schon Millionen
Der Tag für Freiheit und für Brot bricht an.

[Flag high, ranks closed,
The SA marches with silent, solid steps
Comrades shot by the red front and reaction
march in spirit with us in our ranks.
Comrades shot by the red front and reaction
march in spirit with us in our ranks.

The street free for the brown battalions
The street free for the Storm Troopers
Hopeful millions look to the swastika
The day breaks for freedom and for bread.
Hopeful millions look to the swastika
The day breaks for freedom and for bread.]

WADE IN THE WATER
[Act Two, Scene 5, Scene 9]

> Wade in the water, children,
> Wade in the water, children.
> Wade in the water,
> God's gonna trouble the water.
>
> If you don't believe I've been redeemed
> God's gonna trouble the water.
> Follow me down to Jordan stream
> God's gonna trouble the water

THE MOURNER'S KADDISH
[Act Two, Scene 8]

> [May His great name be exalted and sanctified
> throughout the world He created as He willed.
> May he give reign to his kingship in your lifetime and in your days,
> and in the lifetime of the Family of Israel
> swiftly and soon. Now respond: Amen.
> May His great name be blessed forever and ever
> May His great name be blessed forever and ever....]

The sotto voce recitations during the FUNERAL [Act II, Sc. 8] in the Trustus Theatre production were of Martin Luther's adaptation (1522) of the Lord's Prayer, and verses drawn from the sixth (Andante) section of Brahms' German Requiem:

THE LORD'S PRAYER

Unser Vater in Himmel! Dein Name werde geheiligt. Dein Reich Komme. Dein Wille geschele wie im Himmel so auf Erden. Unser tagliches Brot gib uns heute. Und vergib uns unsere Schuld, als wir vergieben unsern Schuldigern. Und fuhre uns nicht in Veruchung; Sondern erlose uns von dem Ubel. Denn Dein ist das Reich und die Kraft und die Herrlichkeit in Ewigkeit. Amen.

EIN DEUTSCHES REQUIEM

Denn wir haben hie keine bleibende Statt, sondern die zukünftige suchen wir.

Siehe, ich sage euch ein Geheimnis: Wir werden nicht alle entschlafen, wir werden aber alle verwandelt werden; und dasselbige plötzlich, in einem Augenblick, zu der Zeit der letzten Posaune. Denn es wird die Posaune schallen, und die Toten werden auferstehen unverweslich, und wir werden verwandelt werden. Dann wird erfüllet werden das Wort, das geschrieben steht: Der Tod ist verschlungen in den Sieg. Tod, wo ist dein Stachel? Hölle, wo ist dein Sieg?

Herr, du bist würdig zu nehmen Preis und Ehre und Kraft, denn du hast alle Dinge geschaffen, und durch deinen Willen haben sie das Wesen und sind geschaffen.

[For here have we no continuing city, but we seek one to come. —Hebrews 13:14

Behold, I shew you a mystery: We shall not all sleep, but we shall all be changed, in a moment, in the twinkling of an eye, at the last trump: for the trumpet shall sound, and the dead shall be raised incorruptible, and we shall be changed. Then shall be brought to pass the saying that is written, Death is swallowed up in victory. O death, where is thy sting? O grave, where is thy victory? —1 Corinthians 15:51–52, 54–55

Thou art worthy, O Lord, to receive glory and honour and power: for thou hast created all things, and for thy pleasure they are and were created. —Revelation 4:11]

A NOTE ON CASTING

In production, many of the characters in this play may be doubled or tripled. For example:

PRIMARY CHARACTERS: played by actors assuming no other roles:

- PRIVATE HENRY: black male, early 20s.
- CETNIK: white male, 20s.
- LIEUTENANT BERGEN: white male, late 20s.

SECONDARY CHARACTERS: played by actors assuming two or three roles:

ACTOR 4: WHITE MALE, MIDDLE-AGED
- Commanding Officer
- Reverend
- Papa

ACTOR 5: BLACK MALE, 30s–40s.
- Sergeant Waters
- Duke

ACTOR 6: WHITE MALE, 30s.
- Lieutenant Reiker
- Agent Marks

ACTOR 7: BLACK FEMALE, 20s–40s.
- Private Abd-al Qaiser (male)
- Gullah Woman

ACTOR 8: WHITE FEMALE, teens–20s.
- Patty
- Anonymous German prisoner (male)

OTHER CHARACTERS: all white males, to be doubled/tripled by the ensemble:

Corporal Müller	Billy
Professor	Del
Corporal Weisz	King
Sheriff Loker	Various prisoners

Holy Ghost from Page to Stage — and Back

Dewey Scott-Wiley

Holy Ghost is a play rich with historical significance, religious juxtaposition, and dramatic action—and a challenge to artists and audiences alike. It's difficult to read, difficult to cast, and potentially exhausting. As I approached the task of directing the premier production at Trustus Theatre in 2005, I knew that to overcome the many obstacles it presents, I'd first have to find the proper focus and emphasis in the storytelling.

I was fortunate to be involved with *Holy Ghost* early in the play's development. I staged a reading of the first act with my students at the University of South Carolina Aiken in March of 2004, while Jon Tuttle was in residence at the university. We made some important discoveries then—the most important being that the first act *alone* ran over 100 minutes. By the time I directed another staged reading of the complete play at Trustus that August, Jon had gutted entire scenes and monologues that I knew were close to his heart. One of the first things to go, as I recall, was the story of Jedwabne, Poland, a town that murdered its Jewish residents—half its population—in order to impress the invading Nazis, who were in fact appalled. It was a fascinating, horrifying story, but it had little to do with the throughline Jon was establishing in his play. He and I continued to work together—I looking for the emphasis in the story, he making the cuts necessary to find it—through rehearsals and the production at Trustus in August of 2005. By then, the script was approaching, but had not yet reached, completion.

As the play evolved, it was clear that Jon wanted to place specific emphasis on the three main characters—Private Henry, Lieutenant Bergen, and Cetnik—by calling for one actor to play each of those characters, while double- or triple-casting actors in all of the other roles. At first glance, then, the play seemed (and may still seem) to have three protagonists and multiple antagonists. We realized that this assumption could potentially muddy the storytelling. My first job was to avoid that and to ensure clarity in the performance.

One question to ask in identifying a play's true protagonist is, "Which character changes the most?" In *Holy Ghost*, two of the characters experience significant human change: Lieutenant Bergen and Private Henry. Bergen undergoes a religious awakening, which ignites a desire to fight on the front lines of the war. He changes from a self-declared pacifist, to a newly-minted officer who enjoys the taste of power, to a man ready to fight and die for his country and his tribe. Henry transforms in the opposite direction. He begins the play loving the Army and wanting to defend his country but is abandoned by and consequently disenchanted by both. At the end, he is a man alone in a cage, with no one to stand up for him, nowhere to call home, no one to call friend. Since both men experience reversals, and since the journeys of both men comprise the throughline of the play, the argument can be made that they are two equal protagonists. But Jon and I eventually agreed that the play had to be Henry's, and so went about making sure that was demonstrated. Jon rewrote the ending so that Henry's reversal is the last to manifest on stage, which makes his change resonate louder and longer with the audience. In fact, in the production draft, Henry appeared at the end with his wrists slashed while the Gullah woman sang in the background. In this final draft, however, Jon has chosen to forecast Henry's suicide (as he also forecasts Bergen's death) by making reference to it earlier on, when he is confronted by Sergeant Waters.

If not for those two characters, the role of Cetnik would have all the makings of a protagonist. He is the one who makes the journey of discovery in the play; he is the one on whom all the forces are working, although he doesn't understand anything that is happening. The audience knows he has a good heart and is someone worth pulling for. Still, Cetnik does not undergo the same level of change as Henry or even Bergen. Although his journey is a rollercoaster of extreme experiences, he greets the ride with innocence and amazement, and at the end of it, he is right back where he started, not much wiser or different than before. Cetnik's dramatic function is twofold: he is the catalyst for the action—the person who unknowingly forces Henry and Bergen into action—and he is the confidant for both as well. It is through their relationship with Cetnik that we get to hear their stories and empathize with them.

The importance of casting these three roles properly is paramount to the success of any production of *Holy Ghost*. Bergen should be an intellectual who is in over his head. The actor needs to portray an icy exterior that we see crack and eventually melt. Our Bergen, longtime Trustus actor Alex Smith, occupied a midrange from steely to tentative and back again, and in his long monologues to Cetnik, he affected the attitude of a man trying to convince himself of something—which he is. Our Cetnik, Dylan Barton, was as Cetnik must be—unabashedly innocent and exuberant—and was committed to making Cetnik's daunting language mean something even to those who didn't understand it. Finally, Private Henry must be the most enthusiastic and likable character in the play. If the audience is rooting for Henry, they will vicariously experience the crushing of his spirit. DeRante Parker, who originated the role, was an actor Jon and I pursued immediately after seeing him in the Trustus production of Athol Fugard's *Master Harold...And the Boys*. As Private Henry, he exuded a youthful goodness even at his angriest, and he registered measures of regret and even horror as he tried to become the soldier he thought he wanted to be. Henry's is the spirit in (or of) *Holy Ghost*; his death is the sacrifice it calls for.

There are several characters who might be perceived as antagonists. Lieutenant Reiker, Sergeant Waters and Papa, for example, all embody the antagonistic role in certain scenes. The danger with these characters is in reducing them to the types that they are not. Reiker is a Nazi thug, but he is also charming and patient and a "damned good officer"; Waters can be a bully and a liar, but in truth he's a man torn between his desires to fit in with his own tribe and to move up in the ranks (as revealed in the different dialects he affects when he speaks to blacks and whites); and Papa, of course, is at heart a redneck in a wife-beater, but he's also all alone in the world, with no one other than a daughter who wants to be as far away from him as she can get.

The real antagonist in this play is the setting: 1940s America. The opposing views about race, religion, and love of country are what provide the major conflicts in the play. The emotional power in the play is the recognition that these conflicts still exist in America. The costs of racial assimilation, the difference between religiosity and extremism, the boundary between patriotism and mindless fanaticism: these questions are just as relevant today as they were when Lorraine Hansberry, Lawrence and Lee, and Arthur Miller were asking them. *Holy Ghost* is a play that depends much more on words than on actions—that uses words *as* actions. We discussed such issues at many of our early rehearsals so that the actors understood what they were saying and why.

Since the play is episodic, it is necessary to identify the dramatic function of the secondary characters in each scene. This is essential because many of the recurring characters serve more than one dramatic function, depending on whom they're sharing a scene with. The supporting characters usually serve one of the following functions in a given scene: foil, confidant, informant, or to provide contrast and juxtaposition. Since Jon has specified much of the double casting in the script, the director must decide what each actor's primary role is, and cast accordingly. It is no accident, for instance, that the same actor who plays the Commanding Officer, whose primary objective is his own convenience, also plays the Reverend and Papa, two other negative characters. Likewise, Reiker and Marks are approximately the same person on different sides of the war and so are played by the same actor.

Language also plays a primary role in both the casting and storytelling. I think it is vital to have a dialect coach who specializes in American Southern, Yiddish, and German in order to realistically capture the musicality of the play. Language, as Jon suggests in his introduction, is practically another character in the play, and the actors' ability not merely to enunciate but to "sell" speeches in languages they may not even understand is crucial. Cetnik's language, Serbian, is meticulously spelled out in the script, but it is very difficult to perform and should not sound like German, or his character will become indistinct. The rhythms and pronunciations of the Gullah woman are also well-indicated in the text. It is such a unique dialect, however, that it would be highly advisable to obtain an aural example of Gullah for the actor to study before attempting a performance.

The multiple locations required in this historical epic provide a unique, if maddening, theatrical challenge. The storytelling should be seamless, so implementing massive scene changes for each locale is inadvisable as it would hamper the flow of the performance. The play is best served on a multi-level unit set that is easily adapted by the actors to quickly and perhaps minimally establish each new environment. Both isolation and expansion in the staging are useful in setting up different locations. Lighting and environmental sound are also vital to creating these realities. Many scenes in the play happen outdoors (e.g., the cotton field, a marsh, a river, a forest), but the specifics need to be carefully communicated with light and sound rather than elaborate set pieces.

Two of the most difficult staging challenges are the boat scene and the depiction of a hanging. Lights and sound can be used to depict the boat effectively on a simple platform; we used a water ripple effect on the actors' faces and subtle sounds of waves beating against a small boat. Too much emphasis on such effects, however, could detract from the subtle transaction being made in that scene. The hanging scene, on the other hand, must appear to be completely realistic. In the original production, we utilized a harness from a flying rig with the clip hidden in the actor's costume at the base of the neck. The hook was hidden in the knot of the noose. The size of the noose was adjusted to provide both believability and safety. At the crucial moment, our Corporal Müller (Charlie Harrell) kicked himself off and away from Cetnik and, suspended in near-silhouette, choked convincingly to "death." Because the play immediately gives itself over to talk, this first scene and image must be powerful.

The most valuable recommendation I would impart to future directors of *Holy Ghost* is to make certain that all aspects of the production are historically accurate. The costumes, props, and sound must work together to construct this multi-faceted world, because this world matters, and because many people in the audience lived in it (you'd be surprised how many) and will care. Specificity of movement is part of this accuracy, especially when exploring differences between religions and military regimes. The audience must completely believe in this world in order to take the emotional journey with the characters. *Holy Ghost* has a profound and lasting effect on both the artists and audience members that have the pleasure of witnessing this golden theatrical experience.

Dewey Scott-Wiley

Dewey Scott-Wiley is an Associate Professor of Theatre at the University of South Carolina Aiken and a Professional Director at Trustus Theatre in Columbia, SC.

Permissions

The Hammerstone

> Dramatists Play Service, Inc.
> 440 Park Avenue South
> New York, NY 10016
> USA
> Website: www.dramatists.com
> Email:postmaster@dramatists.com
> Phone:1-212-683-8960

Drift

> Playscripts, Inc.
> Website: www.playscripts.com
> Email: info@playscripts.com
> Phone: 1-866-NEW PLAY (639-7529)

Holy Ghost

> Samuel French, Inc.
> 45 West 25ᵗʰ St.
> New York, NY 10010
> Website: www.samuelfrench.com
> Email: info@samuelfrench.com
> Phone: 1-212-206-8990

The author is a member of the Dramatists Guild of America.